The Rabbi's Daughter

The Rabbi's Daughter

A True Story of
Sex, Drugs and Orthodoxy

Reva Mann

HODDER

British Library Cataloguing in Publication Data
A record for this book is available from the British Library

ISBN 978 0340 943670

Typeset in Sabon by Avon DataSet Ltd, Bidford on Avon, Warwickshire

Printed and bound in Great Britain by
Clays Ltd, St Ives plc

The paper used in this book is a natural recyclable product made
from wood grown in sustainable forests. The logging and manufacturing
processes are expected to conform to the environmental regulations
of the country of origin

Hodder & Stoughton
An Hachette Livre UK company
338 Euston Road
London NW1 3BH
www.hodder.co.uk

In memory of
Dr Alfred Seyman
(Gershon)
who encouraged me to say it like it is.

The names and other identifying details of the people
in this book have been changed to protect individual privacy.
And certain events have been compressed, expanded,
or chronologically rearranged to reflect my own
perceptions of their importance and meaning.

Contents

Acknowledgements   ix

1. Repentance   1

2. The Test   20

3. Back on Track   39

4. Matchmaker, Matchmaker   54

5. The Find   75

6. *Mazeltov*!   85

7. Pass the Salt   121

8. Oh, Crumbs!   147

9. Mr Fixit Breaks Through   168

10. The Golden Scissors   181

11. Beyond the Mask   195

12. Breaking of the Vessels   211

13. Get a Life   221

14. *Tikkun*   232

15. End of an Era   245

16. The Hidden Light   256

17. Where is God?   273

18. Life after Death   282

19. The Final Release   294

20. Michelle   308

    Epilogue   319

Acknowledgements

Many thanks to Judith Longman and Susan Kamil for their enthusiasm and recognition. Thank you to Robin Morgan, Lisa Ter Haar, Tamara Sole, Judy Labensohn, Eve Horowitz, Muriel Taylor, Paul Taylor, Daphna Small, Naomi Gryn, Niva von Weisl, Neville Shack, Ariel Genadt, Nita Schechet, Yael Unterman, Ilana Weiler and Sharon Goodman for your friendship, support and continued encouragement. With gratitude to Gillian Stern for helping me structure the work, to Jonny Geller for believing in me and finding homes for the book and to Beth Rashbaum for her brilliant and insightful edit. I couldn't have done it without you guys.

I

Repentance

'How do you know if you have succeeded in repenting fully? You find yourself in a similar situation where you sinned in the past but now you do not sin.'
The Rambam, Hilchot Tshuva, Laws of Repentance

I stare through the library window at golden sunlight reflecting off white Jerusalem stone and long to be outdoors soaking up a tan. I want to head down to Tel-Aviv beach, strip off my baggy clothes, stretch out on the sands and take a break from the rigid daily practice of soul searching, prayer and study required of us at the seminary. It is scorching hot and I imagine how cooling the Mediterranean waves would feel against my skin, how they would wash away the perspiration that is gathering on my scalp and dripping down my neck. But I know that sunning at the seaside is a pleasure from my old life, the carefree secular existence that I have willingly exchanged for the absolutes of ultra-Orthodox Jewish doctrine. Now I must keep strictly to the modesty laws and not reveal my body in public. Yet even though I pray and perform the *mitzvot* daily, I still find myself longing to wear blue jeans or, worse, a bikini.

The bikini I brought with me when I moved to Israel is now stuffed into the back of my wardrobe, but I doubt it would still fit me anyway. I have put on weight gorging on the *kugel* served at every *Shabbes* meal and the plates of cakes and sweets at all the engagement parties and weddings which are part of my new life. My slim body is now encased in a layer of blubber and I hardly recognise myself when I stand naked in front of the mirror. My once flat stomach is protruding over formerly shapely legs that now melt into one another at the thigh, and chubby pads of flesh conceal what used to be high cheekbones. I have lost my looks. In the two years since I moved here from London I have changed from a skinny sexy girl into a dowdy matron. Luckily the extra pounds are well hidden under the religious uniform – long shapeless skirt, high-necked, long-sleeved shirt and thick stockings – that I wear even in this August heat. I know I am comfort eating, substituting food for sex, chewing and swallowing for kissing and caressing. I feel a constant need for the solace of foods, even forbidden foods like succulent pink lobster flesh, for which I still have a craving.

My gaze wanders to the far side of the library, past the lines of shelves housing the Five Books of Moses, the Prophets, the Talmud, the Midrash and other scholarly texts to where Mrs Hillman, my idol, role model of the holy Jewish woman, is sitting reading the *Zohar*. Nicknamed 'Hilly' by us girls of the Light of Zion Yeshiva, married by an arranged match and the mother of fourteen children, she is unbothered by outward appearances, never notices the cornflakes stuck to her wig or her mismatched clothes, and devotes her life to teaching Torah. There is an ethereal quality about her that makes her seem disconnected from the material world. I imagine she lives in the world of *Yetzirah* or even *Malchut*, the higher worlds she has taught us about. Rumour has it among the girls here that she is a *lamed vavnick*, one of the thirty-six righteous people on whose merit the world exists. I want to be just like her and become a holy Jewish woman, but I doubt that I will ever be spiritually advanced enough to see beyond the externals to a realm where only beauty of the soul matters.

Hilly looks peaceful as she turns the pages of the sacred book. Watching her makes me forget the oppressive midsummer heat and my desire for the forbidden and inspires me to return to my own study. I pick up the heavy text in front of me, the *Laws of Repentance* written by the Rambam, and read the medieval philosopher's advice with care because here, at the Light of Zion, I am repenting.

The Rambam encourages a repentant to veer to the opposite extreme in order to fix himself. He gives the example of a greedy man who in order to repent should give lavishly to charity. When his weakness is under control, he can return to the golden middle path of balance.

The more I read, the more I feel the Rambam's treatise has been written especially for me, Reva Mann, atoning for a multitude of sins, yearning to change my past ways and live according to Jewish law. I learnt from Hilly that once I rid myself of my weaknesses, God will place me in a situation similar to one where I have sinned in the past. If I withstand the test and do not give way to temptation, I will have conquered my bad traits.

I have been celibate for nine months now and I am determined that the next time I engage in relations with a man it will be with my husband, God willing a Torah scholar, on my wedding night. But today, even though I try to concentrate on study, the pages blur in front of my eyes and memories force their way into my consciousness. My longing for a breath of freedom has brought Chris, my old London boyfriend, into the forefront of my mind and I can see his tall body with its elongated limbs and long, piano-playing fingers, hyacinth-blue eyes, thin rosy lips, cheeks unshaven with a week's worth of beard. His head is bare and he is wearing the fisherman's sweater bought on holiday in Ireland. He is carrying his pinhole camera, the one that filters light in through an angle to give a distorted effect. He used it often to photograph me in the nude so he could enlarge my breasts and buttocks and play with my shape.

I shake my head trying to rid myself of these images and bring myself back into the present. I look around at the other girls here, who all seem to be engrossed in their work. Our common desire for repentance binds us together even if we come from different walks of life and have little else in common. There is Dvorah, my study partner, christened Jane, born into a Welsh Catholic family. She has told me how she was drawn by the stories in the Old Testament, and claims to have heard Moses, Abraham and Isaac calling out to her. In the final stage of her conversion to Judaism, she immersed herself in the *mikveh* waters and surfaced reborn as a Jewess. Then she declared her Hebrew name as Dvorah after the prophetess. She is engaged to Yonatan, also a convert and follower of the Toldes Aaron Hassidic sect. Once she is married she will shave off her long blonde tresses, don a wig and on top of that a pillbox hat to ensure that the synthetic mop will not be mistaken for her own hair.

Even though I am on a similar quest, I am different from her and these other girls from secular families, who, travelling in the Middle East, found themselves at the Western Wall face to face with a yeshiva student offering them a free *Shabbat* meal or a lecture on 'Proofs of God', who got turned on to the buzz of love and esoteric teaching and ended up studying here. I am the daughter of an Orthodox rabbi, the granddaughter of a rabbi who was Chief Rabbi of Israel. This religious world is familiar to me. I already know that only an animal that chews the cud and has cloven hoofs is kosher and that's why pork is forbidden. I know Jews can only eat fish that have both fins and scales. I know how to read Hebrew and recite the prayers by heart. Yet I am also learning that there is far more to this world than I was aware of. I certainly never imagined the intensity of the spiritual pursuit of holiness or the extent to which keeping one's mind on the godly requires shunning modern thought and culture. I always thought that my father's approach of straddling both the secular and religious worlds and integrating contemporary concepts with ancient customs was the Jewish way. But here at the yeshiva this kind of synthesis is frowned upon, as the ultra-Orthodox believe any outside influences will contaminate their carefully circum-scribed and protected world.

Even though most of the girls studying here have a past, I would not want them to know about the memories of Chris that are flooding my mind. I have never told them that I had a non-Jewish boyfriend or that he was someone I met at the backstage bar of the Hammersmith Odeon when he was taking photos for *Melody Maker* magazine and I was tagging along with a groupie who had backstage passes. And I would certainly never let on that he picked me up that night and cut crystal lines of cocaine on a mirror and offered them to me and that I sniffed one up each nostril and pulled him off the bar stool and led him to the ladies' toilet where he entered me from behind. I shudder at the memory and breathe a sigh of relief that I have found this cocoon of purity in which to let go of the past.

My father often preached from his pulpit about the dangers of intermarriage. He used to say that it only takes a lover's tiff to provoke the words 'dirty Jew' to slip from a gentile lover's mouth. But I knew I could never marry a member of my father's community, an empty-headed London Jewish boy who worked in Daddy's business and blow-dried his hair. Chris was independent and deep thinking and I felt sure my parents would have liked him if only he'd been Jewish. But when they found out that I was seeing a gentile, they didn't issue any ultimatums or beg me to give Chris up. Instead they threw me out of the house and threatened to sit *shiva*, the seven-day mourning period for me, as if I had died. I had never believed they would cast me out, no matter how serious my transgression. But my father erected an icy impenetrable wall around himself the night he informed me that I had twenty-four hours to leave, to pack my possessions and never return. There was no way I could get through to him. I felt completely abandoned and feared that I really would be dead to my parents forever.

By that point my parents must have wanted nothing more than to be rid of me, for they had both had enough of the trials I had put them through: the sexual promiscuity, the trouble with the law, the drug abuse. They had suffered through the escapade when I turned canary yellow after contracting hepatitis B from having sex with a junkie who shot wine into his veins. They got me the medical help I needed, nursed me back to health for two months, then sent me off to a kibbutz in Israel to recuperate. Only months later, still in Israel, I had again called for their help, this time when my boyfriend Itai was arrested with ten kilos of hashish and put the rap on me because he was scared of army jail. My parents had helped me then too, arranging lawyers and money to pay the fines. But back in the UK, once I took up with Chris, I had crossed a line from where there seemed to be no way back. I had done the unspeakable. I was dating a *goy*. Only now that I realise the importance of building a Jewish home with Torah values do I understand why my relationship with Chris was so abhorrent to my father. But then, when I felt I had found my true love, I couldn't give him up.

That fateful night when Chris came to collect me and help me lug my bag of possessions down to his car, we bumped into my parents, who had fled the apartment to avoid being present at my departure. In his naivety, and against my advice, Chris tried to speak to my father.

'Could I just have a word, Sir?' he had innocently asked.

My father held his arm in front of his face to block out the sight of the non-Jew who loved his daughter, linked his arm in my mother's and quickened his pace. It was unthinkable for him to accept the idea of his daughter being with a non-Jew. In his mind Jews only married Jews.

I never thought I would marry Chris. I always knew deep down that there was something missing. Still, our first months of living together were blissful. He was the first real boyfriend I had ever had. Despite our sleazy first encounter in the harsh light of the backstage toilet, wastebasket spilling over with bloody tampons and sanitary napkins, toilet bowl streaked with excrement, a sordid ambience that only added to the urgency of our sex and heightened my excitement, our relationship went far deeper than the physical. I could talk to Chris and I felt he understood me. He was a friend and confidant. He didn't judge me for my past, but saw the good in me and wanted to help me develop. He educated me and introduced me to art and literature. With him I frequented the galleries and museums. Our favourites were the Photographers' Gallery in Soho and the Tate, where I fell in love with David Hockney's photographs and oils. I had never travelled far from my father's synagogue in central London and Chris took me to explore the English countryside at weekends. We would ramble along the downs and vales and then relax and eat a ploughman's lunch in a local pub. Chris taught me how to cook. We began with a simple dish of cauliflower cheese; even when I managed to burn the sauce, he didn't give up but continued with my culinary education until it stretched to roasts and apple pies. Chris was my saviour, my Christ, my Messiah. It was under his protective wing that I disentangled myself from recreational drugs and self-abuse. Sure, he would roll a joint sometimes or snort a line of coke, but only on occasion. He wasn't reliant on drugs for a good time.

It was to Chris that I admitted my innermost secret: I wanted to study midwifery. From the day I fully comprehended that the reason my sister Michelle was retarded was because of brain damage that had occurred at birth, I had wanted to become a midwife. Chris encouraged me to fulfil my dreams, for he seemed to understand how important it was to me to find some positive way of responding to what had happened to her during labour. He knew that I wanted to be present at the scene of birth – the very place where a lack of oxygen to the brain had left Michelle with epilepsy, slurred speech and a mind at the level of a child – because I felt that if I could help other babies be born healthy, I could somehow heal myself too. But Chris's sensitivity to me didn't extend towards my parents. He saw them as small and bigoted. Of course, I did too at the time. I was so in need of love and attention that I didn't consider how deeply Michelle's birth had affected them. Later, I would have enough perspective to be able to understand how it had turned the woman my father had fallen in love with – a university scholarship winner, a teacher of modern languages, a strong, innovative person – into the shaking jelly of a woman I knew as my mother, the woman who relied on uppers to get her through the day and downers to help her sleep at night. And gradually I would come to have compassion for my father too, his hypochondria, his anxiety, his constant need of my mother's attention. But growing up, all I knew was that my parents were so far off in their own world that they never seemed to have time for me.

At first, leading an independent life away from home was liberating. I no longer had to answer to my father or lie about my whereabouts. I could come and go as I pleased. I could walk naked in the flat, turn the volume up high on the stereo, cry, laugh, or scream, none of which was allowed in my father's house where I always had to behave with decorum and be presentable at all times to greet the constant stream of callers who came seeking his counsel. It was wonderful not to hear the constant cacophony of the doorbell and the telephone, not to dread the stress they triggered with every ring and the ceaseless interruptions to every conversation.

I loved my new freedom. Nevertheless, my precious time with Chris was clouded by the sadness of my excommunication from home. This played to all my deepest fears. Ever since I was a little girl and Michelle had been sent away I had feared a similar fate. Michelle had been my playmate and best friend and I was devastated when my parents placed her in a home for the handicapped miles outside London. But my mother had assured me that I would have a better life without a retarded sibling around. 'We are doing this for your own good, Reva,' she had said, a phrase that haunted me for years. And now I too had been sent away and my fears of being abandoned had materialised. I felt as if I had been cut off from my source. I was uprooted, floating in the universe without an anchor. I didn't belong anywhere. How would I manage without parental support? I woke up at night in a sweat. My immune system weakened. I had a constant runny nose, a recurring sense of dis-ease. A great emptiness ate at me, but I did not try to contact my parents. I knew I had embarrassed them in front of their community and caused them shame and I was sure they had cut me out of their hearts forever. My only connection to them was through Freda, a non-Jewish social worker, who advised my parents on matters to do with Michelle. Freda had become close to our family and she helped me find the flat in Battersea where Chris and I moved when the lease on his bed-sit ran out.

Chris's parents were kind and adopted me into their family but, despite their efforts, I felt like an outsider. When they sat at Sunday lunch and carved thin slices of roast beef, which they ate slowly in small portions with Yorkshire pudding, I thought longingly of the lavish *Shabbes* meals my mother used to make, the golden roast chickens and roast potatoes that we ate until we were so bloated that we couldn't move from the table. I couldn't contribute to Chris's mother's enthusiastic discussions about gardening, fertilising the strawberry patch and pruning the rose bushes. The only horticultural education I had had was listening to my mother order arrangements of flowers or reading the care instructions on the orchids she received from my father's congregants at New Year. When Chris's parents talked about the church sales and having tea with the vicar, it made me want to see my father dressed in the hexagonal velvet hat and clerical gown he wore to Friday night synagogue services, when he placed his hands on my head and, in the way of the Patriarchs, blessed me to be like Sarah, Rivka and Rachel. I missed the Jewish songs my father sang at the table and the operatic notes of *chazanut* that he practised in the bathtub. My soul was starving. Disconnected from my people and from the Torah that was ingrained in me, the very set of rules I had mocked and rejected, I was unhappy. The severed connection to my parents cast a melancholy shadow that never seemed to dissipate.

Even when Chris and I set up a business together, buying antique cameras and daguerreotypes at auction and selling them on Bell Street Market on Saturday mornings, I couldn't escape noticing my father's congregants, dressed in silken top hats and smart overcoats, striding down the adjacent Edgware Road on their way to Sabbath services at synagogue. Though I had always dreaded the synagogue services, hated the prissy outfits my mother made me wear and suffered having to be on my best behaviour to set an example, I longed for home. I wanted to shout out to the *Shabbes* walkers, 'Wait for me,' but then I would see myself, hot bacon and egg sandwich in hand, and realise just how far away from home I had strayed. I felt what so many Jews before me had felt: the loneliness of exile. But I had exiled myself. Now I am trying to return to the fold.

The independent study session is almost over. Girls are slowly packing up their books and putting them back on the shelves, but I stay seated, reviewing the past in my mind, thinking about how God works in mysterious ways. Now I realise that it could only have been God who put into effect the chain of events that eventually brought me here. My redemption came in the guise of an envelope that fell one morning onto the welcome mat of our Battersea flat. It was addressed to Rabbi Mendel Mann, my father. At first I just looked at it quizzically, not understanding where it had come from, but when I ripped it open to find a letter from the Halifax building society, I soon realised that the flat found for us by Freda was a flat that my father had bought, and that we were not paying rent but a mortgage. My father had not wiped me from his memory but had kept me in the forefront of his mind, worried about me and provided a roof over my head. Even though he hadn't contacted me directly, he was in constant touch through the financial transactions of paying for the flat. He knew where I was and cared that I was safe. I was delighted by this turn around and felt the sweetness of his love enveloping me. I had never felt happier than when I dashed into the bedroom waving the letter in the air.

'He's bought it!' I raved, and handed the letter to Chris.

It took a few moments for the news to sink in. At first Chris said nothing, then he screwed the letter up into a ball and threw it at me. 'I'm not staying. I'm not living in the house of someone who is too high and mighty to recognise my existence. I'm off. I'm history. Look at you, all happy now. How can you let him manipulate you like this, Reva? After all the months you've suffered.'

'He's my father and I love him.'

'Then, Reva, I think it's time you went home.'

It wasn't easy to break up with the man who had shared my bed and my life for a year. But Chris started packing immediately and soon made arrangements to leave. When I saw the back of his green bomber jacket and heard the door click shut, I felt completely alone. I had been living in a non-Jewish working-class neighbourhood on the unfashionable side of the river, far from the centre of London where my parents lived and where all my other friends lived, and the only thing that had kept me in Battersea was my connection to Chris. Nothing was happening for me there, and I knew I had to leave.

However, even if I could have renewed my relations with my family right then, I also knew I could not go back to live with them. I didn't want to be bound by the religious prohibitions of my father's household. I didn't want to return to the place where my parents' constant premonitions of disaster cast a permanent pall over everything. Having no idea of what to do or where to go, I cried out for help, weeping and wailing with grief. Even though I was a rabbi's daughter, I had never thought much about God. The question of whether He existed or not didn't play much of a part in my life. And yet I had experienced Him through my grandfather, Chief Rabbi of Israel, who prayed stooped over with humility and in genuine communication with God, the sound of his prayers filling the room and swathing me in comfort on our annual family visits to Jerusalem.

It was here during *Chanukah* that I remember feeling the presence of God for the first time. I was sixteen years old and Grandpa was lighting the giant menorah at the Western Wall and reciting the blessing over the candles to an audience of hundreds. I was on the women's side of the partition and I pushed my way through the crowd, excusing myself by saying, 'It's my grandpa, let me through.' When I got to the front, I saw him standing on a podium, listening as the congregation answered 'Amen' to his blessing. I caught his eye and he smiled at me radiantly, exuding love and light.

That day in Battersea, I believe Grandpa was pulling strings for me in heaven. He opened the way for me to call upon my creator. God must have answered me, for it was then that I made the decision to ask my parents to help me go to Israel to study midwifery.

Seeing my parents again after a year of separation was not easy. The silence we had maintained ever since I had left with Chris served as a barometer of just how difficult relations between us had been. Returning to their flat caused me to revisit the deep loneliness I had always felt there, the feeling that they had always been too busy, too preoccupied with their own concerns, to give me the love and attention I longed for. When I lived with my parents I felt as though I had fallen between the cracks of their private and their communal lives. But the visit turned out well. Once I broached the subject of moving to Israel, my parents were delighted and gave me both their financial support and their blessing. They were glad to give me a fresh start in a place where it was unlikely I would meet a non-Jewish man and they were relieved I finally had direction. I imagine they welcomed the opportunity to put some distance between us, too.

Because of the many visits I had made to Israel when my grandfather was still alive, Israel has always been my second home. Grandpa lived in Jerusalem opposite the Great Synagogue and Hechal Shlomo, on a tree-lined street in the Rechavia neighbourhood inhabited mainly by *Yekim*, German refugees. He loved Israel and instilled that love in me. I feel at home here as I do nowhere else.

Even when I wasn't religious I always felt that Israel was where I was meant to be. Being there is so different from being in England, where living as a member of a minority group meant that we conformed to the customs of those around us, regardless of whether they conflicted with our own way of doing things. Thus, my father would remove his hat upon entering my school for parents' day, despite the fact that a Jewish man is supposed to keep his head covered at all times. In Israel the social norms are ours. I love it that in Jerusalem the taxi drivers wish me a *Shabbat Shalom* as they drop me off on a Friday afternoon, and men walk down the street wearing a *tallis* prayer shawl on their way to *shul*, and I can pop into any neighbourhood store to buy the *challah* bread and flowers I need for the *Shabbat*.

Chris is still in my mind and I put down the holy book. I need to take a break and get out of here. Maybe I am experiencing a fall from grace. Rabbi Rabinowitz, the dean of the seminary, had warned me this might happen. 'The nature of God awareness is that you can't keep it with you for long. It comes and it goes. You get a glimpse and then a fog covers up the light and you need to work hard until you see it again. That's the real test, to worship God even when you can't feel His presence, when you're sunk in darkness.' Those were his very words.

Lately lethargy is setting up residence inside me and I need to fight myself in order to perform the *mitzvot*. Today, in the bright sunlight, with the outdoors beckoning, the sheer ugliness of my surroundings makes me feel nauseous. The floors need sweeping. The rickety desks are falling apart. Cobwebs hang from the ceiling. Even Mrs Hillman's jumble of mismatched clothes, which I usually find endearing, disgusts me. My mind is turning against me and instead of absorbing the material on how to truly repent, knowledge that I have been thirsty for in order to mend my ways, I can only think about sex and drugs. I know where to get shit, even here in Israel. I won't do anything about this urge, but nevertheless I need something.

The nagging ring of the students' pay phone out in the corridor interrupts my troubled thoughts. Dvorah, my study partner, goes to answer it.

'Reva!' she is shouting from the hall. 'Telephone.'

Who can be calling me? I think, as I heave my heavy body towards the door.

'Hello?'

'Reva? Is that you? I've finally tracked you down. Wasn't easy. Freda had your number. It's Chris. Don't tell me you've forgotten the sound of my voice?'

'Chris!'

'Hello, luv. Guess what, the paper sent me over to cover the Sinead O'Connor concert. Bloody hot here, I must say. Surprised?'

How could this be? I cover the receiver with my hand,

hoping no one can hear the conversation, and whisper, 'Chris, I can't believe it.'

'Feels like yesterday, doesn't it? You sound exactly the same. When can I see you? Brought some good dope; hid it in my toothpaste. They've put me up at the King David Hotel. Come on over for old times' sake.'

I am aware of the element of divine intervention working in the cosmos and I know that God is putting me under the Rambam's repentance test, but all I can think about is how good a hit of weed would feel right now, and how great Chris's lean body would feel against mine.

'Things have changed.'

'New bloke?'

'No. Nothing like that. I'm in a yeshiva, a seminary for girls. I'm studying the Torah and . . .'

'You're kidding, right?'

'Chris.'

'Do tell me you're kidding.' Chris bursts into laughter. 'Daddy's girl is it then?'

'No. It's . . .'

'Whatever happened to midwifery then?'

'It's a long story.'

'Come on over, darling. Just a cup of coffee and you'll tell me all about it?'

Before I can reply, the sound of 'Oy yoi yoi yoi' drifts out of the lounge, a large room at the end of the corridor where we hang out in between classes. Girls are stampeding past me. Another lucky girl has announced her engagement. I imagine the plates of sticky cakes ready to be gorged on, which will surely add another roll of fat around my midriff. I think about us girls dancing around in a circle once again, celebrating the bride-to-be. I can see Dvorah slipping the elastic of her waistband down and belly dancing for the bride. I can hear the blessings the fortunate girl will bestow upon us single and lonely girls and I know I can't take it any more.

'Give me an hour,' I say.

'That's my girl. Room 613.'

I hang up the receiver and look down the corridor. Hilly is standing by the lounge door, beckoning the girls to come inside. Her cheeks flush with joy as she calls, '*A callah, a callah. A bride, a bride!* Come on, everybody – *Mazeltov! Mazeltov!*' I slink past her, through the door, hoping she is not using her spiritual powers to read my mind.

Bella is sitting serenely, like a queen, on a Formica chair draped with flimsy white fabric, a cheery girl who doesn't seem to struggle with her new life and has glided into the Orthodox world with grace. Buxom girls lift her into the air and sing their congratulations as they bounce her up and down. I think about Chris and how I have agreed to meet him, but what I really want is to be the one sitting in the bridal chair having found my soul-mate, building a house of Israel.

Questions about the groom shoot out from every corner. 'Where is he from?'

Bella beams, her lips curl up at the corners as she answers. 'Scarsdale, New York.'

'What does he look like?'

'Tall, dark, and handsome.'

'Does he have a profession?'

'He studies full time,' Bella says smugly, for she has hooked a winner.

All fall silent to hear the answer to the most important question of all. 'Where does he study?' We need the name of his yeshiva to ascertain the extent of his sanctity.

The blushing bride proudly announces, 'The Mir Yeshiva.'

A respectful silence ensues as we nod to each other in awe and grunt approvingly, 'The Mir Yeshiva – top of the line!'

I know that catching a Mir Yeshiva student is a prize. That school is the Ivy League of the Orthodox world. My father was a student at the original Mir Yeshiva, in Poland, and I have heard the stories of his student days: the dire poverty, the housekeeper who swung a chicken through a pot of boiling water and called it soup, the mud and the cold. Despite all this the students studied with fervour into the early hours of the morning. In Jerusalem, the Mir Yeshiva prides itself on students from good families. These boys, who can be recognised by a pearl pinned on the side of their fedora hats, are considered the best possible catch. The snobbism goes even further, but fortunately these girls don't know enough to ask whether Bella's groom learns upstairs at the Mir or downstairs, which would draw still finer distinctions among the students, dividing them into the elite and the mere hangers-on.

The celebrations are over and it is time for me to leave. I pass Hilly on my way out and hope she thinks I am going downstairs to the dining room for lunch. As I walk away from the girls' lounge, the song and chatter still streaming through the corridor, the heat of the summer day reaching its climax, I cross the vestibule towards the exit, excited at the prospect of reunion with my old love.

2

The Test

And God tested Abraham saying: 'Take your son,
your only one, the one you love, Isaac, to the
land of Moriah for a burnt offering.'

Genesis 22:1

Only a step away from the exit, I hear Rabbi Rabinowitz call
my name. 'Reva, can you give me a minute?' he asks. 'I want
to talk to you.'

I nod yes and he returns to his study with another student.
What bad luck. This is not a good time. I want to be out of
here and on my way to the hotel. I stand and wait. I can
already feel the craving for a joint and don't want to delay, but
there is no way I can refuse the rabbi's request. What can he
want? I think, worried that he may have heard about me and
Sally-Anne, an American girl from Arizona. Sally-Anne is
different from the other girls here. Even though she is covered
up like they are, she has a wildness about her. Black curly hair
escapes the confines of the barrettes she uses to clip it back.
Her eyes flicker with the fire of Torah and her full lips and
Cupid's bow entice me. When I am with her I feel intoxicated.
It is not only her zany energy, but her clear vision of the divine
that can whisk me off into a frenzy of spiritual enlightenment.
She lifts the thick veil of the physical and lets me peep at the
glory of God's holy throne, from where He sustains the world,

orchestrates the heavens and the earth and the cycle of nature. Sometimes I find this information overwhelming and hard to contain.

One night in her room we read together from the Code of Jewish law and learnt that from the moment we wake up, every detail of our day is accounted for. We are commanded to arise like a lion and wash our hands, then to adhere to the laws throughout the day, while cooking, eating, praying, until we lie down and say the nightly prayers calling the angels to protect us. I had such fear of God then, realising how mighty He is, that I began to tremble. Sally-Anne took me in her arms to soothe me. I must admit I took comfort there. It seemed only natural then to touch and caress her breasts, lick those rosy nipples that stood erect inside the white cotton of her shirt and kiss her puckered lips, which had only minutes before been spouting holy wisdom. I took the dominant role, relishing the opportunity to experience and enjoy a woman the way a man does, and slipped my finger inside her until her pleasure could be heard on the other side of the thin dormitory wall. When Sally-Anne tried to reciprocate, I pushed her hand away, knowing that it could not compensate me for the hard penetration I craved. I never felt that our love was sinful. There is nowhere in the Torah that condemns relations between women, unlike homosexual relations, which are considered an abomination. But the zealous girl who lives next door and is stricter in her views than the Torah overheard our lovemaking from the other side of the dormitory wall and threatened to tell the rabbis. The fear of being blacklisted from the dating scene put an abrupt end to our affair. We are both afraid of being ostracised by the community, of never finding a match in this

Orthodox society. A rumour about our dual sexual orientation could ruin our lives here forever, nullifying all the spiritual work we have done by performing *mitzvot* and the emotional work that has led us towards our goal of building a Jewish home. So, since then we have plunged into our prayer and study with even more zest.

I am trying to keep to the decision Sally-Anne and I made to improve our religious practice, but she is becoming excessive in her worship. Only last night she refused to let me pour wine into her glass since she feared my observance of the *Shabbes* laws was lax. I know a non-Jew is not allowed to pour wine for a Jew, but I am a Jewess, a rabbi's daughter, and was hurt to be equated with a *goy*. Here at the yeshiva, many girls are inflicted with the Jerusalem syndrome. Whether they contract the messianic fever once they get here or were crazy to begin with, I don't know, but many suffer from delusions of being as holy as the Matriarchs. They amuse me, as they seem committed not only to the religious aspects of a Jewish lifestyle but to many of its cultural idiosyncrasies as well, like the wearing of two pairs of stockings. This custom had its origins in the need to bundle up against the freezing Eastern European winters and it has been passed down from generation to generation, from Hassidic women in Poland and Russia to their daughters here in Israel despite the tropical weather in this part of the world. Even though I think these girls must be crazy, I understand them. They just want God. I too want to be holy, but my religious upbringing keeps me saner than most, as I can differentiate better between Jewish law and the perversion of that law when taken to extremes.

Outside Rabbi Rabinowitz's study, other rabbis, teachers

here at the seminary, are buzzing around. They glance at my long hennaed hair, which falls over my shoulders, and then quickly look away, keeping their eyes on the ground and on each other. They wear white shirts and black suits. Ritual fringes hang like tassels from their belts and shake over the gabardine of their trousers as they move. Most have long beards; all have black velvet skullcaps slipped to the back of their heads visible below the brims of their black borsalinos.

Girls are milling around, chatting to one another. They are dressed modestly in long skirts and shirts that button up under the chin. Yet despite their dull clothes, their expressions are cheery and they are laughing. I am glad there is no sign of Sally-Anne but I am wondering what the rabbi knows. I feel deeply ashamed at the thought of his asking about our relationship and fear he may ask me to leave the yeshiva. I cannot bear the horror of this thought, even though today I need a break.

The tension is mounting inside me and I want to flee, but my feet, firmly laced up in sturdy brown leather shoes, are rooted to the shabby linoleum floor and I wait for Rabbi Rabinowitz to call me into his study.

Rabbi Rabinowitz and a twenty-something girl are saying their goodbyes. She bows as she takes her leave of him. She doesn't shake his hand or touch him because this, of course, is forbidden. She has remembered something, a last detail. He leans towards her to listen. She looks sad. I think she is crying. Rabbi Rabinowitz doesn't put his arm reassuringly around her, but he is comforting her. He tells me with his dark brown eyes that he will just be another moment. I nod. I understand that he is a busy man and there are other girls, just like me, who are also in a state of confusion and have a fury of emotions churning inside them, girls who are repenting their past and trying to start over by only eating kosher foods, keeping the Sabbath day, and living according to the Torah law. Unlike them I have not sought the rabbi's advice. I am taking matters into my own hands.

While I stand and wait, I think back to the first classes I took here with Dina, an old school friend from London, whom I looked up when I came to Israel after breaking up with Chris. Since I didn't have the necessary requirements for nursing school, my A level results being only mediocre, I had been studying at the Israel Childbirth Association, doing course-work that would qualify me to work as a *doula*, a breastfeed-ing counsellor and a childbirth education instructor. It wasn't midwifery, but it answered my need to help labouring mothers and aid in births. Dina lured me away from a key lesson on cervical dilation to a class with Rabbi Rabinowitz. This was my first real encounter with the depth of Torah. My father had tried to teach me, of course, but his lessons always ended up in prohibitions. He'd tell me we were forbidden to turn on the lights or tear the toilet paper on the *Shabbat* but he'd never explain why. Rabbi Rabinowitz clarified everything. As God rested on the seventh day and ceased to create, he said, we must emulate Him and rest from creating on the Sabbath. He explained that switching on the light is a 'creation' as it generates an electrical current and tearing paper creates two separate halves. But what really impressed me was the idea that the performance of even the smallest *mitzva* affects the upper spheres and creates angels to protect us. This made me consider that I might have control over my destiny. Until I came here, I always thought that the Eastern religions had a monopoly on spirituality, that the barefooted, orange-robed Hare Krishna disciples who sold copies of the *Bhagavad Gita* on Oxford Street understood the depths of mysticism, as did the many Jewish kids I knew who travelled east to find God. Once I heard the rabbi speak, I understood that those kids were on the wrong track, that the key to enlightenment is in our very own Torah and that spirituality is in our backyard. All we need to do is cultivate it, pull out the weeds and fertilise the soil. But I cannot connect to all that now. Paradise for me at this very moment would be hanging out and relaxing with Chris.

The girl is walking away from the office, dabbing her eyes with a tissue. Rabbi Rabinowitz is beckoning me to come forward. He is showing me to a chair in his office and asking me to sit down. I sit, careful to pull my skirt as far down as possible and cross my legs at the ankles. I look around the room. The walls are lined with bookshelves. There are photographs and drawings of famous rabbis framed on the wall above Rabbi Rabinowitz's desk. I recognise the Rambam by his turban, the Chofetz Chaim by the sadness in his eyes, and next to him my darling grandfather, Rabbi Yechezkiel Mann. The photo is black and white, but I remember the soft blue of those eyes that used to smile at me and wink whenever I would break the laws of decorum and rush up to his frail body, take his long white beard, the texture of candy floss, into my innocent hands and kiss it incessantly. My father would try to pry me away, apologising for my emotional outburst, but Grandpa soaked up my love and returned it with a full-heartedness that I never felt from my parents. On family reunions, we cousins lined up to be tested on our Torah proficiency. My father was the only one of his brothers to live outside Israel and so my cousins were much more fluent in Hebrew than me. But even though my Torah reading wasn't up to standard, Grandpa would stuff a lira note or a costume jewellery brooch into my hand under the table, reassuring me that my lack of knowledge would not deprive me of his love.

I look at Rabbi Rabinowitz sitting across from me at his desk. He's a big man with a sturdy chest. The top button of his shirt is undone and I can see the milk white of his skin, which looks as if it has never been exposed to the sun. A corner of the ritual fringes he wears under his shirt is also visible. I feel like a voyeur staring at this patch of nakedness. I can see the innocence of him. His hands lie on the book in front of him. They are smooth, hairless. A lock of brown hair is falling over his face and he sweeps it off his forehead. He is leaning back in his chair and tapping his box of Marlboros. I know he wants to light up. I want to too, but it would be inappropriate for him to smoke here with me, for that would create a situation invested with intimacy. I know he has seven children and a devoted wife, but I can still see the boy in him, with short trousers and scabbed knees, and imagine him as a teenager in London, playing truant from yeshiva, smoking cigarettes in secret, leaning up against the grimy wall of the Stamford Hill tube station, pulling his black hat down over his brow, sure no one is looking and eyeing up the *shiksa* girls with their fair skin and upturned noses.

'So how's it going?' Rabbi Rabinowitz asks. He hasn't lost his British accent. It makes me feel at home.

'Fine . . . good,' I answer, and then I add, 'Well actually, I'm having a tough time lately.' I am relieved he isn't mentioning Sally-Anne.

'You need to immerse yourself here, not only in the study but in the lifestyle. It's hard work to make changes, to give up the life you are used to. What you need is to get to know a family, see how they live, get close to them. I'll make the arrangement for this Friday night meal . . . the Rapaports would be a good place to start.'

'OK,' I say, though until now I have felt uncomfortable about attending a meal at a stranger's home and never wanted to go.

'How are your parents dealing with the fact that you've left your childbirth studies?'

'They don't like it. I've given them the run around, rebelling and everything, and just when they were finally proud that I had got myself together enough to be studying for a career, I came here instead.'

'Yes, I've heard about your rebellious days. Quite a name you got for yourself in London.' There is a mischievous lilt to his tone.

I can feel my cheeks flushing scarlet, embarrassed that he may have heard my nickname 'Randy Reva the rabbi's daughter' or the phrase often used behind my back, 'She was only the rabbi's daughter, but she knew how to bench in the park,' a *double entendre* since bench is the Yiddish word for reciting the grace after meals.

'Actually, I mentioned you to Jeffery Rose. He was my study partner in yeshiva.'

'Oh no!' I cannot believe the rabbi has spoken to my old headmaster from Sinai College, the Jewish boarding school in the English countryside that my parents had packed me off to once they heard that the guitar teacher at my posh ladies' college had got my friend Mandy pregnant. At the end of the third term, I had been politely but firmly asked to leave the boarding school because I was, in Rabbi Rose's words, 'a vamp'. I had to complete my matriculation exams at night school in London.

'Rose wasn't in the least surprised that you were here. Don't worry. We've all done things we're ashamed of,' Rabbi Rabinowitz says. I sense he is enjoying my humiliation. 'I was a bit of a rebel myself, you know,' he admits. 'Drove the Gateshead Rosh Yeshiva crazy with my pranks.' He grins a cheeky grin.

He's sexy, I think, and look away. Now that he has stripped me bare of any dignity through his knowledge of my past, I feel close to him. I don't want to imagine wrapping the tassels of his fringes around my finger and then running that same finger under his shirt and over his white skin. But these images have entered my head and I cannot get rid of them. I fidget in my chair, uncomfortable now, ashamed of how easily my mind strays to the forbidden.

'I'll have a word with your parents if you like. Our fathers were colleagues in London before the war. Your father will listen to me. I'll tell him you're just putting your studies on hold. The college will still be there next year and the year after, but this fire that is burning inside of you may not last.'

I wish there was a fire, but today there are no flames, just a few coals smouldering almost extinguished.

'Have you thought about seeing the matchmaker yet?'

Of course I've thought a lot about embarking on the

deepest desire of all the girls here, to get married and build a Jewish home and teach the Torah to the next generation. But I know it is too early. I need to make sure I can fully make the commitment. 'I need more time,' I say sincerely. 'I don't think I'm ready yet.'

'Well, keep me posted, Reva.' The rabbi gets up from his chair and leads the way. 'I think it's time for lunch.'

I steal out of the yeshiva just as I used to creep out of my father's house, lying about where I was going, changing clothes on the stairs of the synagogue building from prim dresses and ballerina flats to mini skirts and long boots, holding a compact mirror in the semi-darkness and making up my face, lining my eyes in kohl and painting my lips burgundy, getting ready for a wild night out. I feel the same knot of guilt as I did then lying in my stomach like a heavy meal; the only difference is that now I know God is watching.

On the bus there is an unspoken modesty code. Men head for the back and women sit up front. Most passengers are reciting psalms from pocket-sized books. They hardly take their eyes off the page and mouth the words, silently bowing back and forth in their seats.

My heart is beating fast and my palms are sweating as I sit next to a pious matron with a bouffant wig. This is the first time in months I will be leaving the safe haven of the very religious Bayit Vegan neighbourhood and I feel a rush of excitement as if I'm going on a trip to a foreign land and not to downtown Jerusalem, a mere half an hour away. I look down at my dowdy skirt and suddenly feel ashamed of my appearance, the extra ten pounds around my middle, and the transformation into a plain girl. Chris is going to have a shock when he sees me, I think, suddenly longing for my old self with the svelte curves and the sexy clothes. I'll just have a few drags of a joint, I tell myself, take a break for an hour and return to the yeshiva invigorated. But I am well aware that the *yetzer hora*, the evil inclination, has got hold of me and that the devil is at work here. I cannot fight back; my need for immediate gratification is too strong.

As the bus travels through Bayit Vegan with its uniform blocks of flats and modestly dressed inhabitants walking along neglected streets, I watch young girls pushing even younger siblings in carriages, young boys holding their father's hand on the way to synagogue services. We ride down Herzl Boulevard. Yad Vashem, the Holocaust memorial, is up on our left but we veer right towards the city centre. Now that we are out of ultra-Orthodox territory, I relax. The scene has changed. There is more greenery, well-tended parks, gardens, planters filled with blossoming flowers hung over balconies. Clusters of teenagers hang out smoking cigarettes, the boys bareheaded, their arms draped lazily around the shoulders of girls dressed for summer in skimpy shorts and tank tops. I am amazed at the amount of skin they expose and the way they flaunt their bodies. Only six months have passed since I wore the same garb, but I have become sensitised to the sight of bare skin, which in the world that I inhabit is always hidden from view.

We pass close to Beit Hakerem and the Israel Childbirth Association premises where I took classes in anatomy, fertility and breastfeeding counselling. Most of all I enjoyed the hands-on work in weekly visits to the labour room, where we helped decide upon the position that would best ease a labouring mother's pain or the herbs that should be used to stimulate contractions. The bus has stopped at traffic lights and I watch students breeze in and out of the gates past security. I stare up at the high-rise building and think back to my second term there, when Dina had introduced me to the yeshiva. She had made *Aliya* two years earlier and by then was heavily into her repentance. She raved about Rabbi Rabinowitz and told me how she had met him on an El Al flight. When his glatt kosher lunch was served, she asked him why the regular lunch wasn't kosher enough. He explained that he was extra strict with the laws of *kashrut* as he wants to protect the Torah by building a fence around it, the same way one would install a security system to guard a precious jewel. At an altitude of 20,000 feet, she fell for him, scrapped her plans to volunteer on a kibbutz and followed him to Jerusalem. 'He's so handsome and so cool,' she enthused, her blonde curls falling about her face, her blue eyes wide open. 'Try a Torah class with Rabbi Rabinowitz. He talks about different spheres and creation. I know you'll love it.'

And finally, I gave in. My friendship with Dina went back years, to school days in London. My father hadn't sent me to a Jewish school but to a posh ladies' college in Harley Street with creamy white pillars in front and an abortion clinic next door. There, Dina and I were among a small group of Jewish girls dressed from head to toe in Cacharel who found a haven in a liberal school without a Jewish quota. My father wasn't concerned that there were no Torah studies or that I would mix with gentiles there. He believed I would receive an adequate Jewish education at home. The rabbis at the yeshiva were surprised to hear of his choice of schooling for me. They didn't realise how easily my father bridged the religious and secular spheres, how even though he was a Torah scholar and son of a great rabbi, he didn't shun the world at large. He wasn't threatened by the theatre and the cinema or by the ways of the gentiles. Science and medicine fascinated him. He read philosophy and psychology and used ideas from these intellectual forays to pepper his sermons. His love of Torah was strong and nothing could influence him away from his daily prayers or performance of the commandments, but ladylike manners and proper articulation were also important to him and he enjoyed hearing me recite poetry in the Queen's English I learned in elocution lessons.

So, every morning I walked the ten blocks from my father's house with its strict adherence to Jewish law to the foreign world of school where many of the girls were daughters of diplomats from India and Greece, daughters of Members of Parliament, society girls, and the honourable so-and-so's. There I was an outsider. Unable to eat the delicious smelling lamb in mint sauce they served in the dining room, I ate smoked salmon sandwiches made by my mother. I was not allowed to perform in a recital of experimental opera at the BBC studios with the rock star Kevin Ayres as it was scheduled for a *Shabbes* afternoon. Surrounded by daughters of lawyers and surgeons and diplomats, I dreaded the question 'What does your father do?' When asked, I stuttered that my father was a member of the clergy, the most shameful profession I could imagine, and I went out of my way to dispel any connection to that identity. It was the unbearable expectation of others, people looking at me as if I were supposed to be some kind of an angel, that made me ashamed to be a rabbi's daughter. I didn't want that. I wanted to blend in with the other girls, those whose fathers played golf on Sundays and took their kids for a drive in the country. But the only place my parents had taken me on a Sunday was down to Berkshire to visit Michelle in her new home for the handicapped. Those visits were hard, for even though my sister looked normal to me despite her spastic arm and the strange noises she made, her new friends, kids with all kinds of deficiencies and deformities, terrified me and filled me with anxiety.

Perhaps it was because I had so little chance of blending in at school that I chose for my bosom friend a Hindu girl, Amita, who was also bound to a life of rituals different from everybody else's. I was attracted to her graceful manner and generous spirit and I loved the after-school visits to her flat with its curry smell and the beautiful saris her mother let us try on. Amita's family gave me my first taste of India. But unlike Amita, who respected her heritage, I was always rebelling against mine. I began by succumbing to the temptation one lunch break of eating a pork sausage, which I considered the ultimate in forbidden. I was testing God. Seeing that His wrath was not unleashed, thunder didn't roll in the heavens and God did not strike me down, I confidently ventured further into the illicit.

Soon, Dina and I were playing truant from Jewish prayers. Instead of going to the small gathering upstairs in the Floyd Room, we walked arm in arm up the regal staircase, past the oil paintings to the main Hall, where we attended Christian prayers and sang to sweet baby Jesus, crossing ourselves and singing hymns with devotion. As we recited the Lord's Prayer and stood in respect with eyes closed, I felt I was finally communing with God, who was inaccessible to me at my father's synagogue.

When I came to Israel, I was curious as to how Dina had made such a drastic life change. She didn't come from a religious family and had never shown any interest in spirituality. But she had been heavily influenced by Rabbi Rabinowitz and it didn't take long for me to understand why. In that first Torah class Dina took me to, Rabbi Rabinowitz spoke about the sanctity of marriage, using the numerology of the holy tongue and showing the power of each individual letter. He told us that words for both man (*iysh*) and woman (*ishah*) have a letter of God's name in them. If that letter, the y (*yud*) or h (*heh*) respectively, were taken away, the word that would be left, bereft of a y or h, would be the Hebrew word for fire. So, he explained, if a man and a woman don't keep to a Jewish marriage according to the law, they will be consumed by the fires of lust, jealousy and greed. But if they do keep to the law, they will bring God into their lives and their union will be blessed.

It was not only the way Rabbi Rabinowitz delved into the esoteric that hooked me immediately, but the atmosphere of sanctity in the yeshiva. As I sat there in class, all the puzzle pieces of my life, my upbringing, the Torah I had heard at home and from my grandfather, seemed finally to fall into place. It was such a relief to discover that this was my world and I belonged. I continued studying Torah that summer and then stopped when my childbirth classes resumed in the fall. Once back at the Childbirth Association, however, I found my head wasn't there at all. I had tasted the delicacy of the Eden of Torah study and I wanted more; I wanted to immerse myself in it totally.

But now, as I look out of the bus window and watch the

childbirth students milling around, I envy them suddenly, wondering if I have made an irresponsible move by putting my career on hold. I feel stupid for having left my studies. Surely it is doing God's work to help bring forth life, I think. Instead I am focusing on toilet paper and the rabbinic debate about whether one should prepare cut toilet paper squares before the Sabbath or if it is permissible to tear the tissue on the perforated lines.

Yet I cannot turn my back on the moment when I caught my first glimpse of God Himself. I will never forget the events of that day, which happened only a month after Dina took me to Rabbi Rabinowitz's class, thirty days after I decided to start reciting the blessings before eating and lighting *Shabbes* candles again. I'm not sure what made me perform these *mitzvot*. It was a combination of the taste of sanctity the rabbi imparted to me and the connection I have always felt to the Jewish homeland. Just being on holy ground made me conscious of the Lord above. My prayers must have had an effect. Like a chain reaction they put into motion a supernatural force that caused a revelation. I was sitting in the college cafeteria at the Childbirth Association, in a dimly lit, open-plan foyer, munching on a chocolate snack, when I looked up and saw fairy lights strung across the ceiling. I felt as if I were transported back to the London Planetarium, gazing up at a star show of distant realms of time and space. The glowing specks looked like a child's puzzle of join-the-dots, forming all kinds of different shapes. They were so beautiful, so bright. I have never seen anything shine like that before. All the lights came from a single central source above, a blazing nucleus. At first I was frightened. Maybe I was hallucinating, having a flashback after all the hits of acid I'd taken in the past. But this was no drug-induced vision. I knew I wasn't delirious. I was perfectly aware of my peers drinking coffee at the next table and I could see students walking from class to class. It was obvious to me that God was speaking only and directly to me. He was showing me a diagram of how everything in creation emanates from Him. When I realised the enormity of this phenomenon I felt giddy, like the children of Israel did at Sinai when their senses became mixed up and they 'saw' the voice of God. Like them, I felt I was going to faint, as it was impossible for my mortal mind to contain a revelation of this magnitude. It wasn't as spectacular as the Red Sea parting and manna falling from heaven, miracles which the Israelites merited by the very act of leaving the spiritually impure land of Egypt, but it was a genuine experience of the transcendental presence of God that I believe was a direct result of performing the mitzvot of lighting *Shabbes* candles and reciting the blessings before eating.

The cafeteria was reeling. I heard an incredible silence. My body turned cold. I clung onto the table in front of me for support. I knew I had to act immediately and there was no time to waste. A surge of energy propelled me to walk towards a payphone. There was only one person I could turn to who would understand. I called the Light of Zion and asked for Rabbi Rabinowitz. It took time for the secretary at the yeshiva to find him and I remember trembling in awe of God as I waited for him to come to the phone, knowing I was on the brink of something new, on the cusp of enlightenment. It seemed unbelievable: me, Reva, the unbeliever, the sceptic, seeing God. I wept when I heard Rabbi Rabinowitz's voice on the other end of the receiver, for I knew I was finally on my way home.

Rabbi Rabinowitz listened to my incoherent babble. His voice stayed calm as he explained, 'You had a moment of clarity. You're very lucky, Reva. Some people walk around blind their whole life. Now you need to decide what to do with that knowledge. You can come and study here full time, take a year off and really devote yourself to a new path. But if you don't, the vision you have seen will wane and pale and will soon get covered up with doubt and fog and you will have missed your opportunity.' I didn't hesitate. I walked out of the Childbirth Association and immediately took a cab to the yeshiva. I never wanted to lose the clarity I felt that day. It was the highest I had ever been, a state of ecstasy far superior to the effects of any drug I had ever taken.

Ecstasy doesn't last forever, but it is a state that I always crave. Unable to obtain it now from prayer and Torah study, as I feel God has hidden His light from me, I am hoping that I will find it in room 613 at the King David Hotel. But deep inside I know I am running away again.

By the time the bus stops outside the hotel and I step down into the sunshine, I am in a state of confusion. I stand outside the large boulders of white Jerusalem stone, debating whether or not to enter. I spin through the revolving doors into the lobby and am taken aback by the opulence and splendour. The lounge is large and spacious. The domed ceilings are hand painted in blue and gold with geometrical Eastern designs. Velvet and brocade upholstered couches and armchairs are set together to make intimate conversation corners. I step onto the thick blue carpet. Above me a crystal chandelier gives off subdued light. American tourists stand by the reception desk wearing the latest Paris fashions. Their Louis Vuitton luggage is piled on trolleys. I look ahead to the far end of the lounge. Through the large windows I can see the ancient walls of the Old City. Chris is not here. He must be waiting for me in the room.

At the far corner of the lobby, I notice the *shidduch* dates. It is easy to spot them, yeshiva girls and guys sitting on plush velvet armchairs across from each other. The girls are decked out in their Sunday best, legs crossed and lips glossed. The men in their black suits and black hats are twiddling their beards, rocking back and forth as they speak. I know this rocking habit originated in the Ukraine, when times were hard and many students shared a single book; that they had to alternate with some of them rocking forward and others back in order to give each other turns to read and memorise the page.

I stand and stare. This is what I really want, I tell myself – to meet a yeshiva student with a view to marriage and building a Jewish home. I look on at how they talk and smile, how shy the girls are, how sensitive the boys and how pure their purpose. I know I cannot go upstairs now. I cannot ruin everything I have worked for. God is surely helping me pass His test by orchestrating this idyllic scene. I stand for a moment and let this realisation sink in. I take a deep breath. I can let go of this need to see Chris and smoke a joint. I can leave now. I turn on my heel, step back into the revolving door and leave the hotel. Outside in the scorching day, I breathe a sigh of relief. I have passed the repentance test. I am ready to take another step up on the spiritual ladder towards holiness.

3

Back on Track

Yerida l'Zorech Aliya – *falling from a spiritual height is necessary to enable an even higher ascent.*

Rabbi Nachman of Breslov

It is six o'clock, the following Friday evening, and I am on my way to the Rapaports' home, just across the road from the yeshiva. I climb the slummy steps of the neglected building in Uziel Street, walk past the heap of strollers piled under the stairwell, through the litter strewn in the lobby, and knock on Shlomo and Chani Rapaport's front door. I am wearing my *Shabbes* clothes, a long skirt and knit top, and carrying a bottle of grape juice. Usually I feel embarrassed joining strangers for dinner but tonight, since Rabbi Rabinowitz has made the arrangements and I didn't have to sign up on the hospitality list to be placed for a *Shabbes* meal, I feel more comfortable. This is an opportunity to strengthen my commitment to the path I have chosen. It is in the interests of the religious families to open their homes and help us girls keep the Torah laws as we Jews are all part of one soul body joined together in the collective destiny of bringing the Messiah and rebuilding the third temple.

A five-year-old child answers the door. Long dark sidelocks fall down his cheeks. A blue velvet *kippa* with two cherries embroidered on the side is clipped to the bristles on his head.

His white *Shabbes* shirt is hanging out of dark trousers. Large black eyes stare at me.

'Hello, I'm Reva,' I say. 'your *Shabbes* guest.'

The child runs back into the apartment leaving me stranded in the doorway. I feel like a charity case with no home of my own.

'*Gut Shabbes. Gut Shabbes*,' Chani Rapaport is coming towards me. She seems breathless. 'Come on in.'

I walk inside the room. There are two dining tables in the room. Both are set with starched white linen *Shabbes* table-cloths covered with disposable plastic squares and *Shabbes* crockery. In the centre of the larger table the candles radiate a yellow glow. There is no other furniture, no couch or easy chair to sit on. I notice the walls are lined with shelves filled with holy books. Three young children sit under a table reading a picture book. An older girl is praying in the corner. The aroma of roasted chicken and potato *kugel* fills the tiny apartment.

I hand the bottle of grape juice to Chani and she places it in the centre of the larger table. She pulls out a dining chair for me to sit on and she sits opposite. She is wearing an apron over a white silk shirt and black tailored skirt. Her shoulder-length synthetic wig is pulled back and fastened with a diamante clip at the nape. I notice a few strands of her own hair have come loose at the back. I don't think I will ever be able to wear a wig to cover my hair if I get married. I will wear a kerchief, which I consider to be more modest.

She smiles warmly. 'So how do you like the yeshiva?' she asks.

'I love it. I'm learning a lot,' I answer, but my mind is still on the two tables. Why two?

'*Baruch Hashem*.' she says, 'What are you learning?'

'The laws of *Shabbes*. There is a lot to learn.' I think about how many of the girls take their observance slowly, adding to their practice week by week, but from the first day after my epiphany vision of the godly lights on the cafeteria ceiling, I have been meticulous about not abusing any of the thirty-nine categories of work used in building the tabernacle that are the paradigm for forbidden actions on the Sabbath. I am proud that I don't switch on the electricity, travel in a car or light a match. I dedicate the day to study, trying to access the *neshama yetera*, the extra soul promised on the Sabbath.

'Apart from the studies, it must be challenging? No?'

'Yes, but the other existence doesn't interest me any more.' I've put the Chris episode behind me and I really mean what I'm saying. 'It seems so empty.' Listening to myself, I know that I have gone to an extreme, cutting myself off from life outside the yeshiva, so unlike my father's way of integrating secular life into his religious world. But now that I have re-experienced God and the truth of His Torah, there seems no other way for me. If I followed my father's path, I would become easily distracted once again by the impure, unable to sift out the holy from the profane the way he does. I think about all the years wasted when I paid no attention to a higher being and lived without God consciousness. If I had been aware of Him, I might have ended up pure and innocent like Chani.

'You must have a strong will to change your life. I admire that,' Chani says.

I'm sure she can't imagine what the change involves, but I'm pleased she appreciates the struggle.

I fidget in my chair, feeling uneasy about the obvious gap

between my hostess and myself. Even though I am dressed modestly, not like some girls at the yeshiva who only gradually change their mode of dress, trading tank tops for T-shirts, tight jeans for baggy pants, I still feel that I look slutty next to Chani. But at least in terms of my clothes there is nothing further I can do. I have been as punctilious as the holy Mrs Hillman in keeping to the modesty dress code and now wear shapeless garments borrowed from The Niche, a cellar filled with hand-me-downs that we girls are free to borrow. The designer models that I have always loved, bought often in the trendy South Molton Street shops in London, are of the past and now I laugh when I look in the mirror. Workmen don't whistle at me any more and cab drivers don't honk. Until tonight, I thought I had regained some dignity by keeping myself hidden and not showing off my curves, but now, sitting next to this pious young woman, I feel all my efforts are in vain. My soul has been stained by sordid sex and drug abuse. Long sleeves and hems cannot deny who I really am, they are only superficial accessories. Real modesty is inbred. It comes from a life of keeping to the Torah. Only by adhering to the *mitzvot* can one achieve a genuine and deep purity. It cannot be attained by a few months of repenting or a few extra layers of clothing.

I notice Chani's hands; nails that have probably never seen varnish are cut short, delicate fingers that surely have never held a cigarette or cut a line of coke are holding a white linen handkerchief. I look down at my own hands and remember how they have been instruments of sin, chopping sulphate with a razor blade, rolling joints and laying brown powder in a piece of silver foil, lighting it from underneath, chasing the dragon and smoking the heroin.

I feel vulgar when Chani speaks in subdued tones from a mouth that I am sure has never let out a curse and I feel like a whore sitting next to a body that has never been defiled. I have desecrated my body, desperate for that one split second when men would lose themselves inside of me. That was the only way I knew to counteract the loneliness I felt at home. After Michelle was sent away, my parents drifted off into their own private suffering, my father rigid with denial lest any feelings crack his external composure, my mother using prescription drugs to keep her feelings at bay. The fact that I too had feelings, that I missed my sister, that I felt threatened by the silence around her absence, so carefully maintained lest any mention of her cause my mother to slip into another depression, was just another thing that my parents didn't want to know about. All I could do was to follow their example. So, like my mother, I turned to drugs. But my drugs were of the recreational variety, and I took my self-abuse one step further and used anonymous sex to numb me.

The experimenting with drugs, and sex, began in Compagne Gardens, at the home of Nick Morgan and friends. They were a group of musicians who shared a run-down house in West Hampstead, which became my refuge. It was a place without any rules. Free love and peace were the motto. Bright coloured Indian scarves hung as curtains and covered the mattresses where I lay listening to Nick practise his songs. My favourite was 'I'm high on a highway baby, high on a highway baby now'. There, in the cosy living room, a guitar being strummed in the background, crystals hanging on the window frames reflecting rainbows onto the walls, a collection of potted plants on the sill, a large wooden coffee table in the centre, fresh pots of tea constantly being poured, I relaxed. I was cool and I was free enough to allow any strange hand to grope me. The members of the gang were at least five years my senior and I envied them living an independent life. The love that was hard to come by at home was available there with Rob and Pete and many other nameless faces. Joints were continuously being rolled, white powder sniffed and generously shared. I would sit back in a stupor, feeling that I finally belonged somewhere. They were my real family and their pad my home away from home. My parents thought I was attending a Jewish youth club arranging charity events for Israel and in their presence I still wore the *Shabbes* outfits my mother insisted on and brushed my hair back into a ponytail. But anyone who looked deep into my pupils or noticed the few crumbs of white powder stuck on the inside of my nostrils knew that it was only the very shell of me that was turning over the pages of the prayer book in synagogue and not for even a single moment was I thinking about God. My mind was elsewhere. Mainly on figuring out how many more unbearably tedious minutes there were till the end of the service and the end of the Sabbath when I could leave the house and escape to my safe haven.

I was addicted to the false sense of intimacy that I reached when I was stoned out of my mind; I enjoyed the flirting and the getting close. And like any addiction it fed on itself. As soon as the sex was over and I was left discarded like a snake's shed skin, humiliation seeping into me, I would become desperate to grab the attention of another man. The cycle went on and on. Before Chris, I was unable to make any real connection to a man, as I feared he would soon abandon me for another girl. To avoid the pain of rejection, I would sleep around, giving off the vibe that I wasn't interested in a steady boyfriend.

I look at Chani and shudder as a painful memory slips into my mind. I am sixteen years old. A tab of acid is dissolving under my tongue as I head for the squat in Warwick Avenue where Tim my dealer lives. He hands over the stash of Thai sticks. I stuff them deep into my pastel blue cowboy boots, innocently reach into the scalloped neckline of my shirt and retrieve a few bank notes from my bra to pay him. The atmosphere is changing. I sense sex in the air. The acid is kicking in and I lie back on a tattered beanbag and Tim and the other squatters stand around me in a half moon. I see them swaying in psychedelic colour. I know what they want. I want it too. I tease my DD tits out of my Wonderbra. I am only a child, but I feel powerful, in control, for I am the one who is choosing. I shudder as I remember that night. It's no longer enough to be loved for only as long as a hard-on lasts. I want to be wanted for my self and for my soul. I want to connect to a man on a higher level than just the physical. I look back at Chani enviously. I want to wipe my slate clean and be just like her.

We sit in a comfortable silence for a few minutes and I soak in the holy atmosphere.

'Why are there two dining tables?' I finally ask, as I have been wanting to do since I came in.

'One for the men and one for the women. We're expecting another two girls.'

'I've never seen this before.'

'It's a Hassidic custom. The men sit with the men, the

women with the women. My husband feels it's more modest this way.'

Chani looks at her watch. 'My husband will be back soon. I still have to check the eggs and the lettuce.'

I have no idea what she means but I follow her into the kitchen. She cuts a hard-boiled egg into half. Then she holds up the whites and scrutinises them. 'See this?' she says pointing to a pink vein the size of a pinhead.

'Yes.'

'It's a blood spot.'

'Isn't that why we boil three eggs together?' I ask, puzzled. 'My mother does that so that any blood will be invalid.' An image of my mother in her kitchen comes to mind. She is koshering liver. She places raw meat on a grid and smears it with coarse table salt. Blood drips from the meat onto a tray below. Even though she doesn't have much patience for many of the *Shabbes* laws and often repeats the phrase 'It's just so archaic; I mean really, not putting on a light in this day and age', she is punctilious with the dietary laws. She separates the milk and meat dishes, careful never to stir a meat pot with a milk spoon and always cracking eggs into a glass so she can examine them for blood from all angles. When my grandfather came to England to visit my parents as newly-weds, he made an inspection of the kitchen and, satisfied with my mother's kosher standards, ate heartily of her food at dinner. But even though he was Chief Rabbi of Israel, I know his standards would not have been high enough for Chani. She probably has her own Hassidic rabbi whose rulings she follows and anybody else's seal of approval is insufficient. When I first came to the seminary I found this gap between the customs in my father's household and those in the yeshiva ridiculous, but now I understand that my father is paying a price by trying to span the religious and the secular worlds. He cannot achieve the holiness that is here in this home, where only the sacred has a place.

'We want to be extra careful,' Chani explains. I can tell she feels sorry for me. I can also tell she doesn't think much of my mother's level of *kashrut*. 'My dad's a rabbi,' I want to say, 'I'm one of you,' but somewhere deep inside I know that Chani wouldn't think much of my family's level of observance. My father's secular library, his custom of kissing the cheeks of female congregants to wish them a *gut Shabbes*, and so many of his other worldly practices, would be out of place here. Chani is holding a lettuce leaf up to the fluorescent strip on the ceiling. 'I'm checking for bugs,' she says. 'Just hold each leaf up to the light and make sure nothing is moving.'

I do as she says, hoping I won't see anything.

'There's a really good movie about checking for bugs,' Chani tells me. 'I saw it last week. Can you imagine even carrots have bugs? And dried fruits – you have to open dates and apricots before you eat them and check.' The idea of a movie about creepy crawlies in food makes me feel sick. I flip back momentarily into my secular mindset, thinking Chani must be some kind of religious fanatic.

The meal ready, Chani suggests we pray the evening service before her husband comes home from shul. She hands me a *siddur* and I return to the dining room, face east and place my feet together. I try to concentrate on my prayers and ignore my rumbling stomach and the itch of a mosquito bite on my left ankle. I close my eyes and meditate on the four letters of

God's name. I image them in my mind's eye written in fire, glowing red and orange. I see flames lapping at the *yud*, *heh*, *vav*, *heh*. The image is so real, I feel like Moses at the burning bush. I take three steps forward to place myself in the presence of the King and then bow to Him, beseeching Him to open my lips and let my supplications flow. I bow down low. As I pray, I sway back and forth as if using my body to break through the gates of mercy. I recite the ancient liturgy carefully, hoping each blessing will draw me closer to my creator. Even after years of silence, I still remember the prayers by heart. It is as if they have been engraved upon my soul since childhood. When the prayer is over, I step backwards and take leave of the King. I close my book, kiss the maroon leather cover of my *siddur*, hold my lips to the smoothness of the hide and then hug the book to my bosom with love.

'*Gut Shaaabbees.*' There is a voice from the hallway. Chani takes off her apron and smoothes her wig. In her modest way, she is making herself beautiful for her husband. I have learnt from Hilly that Friday night is the time most worthy for sexual relations. I feel a pang of jealousy as I watch her. Suddenly I feel so lonely. Emptiness is gnawing in my heart. I think briefly of Chris but then banish him from my mind. I am ready to be in a truly committed relationship, wanting that bond of love within the sanctity of marriage. Even though husband and wife don't embrace or hold hands in public, I can feel the intimacy between them from the way Chani stands close to Shlomo and then warmly says, '*Gut Shabbes*, the *Shabbes* bride is here,' her face aglow, the light of the candles reflected in her eyes and on her peaches and cream complexion. 'This is our guest, Reva,' she introduces me. 'She's new in the yeshiva.'

'Welcome,' Shlomo says. I can tell he is not looking straight at me but past me at a speck on the wall. I am not offended. I understand why men don't look at women. When Rabbi Rabinowitz is in a confrontational mood and picks on me in class to expound on an argument between two opposing commentators, I can feel the sexual energy unleashed by our debate. Even though he is so much better versed than I am, I try to hold my ground in the argument. He humours me, lets me ramble on and then, in his flirtatious way, with his wit and sharp tongue, cuts me down to size. It is then, when I feel small and in awe of the breadth of his knowledge, that an animal longing takes hold of me and my thoughts are pulled away from what is pure and it takes all my control not to allow my eyes to sweep over the tilt in his gabardine trousers or to imagine how at my lightest touch he would rise and carry me off to a heavenly sphere.

The level of modesty here makes me feel so clean, as if I am wrapped in God's light and glory. I feel lucky to have been stationed with this family tonight. I think about Mrs Hillman's teachings about being modest even with ourselves. She has confided that when she is alone and changes into her night-gown, she goes into the bathroom and undresses under a robe. 'God is always in front of us at all times,' she says, and expounds on a story in the Talmud of a woman who merited having seven sons who each became the High Priest because the walls of her house never saw a hair on her head. She explained that the walls of one's house come to give witness on the Day of Judgment. It reminds me of the saying, 'walls have ears', but here, in the Jewish world, walls have eyes too.

The children line up to be blessed by their father. I feel like crying when I see how lovingly Shlomo places his hands on their heads, closes his eyes, and blesses his daughters to be like Sarah, Rivka, Rochel and Leah and his sons to be like Ephraim and Menashe. The children lean into him, cuddling, and I think of my own father and how I want his blessing now. But he is not happy I am in the yeshiva. He thinks this community is too extreme in its religious practice. All his life he has been fighting to get out of the ghetto, and my coming here reignites fears in him left over from the war when the Nazis invaded Poland and killed three million Jews. He cannot bear how the ultra-Orthodox close themselves off. There is no pleasing him. I was sure he'd be relieved with my decision to study Torah but instead, during our weekly phone calls, he insists I return to the college and finish my degree.

Two other women have arrived. One I recognise from the yeshiva and the other, an unmarried woman in her early forties, is a social worker in the community. As we stand around the women's table, I say a silent prayer, hoping I won't end up an old maid, having to invite myself to other people's houses.

At the men's table, Shlomo is singing a welcome to the *Shabbes* bride. He takes his time, bowing and singing in a sweet voice. I imagine angels flying around his head in a halo. His light has transformed the poky little flat into a palace where he is king. Joy emanates from him. I can feel God present here in this humble abode. Shlomo picks up the silver chalice and looks at his reflection in the wine before it spills over the cup onto the plate below. I am mesmerised by his voice and his sincerity as he sanctifies the *Shabbat*. I have forgotten about the pink stains in the eggs and the insects in the lettuce now that I am transported to the Sabbath sphere. I can feel the presence of my extra soul. This is something I never experienced with my family.

At home there was no peace, just tension during our evening *Shabbes* meal. My father was always lost in anxious thought about the weekly sermon he had to deliver the next day and my mother, trying desperately to prevent an escalation of his irritability, emotionally blackmailed me into silence by threatening that if I didn't keep my opinions to myself I could cause my father's already weak heart to collapse. Even though I knew she was exaggerating, this scared me enough that I remained quiet throughout the meal. The following day when my father mounted the *bima* to address his congregation, I was always in a state of tension about whether anything would happen to disrupt his sermon. I waited anxiously for speculations on the stock exchange from the downstairs hall and gossip about the latest fashions in millinery from the women's gallery to die down, for my father would begin to speak only when he had everyone's attention. I can hear him now, delivering one of his perfectly timed speeches, whispering the emotionally charged messages and raising his voice to high decibels when quoting from the Torah. To ensure that the congregation remained completely still, I would borrow my mother's friend Bettie's diamond rings and dangle my hands over the smooth chestnut tier of the ladies' gallery, believing that by reflecting a prism of light from the cut diamonds onto the Holy Ark I had the power to muffle any sneezes, coughs or clearings of the throat.

My father was a great orator and his sermons legendary. But the fact that yet another successful sermon had been delivered never resulted in a lighter mood during the *Shabbes* day meal. Synagogue politics, who said what about the sermon, who came to shake hands in gratitude after services and who snubbed him by walking away, these were the subjects of those Saturday lunches. The only words my parents directed at me were criticisms of my deportment and table manners. I couldn't wait to escape and my chance always came when the ear-shattering sound of the weekly rock concerts in Hyde Park drowned out the traditional *Shabbes* melodies my father sang after the meal. Then, while he took his *Shabbes* nap, I would change into a psychedelic T-shirt and long hippie skirt and leave the house. My mother was my secret ally in these outings. She sympathised that my father was often too strict with me and turned a blind eye as I ran down Oxford Street, down the underpass that exited into Speakers' Corner and beyond into the park. There, I joined an audience of flower power freaks sitting on the grass, while passing around joints, hanging out and listening to the groove. That was more my idea of Sabbath rest.

This meal is simple, yet it tastes like nectar to me. I am listening to Shlomo and his rendering of the weekly Torah portion, fascinated by the way he explains the esoteric meaning of the text, how he includes the children, even the smallest one, by asking simple questions about the Bible stories they have learnt in nursery school. This is a happy family, I think. This is what I want, to build a family like this with a man who will elevate me to the paradise of *Shabbat*. But tonight, experiencing *Shabbes* with these holy Orthodox Jews, I am aware that my tainted past is embedded deep within me, apparent in every nuance of my being. I don't believe that I deserve this kind of wholeness or that anyone as holy as Shlomo would be willing to give me a second chance. Yet, I gather up my faith and courage, believing that my God is a compassionate God. I feel sure that the time has come to begin the search for my true soul-mate and I decide to pay a visit to the matchmaker at the yeshiva the very next week.

4

Matchmaker, Matchmaker

It is not good that man should be alone;
I will make a helpmate for him.

Genesis 2:18

It is the following Sunday and I am walking down the rickety staircase to the yeshiva basement where the matchmaker has a private office. I hesitate for a moment in the hallway. Once I cross the threshold, I will step into the Orthodox world for real. But I am sure of my path and I knock firmly on the door.

Mrs Frankel greets me with a beaming smile. 'I am so pleezed you hev finally come to see me,' she says, making way for me to enter.

Originally from Czechoslovakia, she is a pretty woman with delicate features, someone who has kept her figure despite the many pregnancies and umpteen meals she has cooked and served. Mother to nine children, she is the most glamorous female at the yeshiva. Today she wears a purple chiffon dress enhanced by two strands of cultured pearls and a fashionable chestnut wig styled after Mia Farrow's hairstyle in *The Great Gatsby*. The room is as small as a confessional. A table and two chairs are the only furnishings and the walls are bare save for a prayer for *shalom bayis*, written in flourishing calligraphy and embellished by a border of pink and gold leaf.

A large diary, a Rolodex and an assortment of pens are scattered on the table.

'I've been vaiting for you . . .' Mrs Frankel says. I feel proud to have made it down to the legendary room the girls here are always talking about and to finally be a member of the dating club.

'Yes, well . . . It took me a while. I'm not used to dating like this . . . I . . .'

'Don't I know,' she sympathises, trying to put me at ease. She has obviously heard the same story so many times.

'So tell me, darlink. How old are you?'

'I'm twenty-five,' I reply, aware that most girls from religious homes have at least four children by the time they are my age.

'And vat kind of a husband are you looking for?' Her voice is soothing.

In my old life I would have answered, a raw, sexy man wearing button-down jeans, tight at the crotch, exuding irresistible charm and who can woo me off my feet onto the nearest couch, but today, in all sincerity, I answer, 'I'm looking for a scholar, a spiritual guide to help me get closer to God.'

Mrs Frankel beams with delight at my progress. It is less than a year since I arrived at the yeshiva with the 'outside' ingrained in every pore, mascara thickly applied to my lashes and tight clothes accentuating my figure. Now I sit in front of her like a daughter of Israel with my hair tied back and my face scrubbed clean.

'Blessed be the Lord who heals the sick and releases the bound,' Mrs Frankel mumbles. 'Do you realise the commitment you hev to make – to your husbant, to *clal Yisroel* and to God?'

'With God's help, I hope to have many children and will teach them how to keep the *mitzvot*.' I glance up at the prayer on the wall, sure that my home will be a sanctuary for peace. 'I've almost finished my studies. I'll be able to work in the labour room as a *doula* so my husband can devote all his time to studying Torah.' I only want a man immersed in Torah who will come home from yeshiva at night and share the Torah he has learnt, not a man who brings the office home and all the profanities that go with it.

'You were studying childbirth? I didn't know that.'

'My sister Michelle was born severely retarded . . . I always hoped I could help . . . you can understand.' I think of my sister with her red hair tied in bunches, her lower lip dry and swollen from medication and a line of drool running down her chin. How I loved it when she lived at home and we played games together, games in which I could take the lead and boss her about even though I was five years her junior.

'Oy! Vot a tragedy!' Mrs Frankel pats me on the shoulder and then in a cheery voice she says, 'Helping in birth is a great profession, just like Yocheved, the mother of our greatest prophet Moses, but tell me, Reva, vat about your own connection to God? Being a *Kollel* wife isn't for everybody you know.'

'I will reap the reward of my husband's study in the next world. In this world I will have the honour of living with a *ben Torah*.'

'*Gevalt*!' Mrs Frankel is impressed at how quickly I have seen the light.

I am not sure what a *Kollel* life entails, but I am thinking purely of the spiritual dimension to marriage; the financial burden of day-to-day life doesn't even enter my head.

'There is just one more crucial question, Reva . . . I need to know if you ever hed sexual relations mit a non-Jew.'

I blush and lower my head.

'Is that so important – relations with a non-Jew?' I ask.

'If you hed relations mit a non-Jew, then I cannot introduce you to a *kohen*, a man from the priestly tribe, as he is forbidden to marry you.'

I stay silent. I think about Chris and the foreskin on his uncircumcised penis that slipped back and forth with ease, making my job of caressing him so much easier than with the Jewish boys. It looked beautiful erect, with the head hiding and revealing itself. But once his erection would wane, I didn't like the way it hung in a hood of skin. Then I preferred the steady stick of those who had adhered to the covenant of Abraham.

'Reva?' Mrs Frankel is waiting for an answer.

'No *kohanim* for me,' I reply.

Mrs Frankel nods. I spot her upper lip curl in distaste. She must have thought as much. I had never realised the repercussions of having a foreskin enter me. I always knew there was something un-kosher about that extra notch of flesh and the foreign tang of its taste in my mouth always made me fear germs lurked inside. Now, not only am I impure, but I have disqualified myself as a match for a small but significant percentage of the male Jewish population.

'Are you going to introduce me only to someone from a secular background who has become religious – a *ba'al tshuva*?' I ask. I have been hoping to meet a holy man who has never been tainted by a secular lifestyle even though I know that as a *ba'alat tshuva* myself, I am damaged goods in the Orthodox world. However devout I am in my search for God and however serious about the keeping of His *mitzvot*, I cannot join the ranks of the FFBs, *frum* (religious) from birth. They may claim that they themselves are not nearly as holy as the newly repentant, that they cannot come close to the spiritual level we have attained by changing our lives around, and they may welcome me into their community, but if I am suggested as a potential daughter-in-law, the FFBs will politely refuse the match. They will take into account that I am not a virgin, that I have eaten non-kosher foods and immersed myself in an impure world, and even the fact that I am a rabbi's daughter will not outweigh those negatives.

'Darlink, you need someone to hev things in common with – someone who can understand your past,' Mrs Frankel replies, giving me a pitying look. Her job is obviously hard, matching up a bunch of lunatics like us girls who come from a world she shuns. She writes down the name of the first suitor on a yellow Post-it. Chaim Dovid Levinson.

She raves about his personality. He has all the right attributes: studious, responsible and devoted to Torah. He studies at the Ohr Somayach Yeshiva, a yeshiva designed for secular men who have returned to the fold. I would have preferred to meet a guy who studies at the Mir Yeshiva, like my father did, but still I am excited. Yet it is so bizarre – a blind date – no touching allowed. What if he is fat and ugly? I ask myself. How will I manage then? Will my newly acquired spiritual aspirations still hold?

'Now, Reva, you vill meet Chaim Dovid on Tuesday night in the lobby of the King David Hotel. Hev a cup of coffee or go for a stroll. Afterwards call me and tell me if you vant to meet him again.'

'The King David Hotel!'

'Yes, be there at eight. Prompt.'

'What do I say? Talk about?' I ask nervously, wondering if Chris will still be there. I imagine the horror of having him catch sight of me in the lobby with Chaim Dovid.

'Just relax, Reva. Let him take the lead, and remember – cross your legs and make sure your skirt doesn't ride up.'

All during *Shabbes*, I repeat the name written on the Post-it and try it out for size. Reva Levinson. I extend my hand, flipping it this way and that, imagining it enhanced by a diamond ring and a wedding band. On Sunday, Monday, and Tuesday, I skip lunch hoping I can wear my grey dress, which is getting tight round the hips.

On Tuesday afternoon, after reciting prayers, I take a bath and set my hair. I apply a faint glimmer of eye shadow and colourless gloss to my lips. The grey dress is still too tight, so I wear a simple cream dress that seems to me to strike the right balance: modest but becoming, virginal but not too innocent.

Only a week after my earlier visit to the King David Hotel, I spin back through the revolving door at exactly eight o'clock and scan the various men in the lobby. Which one is Chaim Dovid? I wonder, as I plop myself down in a velvet armchair. I cannot see a possible candidate. No one fits his description. My watch now reads ten past eight. Where is he? Have I been stood up? I wait, anxiously biting my nails. I am nervous. Despite my extensive history with men, I'm not sure how to behave when no flirtation or touching is allowed. I have always relied on my sex appeal to connect. Now I will have to work harder, count on my brain and conversation.

Minutes pass and still no Chaim Dovid. Memories of Chris flash through my mind. I remember how anxious I felt meeting his family for the first time, hoping they would accept me. 'How will your parents feel about my being Jewish?' I had asked.

'Don't worry, luv. They'll love you for who you are, not for your religion.' Chris pulled me close and teased, 'Bet my dad'll love those big Jewish tits of yours.' Oh God, I mustn't let my mind wander back to Chris again. Without the commitment of a Jewish marriage, it isn't love but hedonism, debauchery, mere self-love. 'True love,' Mrs Frankel has told me, 'is the love that comes from giving to someone else. Love grows through responsibility and action, not some lustful Hollywood dream that shatters the moment one partner gets bored.'

I feel someone eyeing me. I stay seated and quickly cross my legs before looking up at a clean-cut young man.

'Might you be Reva?' he inquires in a southern drawl.

'Chaim Dovid?' He is well built, with corn-coloured curls that spill out from under his skullcap.

'I'm sorry I'm late. My Torah class finished later than scheduled,' he apologises.

Even though I am annoyed that he kept me waiting, I understand that Torah study overrides all other responsibilities. Every day I read in the morning prayers that we must honour our parents, perform deeds of loving kindness, attend the house of study, be hospitable, visit the sick, help a bride with her dowry, accompany the dead to their grave, concentrate on the meaning of prayers, make peace between men – and the study of Torah is equal to them all.

'Don't worry,' I say. 'I haven't been here long.'

'Would you like to go for a walk?'

I would rather go to a bar and order a bottle of red wine. Instead I get to my feet and follow him out of the hotel.

We walk towards Yemin Moshe, careful not to brush against each other accidentally. He's handsome, I think, snatching glances at his tall physique, well-built chest and baby-blue eyes. Not the heroin chic type I used to like – he's too healthy looking for that – but maybe my new type. Walking down the majestic King David Street, where luxury apartments remain empty save for the few weeks a year when their wealthy owners fly in for the high holidays, I close my wrap around me, protecting myself from the cool Jerusalem evening and an overwhelming need to be held.

We walk until we reach the Montefiori Windmill. Chaim Dovid motions for me to sit down on a bench. I place my handbag between us as a buffer.

'I want to get married as soon as possible,' he admits. 'I'm not used to this segregation of the sexes. Back home in Alabama, I used to party all night.'

I nod my understanding, disappointed by his conversation. I was hoping for a few uplifting words of Torah, maybe some thoughts from the lesson he attended before meeting me or more details about the spiritual path he has been seeking. His banter makes me aware of my own flaws and I sadly understand why Mrs Frankel thought we would have so much in common. My dream of marrying a holy man is fading rapidly and my disappointment rises from the pit of my stomach in a wave of nausea.

'But now, living in the yeshiva and sleeping in a boys dormitory, I'm finding it especially hard. To prevent turning over onto my . . . my organ . . . I tie a cord around my ankles and attach it to the bed frame so that in my sleep if I try and turn onto my side, I will feel the pull of the cord and be reminded not to roll over.'

I cannot believe what he just said. Even though I know masturbation is prohibited, as spilling seed is a sin that some Rabbinic authorities equate with murder, I am mortified by the graphic detail.

'You're kidding!' I think the guy must be crazy, brainwashed by the rabbis into sleeping in this unnatural way. I want to get away from him. Again, I feel this yeshiva world is too extreme for me. I'm worried that I've fallen in with a bunch of madmen.

'No, many of the boys do this; it's a known thing.'

'Do you think we should be having this conversation?' I ask. 'I mean, isn't it a bit too intimate for a *shidduch* date?'

'You're right, but I feel comfortable with you; I feel I can tell you anything.'

I do not feel comfortable with Chaim Dovid and am shattered to realise that my attempt at modesty is so clearly just a front. I want to tell him that I don't want to see him again but the dating protocol is to talk to the matchmaker first.

'I'm sure Chaim Dovid isn't Mr Right,' I tell Mrs Frankel the following morning. 'I don't know if I should say anything, but he told me he ties himself up to the bed!'

'This shows vat a God-fearing Jew he is,' she reprimands. 'You still have a lot to learn, my dear.'

I sense a nastiness in Mrs Frankel I have not noticed before. She is speaking to me in a condescending tone. I feel small and stupid. I had always thought of her as someone to trust and confide in. I want to get up and leave but she is already discussing the details of my second *shidduch* date with a man named Shimon Schwarz and I can't afford to pass up this new opportunity.

Shimon is from a rabbinic family. He has always lived in the religious environment, yet is ready to meet a girl with a past. This information sounds suspicious but Mrs Frankel tells me to be open-minded.

We meet at the Laromme Hotel, just down the road from the King David. The first thing I notice is that Shimon is shorter than me. I feel uncomfortable, especially since I am also heavier than he is with my figure so swollen from overeating. We sip soft drinks in the lobby, which isn't as plush as the King David, or as quiet. Groups of American tourists bustle around. Shimon wins me over with his charm and takes me to dinner. Half an hour into the date, I have forgotten about his height and am laughing and relaxed. This has potential, I think. We could merge two rabbinical dynasties. Our children could be geniuses, combining genes from both. He asks about my family and is taking a great interest. Out of the corner of my eye I can see Chaim Dovid sitting across from Sally-Anne. Seeing last week's date with my girlfriend makes the *shidduch* scene seem as incestuous as the secular world.

* * *

I am back in Mrs Frankel's office. I am wary of her now and don't want to get on her bad side. She is an important person in the matchmaking world and I know that she could easily blacklist me. But today I will please her and tell her that I liked her match. Before I even sit down she is telling me, 'Vell, I don't have good news.' She sighs deeply. Her bosom and gold necklace heave up and down. 'Shimon doesn't vant to meet you again. He was put off by the vay you ate the entire plate of avocado salad at dinner. He feared your appetite might spill over into other areas as well.'

'What . . . ?'

'He also told me you told him about Michelle, your sister. Reva, this is such a mistake – and on the first date!'

'What's wrong with talking about my sister?'

'Men are concerned for the health of their future children. Anyvay, I've called England to verify your sister's handicap is not congenital – just a birth accident. You're lucky that it won't mar your possibilities for a match.'

I feel as if I've been raped and Michelle defiled. I want to snatch Mrs Frankel's wig off her head, throw it on the floor and stamp on it. What a mistake I have made telling these people about my sister, but I didn't want to hide her existence any more, as I used to when I was asked if I had siblings. Then I always said I was an only child, not wanting to open up a Pandora's box of feelings and see the embarrassment on their faces or their pity, or, worse, my mother's nervous twitching if she was also in the room. I can feel the anger bubbling inside of me. Mrs Frankel with her entourage of healthy children and grandchildren could never understand the trauma surrounding Michelle. She could never imagine how my mother's world fell apart, smashed into thousands of fragmented shards, when she found out what was wrong with my sister. Michelle had seemed completely healthy at birth, possessed of all ten fingers and ten toes and an adorable mop of curly red hair. But when it became obvious that she couldn't hold a biscuit like other children or say mama or papa, my parents took her to a specialist and shortly after her first birthday were told that she had learning difficulties. Mrs Frankel could never understand what it was like to take care of such a child, or to have to send her away. She has reduced Michelle to a biological study, completely ignoring my feelings. I can't believe how cold and clinical she is.

'I'm taking a break from dating,' I say, on the verge of tears and sickened by the whole sordid business. I don't want anything more to do with this matchmaker. I think of poor old Michelle and how she hangs her head, scuffs her shoes, grinds her teeth, drools, waves her arms, walks around in circles and talks to herself in her own made-up language.

'Reva, darlink, this is not the time to take a break.' Mrs Frankel puts her arm around my shoulder and pulls me close. Suddenly she is my best friend. 'Making a match is harder for God than parting the Red Sea,' she explains, quoting the Midrash. 'Anyvay, I hev good news,' she says, perking up. 'The holy Biale Rebbe has a fine young man to match. I think he'd be perfect for you.'

I imagine another contortionist, maybe one who shakes chilli pepper onto his hand so as not to succumb to masturbation.

'The Biale Rebbe, a famous Hassidic rabbi and leader of a large following, admires this man Alan Lowe. He's from

London, just like you. He's a *ba'al zedaka*, gives generously to charity and . . . he's in the diamond business.'

'Diamonds . . .' I begin to sing in a breathy voice, trying to sound like Marilyn Monroe, still furious at Mrs Frankel's insensitivity towards Michelle and towards me. I am pouting sexily to annoy her, 'Diamonds . . . I don't mean rhine-stones . . . are a girl's best friend.'

'Reva, pull yourself together! Don't you know that a voman's singing voice is considered nakedness? One of the rabbis might hear you. Tomorrow appear at the Rabbi's Court for an interview. Be there promptly at four o'clock and behave like an Orthodox Jewish Voman.'

The following day, I trek out to the ultra-Orthodox Mattersdorf neighbourhood of Jerusalem. It seems even dirtier here than in Bayit Vegan where I study. Four-storey buildings flank the dusty streets on either side. Women push strollers. Their faces are blank. Clothes and hats are imported from the States and sold out of spare rooms in the run-down apart-ments. There is a *sheitel macher*, who fits and styles human hair wigs. Every few blocks there is a small grocery store sell-ing basic staples. Small children run errands for their mothers and walk around holding a loaf of bread or a bag of milk. I walk at a swift pace to the haven of the rabbi's home. This is more like it, I think. I'm moving away from the *ba'al tshuva* yeshivas into the inner circle of the *frum* community, to the Biale Rebbe himself.

The rabbi's wife greets me warmly. She wears a honey-blonde wig and tailored dress. 'You're just in time for tea,' she says and leads the way to the dining room. Their apartment is clean and neat and furnished just like all the other religious homes with a large central table surrounded by bookshelves filled with holy books.

The rabbi is a tall man. He is wearing a midnight-blue caftan belted on the hips and a large black hat. His smile is warm and open. The way he stands with his hand on his hip reminds me of my grandfather. Mrs Frankel says he's a true *zaddik* and I can see why. Light emanates from him as he blesses quietly before sipping his tea. He seems so at peace with himself and he reminds me by his very presence that God is everywhere. As is the custom, the rabbi speaks about the Torah portion of the week at the table. This week the portion is *Re'eh*.

'*Re'eh* means see – have vision. God tells the Jewish people "*Re'eh*", I put before you a blessing or a curse. If you choose blessing, the rains shall fall and irrigate the land.' He pauses and looks at me lovingly, like a father as he speaks to his child.

I want him to know I understand that we need to make this choice every day anew. 'I have chosen blessing, rebbe,' I say. 'You can be assured that I am ready to build a Jewish home.'

The rabbi asks me about my family and my studies and after a while I feel comfortable enough to ask, 'What does Alan Lowe look like?'

As the words leave my mouth, I am embarrassed to have revealed how much I care about looks and exteriors. But they understand. His wife exits the room, leaving the door wide open, and I presume she has gone to fetch a photograph of Alan. The rabbi signals me to look down the hall and I peer out. A Hassidic teenager dressed in a silken coat glides in slow motion across the corridor like an elegant model down the catwalk.

The rabbi turns to me. 'Alan Lowe is about as tall as our son.'

It takes me a few moments to decipher the meaning of the show. This is their answer to my question. Of course it would be inappropriate for the rabbi to introduce his son to me personally, but couldn't they just give me the vital statistics? Enthralled by the modesty and the theatrics and relieved that at least my date is of average height, I nod my consent. I will meet their match.

Back again in Mrs Frankel's office, I tell her there is something seriously wrong with Alan Lowe. Our date lasted all of half an hour in the rabbi's study, just barely long enough to eat the light refreshments the *rebbetzin* brought us before leaving us alone. I wanted to get away immediately, but out of politeness to the holy rabbi, I tried to engage in a conversation. Alan Lowe was a sickly young man who spoke with a slight lisp about his jewellery designs and was almost certainly gay. Underweight, with a sallow complexion, he had dark eyes sunk deep into his head. It seemed strange to me that after interpreting the first word of the Torah portion *Re'eh* as having vision, the rabbi himself has so little insight into Alan Lowe. 'I think he's ill,' I say.

'Ill, shmill, Reva. Vat are you talking about? He's fine. It's you who aren't well, rejecting all my matches.'

In my despair that I will never find my match, I seek help from Mrs Hillman. I sense she will understand me better than the matchmaker. In a private meeting in the yeshiva library after philosophy class, Mrs Hillman looks deep into my eyes with compassion.

'Yes,' she says, 'it isn't an easy thing.' Her wig is wobbling off her head as she nods in understanding.

'The only one who can help you is the *Abeshter*, God Himself. Regular prayer may not be enough in your case. Go to the Western Wall every day for forty days and beg.'

'Forty days? What, in succession?'

'I'm afraid so,' she says smiling at me now. 'It's a *segula* for finding a soul-mate. There is a great significance to the number forty. The Israelites spent forty years in the wilderness before entering the Promised Land. Moses went up the mountain for forty days before coming down with the two tablets. Forty is a very important number. Something big could happen for you too.'

I say nothing, but think it over. From the yeshiva in Bayit Vegan to the Kotel is a long way. 'What about on *Shabbes*?' I ask. 'How will I get there?'

'It's an hour's walk. I've done it many times. The exercise will do you good. I think there are other girls walking too. You could all go together.'

I have taken Mrs Hillman's counsel and am standing in front of the weather-beaten stones of the Western Wall, ancient boulders that date back to the Second Temple period. The Jerusalem air feels cool against my cheeks. It is quiet here now. There are only a few others on the women's side of the partition. Spotlights cast on the Wall reflect an orange light. I can hear the crying of a woman at the far corner near the booth where the shawls are kept to cover the immodest. This is the centre of the earth, below Har Habayit, the Temple Mount, the most controversial site on earth, known as the navel of the world. According to our tradition, Abraham was instructed to sacrifice Isaac here and this is where the two tablets inscribed with the Ten Commandments are buried. I walk back twenty paces to look up at the gold-leaf dome of the mosque in the distance. It glitters in the dusk. Turquoise-patterned tiles decorate its exterior walls. I remember studying Yechezkiel's prophecy that on this exact spot, the holy site from which Muslims believe Muhammad ascended the heavens, the third temple will rise. And once it has been rebuilt, Mrs Hillman has taught us, the ritual of animal sacrifices, which ceased with the destruction of the second temple in AD 70 will be reinstated. The High Priest will officiate and offer up sheep, cows and doves in atonement for our sins and sprinkle ashes from the Red Heifer for our purification, helping to prepare us for the end of days. I retreat further from the courtyard and scan the horizon beyond the Wall. Down the block from the Mount is the Temple Institute, where blueprints of temple architecture have already been drawn up, vessels have been reconstructed, clothes of the High Priest have been fashioned according to biblical design and plants have been collected to make incense, all in preparation for the coming of the Messiah. I learned about this place from Sally-Anne. She is now dating Chaim, a student there, and hopes to announce her engagement to him soon. As his wife, she too will be expected to dedicate herself to bringing the redemption closer, a task for which she seems well suited, as the end of days is a subject that has always been in the forefront of her mind.

Returning to my place at the Wall, I bring my focus back to my reason for being here, to pray for a mate. Thousands of notes with wishes and prayers of those who have come to the Wall seeking godly aid have been stuffed inside the cracks between the large boulders. They look like little coloured jewels in the light. I want to pour out my heart, but tonight, the first night of my pilgrimage, the words don't come easily and I recite the evening prayers by rote.

Day after day, I make my way to the Wall. I am slowly opening up. The Wall has become a home away from home. But still I fear there is an obstacle to the depth of my prayer. I know I can connect in a deeper way with my creator. But how to break through the gates of prayer? I want my mate and I want him now. I cannot bear to be alone any longer. Mrs Hillman has told me that there are rabbis in Jerusalem who can perform cabbalistic magic and remove blockages in the spiritual works. Some write amulets to ward off the evil eye and others give blessed water to drink. When I ask her which of them could help me focus on my prayer, she suggests I see Rabbi Ben Tov, better known as the 'Mezuzah Rabbi', and let him check my *mezuzah* for any errors that might indicate a spiritual flaw. He'll need to examine the contents of the *mezuzah*, the small scroll of parchment bearing the words of the Shema, a prayer that declares the unity of God. I remove the parchment from the *mezuzah* on the doorpost of my door, slip it into a sandwich bag and trudge to the house of the Mezuzah Rabbi.

The waiting room is packed. It could be hours till the rabbi will see me. Books of psalms are stacked on a coffee table. I take one. The poetic Hebrew of King David's words is hard for me to understand. I look around at the people waiting. The majority here are women, some religious and modestly dressed, others secular but wearing long-sleeved shirts over their tank tops for the purpose of their audience with the rabbi. Many are mouthing the holy psalms.

Two hours later my turn has come. I take a seat in the rabbi's study. I've been told that he doesn't need the intermediary of the *mezuzah* to give a prognosis on the soul and its ailments, but this is the vehicle he has chosen to interact with the public. He takes out a magnifying glass and flattens the scroll in front of him. He is checking for flaws and takes his time. He shows me how the first letter of the Hebrew alphabet 'Aleph' is smudged in the word 'Echad', which refers to God's oneness. He has found the problem.

'The imperfection in your *mezuzah* reflects that you worship other gods.'

'Worship other gods? Of course I don't,' I say, horrified at the thought. What can he mean?

'Do you own any books on idolatry?' he continues.

'Idolatry? No.' I am surprised. I know I've sinned in my life, but I have never been drawn to other religions.

'What about yoga books?'

I think about the Ashtanga book sitting on my bedside table. I nod.

'You must burn it,' he says, 'immediately.'

Even though I know the defect in my *mezuzah* must be a mirror for the blemish in my soul, I am unprepared for this advice. I have never considered yoga as idolatry. I am only interested in the poses, the stretching and the concentration, meditation in movement, a routine that keeps me flexible. It is true that travelling to an ashram in India for a yoga retreat has been a dream of mine for years, but it is only the body work that I'm after, not the Hindu religion. I don't want to burn John Scott's primary series, a book I have kept with me for years, but I have no choice. This rabbi can see through to my soul. If I am to make every effort to meet my soul-mate and not let anything stand in the way, I have to do as the rabbi says.

I rip out page after page of my beloved yoga book and burn them in the vacant lot next to the yeshiva. I look at the pile of ash settling on the ground, the remnants of the book, and feel the waste of it. But what do I know? I am just a small and insignificant Jew. The rabbi is a Cabbalist, a holy man of God, and he knows more than I do. I decide to look upon the cinders as my sins and my past. They symbolise the men, drugs, lies, cheating, the breaking of the Sabbath, the pork, bacon, milk after meat and eating on Yom Kippur – all the laws I have broken, the sins I am guilty of committing.

It is only a day later and I am feeling the results. There is a shift of energy. I feel well and strong. I have a handle on the cravings. I long to clothe myself in humility and charity, the garments of the soul. I am no longer hungry for shellfish and other non-kosher delights, but only for prayer and contemplation. It is in this pure state that I leap out of bed at five thirty in the morning on the fortieth day of my prayer marathon. I want to reach the Kotel in time for sunrise, when the gates of prayer are said to be wide open. In a jubilant mood I march through Jerusalem towards the Old City, turn into Jaffa Gate and then left at the Holy Sepulchre Church, into a deserted street. The vendors have not opened their colourful stalls yet, otherwise I would be offered tea and coffee, carpets, trinkets and carved wooden boxes. I continue down the dark cobbled alleyways of the Arab souk, passing a lone donkey laden with wares and pulled along by a young boy. The stench of dung evaporates as I come out of the dark tunnel-like streets into the first light of the day.

The ringing of church bells and the wail of the muezzin from the Temple Mount serenade me as I walk into the grand plaza of the Western Wall. The place is already packed. Men in black panamas and long coats rush about organising prayer groups. Bar-mitzvah boys prepare to read from the Torah for the first time. Beggars wind holy red strings around wrists to ward off the evil eye in exchange for a few shekels. Weeping women bow and bend themselves in despair and girls like me are praying with fervour.

I take my prayer book out of my bag and run up to the women's section of the Wall, feeling that each step is bringing me closer to God. Bird droppings splatter my shoulder as I embrace the Wall, but I take it as a lucky omen. Even the ecstasy I felt when I saw the vision on the cafeteria ceiling doesn't compare to the clarity I feel now, when I feel His presence in every pore of my being. On this final day of my pilgrimage, the prayers spill out of my mouth like honey.

I stand in the morning light feeling cleansed and purified, sure that the number forty has played out its magic and that God is sending His angels on a mission to bring me together, at last, with my true soul-mate.

5

The Find

Forty days before conception, a heavenly voice announces, This woman and this man will marry.

Talmud Sotah

Downtown Jerusalem is bustling this Saturday night as I pass Zion Square, the favourite meeting place for drop-outs and dealers, which ironically is just across the road from the police station at the Russian Compound. I am headed to the Anna Ticho House, a delightful restaurant set off the main road in an Arab house surrounded by a private garden with a lawn and palm trees. There is a terrace where tables are set outside in summer, and on winter nights a log fire burns, creating a warm and cosy atmosphere, but on this autumn night neither of those delights is available. This is where the artist Anna Ticho lived with her husband, the renowned ophthalmologist Avraham Albert Ticho. He established an eye clinic in the house and she painted there. As a token of her love for Jerusalem, Anna Ticho bequeathed the house, all of its collections and its library to the people of the city, to serve as a public centre for art.

I stand in the foyer waiting to be claimed, admiring the Anna Ticho landscapes drawn in ink and watercolour hanging on the thick walls. It is a relief to get away from the hotel lobby *shidduch* scene and I am impressed that Simcha

Lewinsky has suggested this venue. Mrs Frankel has assured me that Simcha is different from the other dates. 'He devotes himself to Torah and *mitzvot* – a real *zaddik*!' she boasted. I don't hold out much hope and haven't bothered to get dolled up to meet him. I have come straight from the Childbirth Association where I have resumed my studies. Now I only attend the yeshiva part time. I am wearing an old sweater and a denim skirt that is tearing at the pocket, and have pinned my lank hair into a bun. I pray the evening won't be a waste of time with yet another weirdo.

A tall man, stooped over with humility, approaches. His sea-blue eyes peer at me through thick prescription bifocals.

'Hey, Reva?' I hear him whisper hopefully.

'Simcha?' Jesus Christ dirty-blond hair falls to his shoulders and a shaggy beard and sidelocks give him an ethereal aura of holiness. The only thing I can think of is how awful I look and I curse myself for not making more of an effort.

He stands next to me for a moment without speaking and then in the gentlest of voices suggests, 'Let's take the corner table,' pointing to a round table at the back of the teahouse.

Walking across the room, I notice how Simcha glides along gracefully as if his feet do not quite touch the ground. He keeps his distance from me and I can feel him contract into a tight package, so as to be sure not to touch me. He seems sincere, so unlike some of the other dates, who made a show about being *shomer nigiah*, but would have easily jumped at the chance to break the rules. I sit down at the table. Simcha takes the chair opposite and sets his briefcase on the floor.

'What would you like to drink?' he asks shyly. I notice the streak of turquoise threaded through his ritual fringes. It is worn by those who want to be reminded of the sea and then of the sky that is reflected in the sea, and then of God's holy throne, which leaves no room for temptation.

'Cocoa please,' I reply.

A waitress takes our order – two hot chocolates with whipped cream.

'So . . . Reva,' he pauses, rocks back and forth, holds out his long and sensitive hands like Moses holding the two tablets. 'How did you get here – to Israel I mean?' He speaks in the sing-song tone of voice that men use when they learn the Talmud.

I need to sift through the memories in my head and find something to say that will not put Simcha off. The first date is not the appropriate time to confide the details of my history in Israel, picking oranges on a kibbutz where I had an affair with the Druze guard, or getting busted for drugs and spending the night in a cell just down the road from this teahouse. I don't think this Simcha Lewinsky would be impressed to hear that I was caught with ten kilos of Lebanese hashish. I play it safe and say, 'My grandfather was Chief Rabbi of Israel. I travelled with my parents to visit him every year. Israel has always been like a second home for me. It was the obvious place to move to.'

'Chief Rabbi of Israel!' Simcha leans forward, animated. 'That's a *gevalt*. Tell me about him.'

I can see my beloved grandfather in my mind's eye and say, 'He used to wear a silky dressing-gown and interlace his hands behind his back when he prayed. It was a gift to have seen someone pray with such devotion.'

Simcha smiles. 'Wooh,' he says. 'Did you study with him?'

'He was busy most of the time. But I insisted on sitting next to him at meal times and I would hold his hand under the table.' I omit telling him that when Grandpa was busy, I sat on the balcony of his apartment and flirted with the naval marines living upstairs. Instead I ask, 'So where are you from and how did you get here?'

'I'm from Colorado. No rabbis in my family, only cowboys! My parents don't know much about Judaism; they didn't bring me up to be religious.' He looks pained by the fact that he hasn't always been observant. 'I was travelling in the Middle East in my gap year, hanging out in Jordan, and I hooked up with a couple of guys who were on their way to Israel. I hadn't planned on coming here. I had no interest in Israel or the Jewish people. The Arab countries seemed far more fascinating to me.'

I like him, I like him, I think.

'When I got here I stayed in a run-down hotel in east Jerusalem, smoking narghiles in the souk at night, not realising that I was so close to the Western Wall – yet so far. Then one day as I was strolling down the Arab market, I heard what I thought was tribal singing and followed the sound to check it out. I went over to the men's section and looked around at the guys in the long black coats swaying and kissing the stones. I thought they were the weirdest bunch of freaks I'd ever seen. Then a young guy approached me and offered me lunch. I was kinda going with the flow and I followed him up the steps to the Aish HaTorah Yeshiva where I heard Rav Noach Weinberg talk about repairing the soul . . . Reva . . . well . . . the rest is history.'

'Unbelievable,' I say, already lulled into an alpha state by Simcha's mellow drawl.

The waitress brings our order and Simcha picks up his hot chocolate and disconnects from the world around him. He seems to be in a trance as he looks intensely into the ceramic cup at the chocolate sprinkles. He closes his eyes and slowly says the blessing, articulating each word, speaking directly to God. 'Blessed art Thou, O Lord, King of the universe, by whose word all things exist.'

I am overwhelmed by the way he recites the blessing with such reverence. I am sure that with his blessing, Simcha has created celestial angels who are now dancing above him in a halo of light.

'I was born Sheldon Lewinsky. I have taken my true Hebrew name, Simcha, after the Hassidic rabbi Simcha Bunim of Pshiskhe. His teachings are awesome. My favourite is "The Wedding Ring". Know it?' Simcha lowers his voice. 'The Torah compares this world to a wedding.'

I lean forward, excited. He is already talking about marriage.

He continues in the same sing-song voice. 'If a man makes every preparation for his wedding but forgets to purchase a ring,' he says, flipping his thumb upwards like the rabbis do, 'then the ceremony can't take place. In the same way, a man may work his entire life but forget to sanctify himself through Torah and *mitzvot*. When he comes to the next world, he can't enter. Imagine, his whole life has been a waste.' He pauses, looking straight into my eyes and continues in earnest.

'Reva, I want to devote myself to God in this world. I really want to attain the world to come . . . Do you understand?'

'I do,' I nod in agreement. 'I have had enough of the material life I grew up with and I want to be close to God. I'm prepared to work so my husband can devote himself to studying Torah,' I say boldly. 'I'm a qualified childbirth educator and coach. I'm considering beginning midwifery studies. I've already done an apprenticeship at the Misgav Ladach maternity hospital. I'll be earning soon.'

We are quiet. A lot has been said and we have bared our souls.

'Reva, would you be interested in learning something together . . . I brought some books . . . if you'd like that?'

'Sure.' I am delighted at this unusual request and settle into my wicker chair. I hold my glass, warming my fingers, while Simcha springs open the rusty lock of his briefcase. It is filled to the brim with esoteric books. Worn from use, with worm-holes in the yellowed corners, the pages look as ancient as the texts. He takes a few moments to decide which book to select. There is a hesitation in his manner that makes each move seem deeply thought out. Finally, he takes out a large book and caresses the peeling leather binding with love.

I am aroused by this sensual movement and can imagine the wells of emotion seething within this man. I sense that Simcha is someone who can merge the physical with the spiritual. If he treats a book with such care, he would surely make love to his wife just as tenderly. I have imagined intimate life in a holy Jewish marriage. The act itself embed-ded with meaning, bringing godliness into the world with our love and conceiving new life. It would be so different from purely physical sex in the secular world, the condoms and spermicidal creams, the worship of the body, the physical satisfaction and then the inevitable aftermath of loneliness. Even in my closest times with Chris, he would fall asleep after our lovemaking and I would lie there feeling empty and soul-starved, because our relationship was going nowhere and our love existed only in the now. Here is the combination I have been longing for, the union of body and soul that will finally satiate me. The depth of feeling I had with Chris will be nothing compared to what I will have in marrying a Jew, a Torah scholar, one who searches for truth. I watch how Simcha's fingers slide gently up and down the spine of the book before opening it, how those fingers with their neatly trimmed nails go flipping through the pages in search of a specific passage, and as I watch I can almost feel them threading through my hair, reaching for me.

He points to the first word in Genesis. 'Reva,' he says softly, 'let's begin? *Bereisheet* . . . In the beginning.' He lifts his hands and shakes them heavenward as if he too is about to create a world. 'Why does the Torah start with the letter bet, the second letter of the alphabet that has the numerical number of two, and not with *aleph*, the first letter?' His voice rises a few decibels.

For the past year, I have been turned on by stimulation of the mind rather than the body, by dissecting commentaries rather than caressing flesh. My cerebral muscles are now flexed from the constant *pilpul*, while my clitoris is slowly shrinking, and I eagerly listen to Simcha's answer.

'The Torah starts with the second letter to hint that there are two beginnings,' Simcha explains. 'The first is in Genesis, the creation of the world; the second is in Exodus, the creation of the Jewish nation at Sinai.' Simcha twirls his sidelocks around his thumb and forefinger as he speaks, swinging back and forth in his chair.

I wonder if there could be a second beginning for me with this man and I fantasise about him rocking back and forth with me, in prayer and in love.

'Every letter has meaning,' Simcha teaches. 'Torah is written black on white – black fire on white fire.' His hushed tone weaves a web of intimacy around us.

This is what I have been waiting for – the deepest of the deep, the light, the fire and the holiness.

'He's the one,' I tell Mrs Frankel the following morning. 'I just know it.'

'Vunderful! At last! I know I shouldn't tell you this but Simcha already called and told me vat an honour it would be for him to marry the daughter of a rabbi and fulfil the words of the Talmud, "It is worthy to marry the daughter of a *talmid chocham*." He also feels that you understood the maxim of toiling in this world and reaping the rewards in the world-to-come.'

'So how do we meet again?'

'I'll give him your number and he'll call you direct.'

I give Mrs Frankel a hug. I feel elated. I can't wait for the next date.

I study with fervour, preparing texts for my dates with Simcha to impress him with my knowledge, taking care with my appearance and sitting demurely, repressing my fiery nature. Each time we meet, Simcha brings a different text to study and we submerge ourselves in the spiritual spheres and the creation of the world. We study esoteric commentaries on the Torah, the Sefat Emet, Midrash Tanchuma on the weekly portion, morals and values from the Mussar schools. We discuss the meaning of life and how to cleave to God.

After two months of dating we meet this evening in the King David lobby. Thoughts of Chris couldn't be further from my mind as I sit spellbound by Simcha's stories of Hassidic masters and *lamed-vav zaddikim*, the thirty-six righteous men on whose merit the world exists. Of all the material that we cover tonight, I love most the Hassidic tales of the threadbare down-and-outs, men who are satisfied with their lot, aware of the enormity of the repercussions of their *mitzvot* on the upper worlds and longing for one thing only, the Messianic redemption. Simcha is just like these men, I think. He is a modern-day Siddhartha, pure of heart and soul, who would give the shabby shirt off his back to anyone in need.

He puts the book aside, takes off his glasses and looks at me with great intensity. 'Reva, do you want to dedicate your life to God – I mean really dedicate your life?'

'Yes, of course I do.' I melt inside at the way he is looking at me, not with lust or desire but with love and recognition.

'I feel we could be partners in bringing God into the world. Reva, will you build a house of God with me?' He clasps his hands together, yet I know that it is my hands he wants to hold.

'Simcha . . . yes . . . oh my God . . . yes.' I want to hold him, love him and caress his sensitive fingers.

He rummages around in his briefcase, takes out a package and places it in front of me. 'This is my engagement present to you. I was hoping you would say yes.'

It looks a bit big for an engagement ring. As I untie the silky bow, I comfort myself with thoughts of a necklace, a string of pearls, a family heirloom. Instead, a leather-bound prayer book weighs heavily in my hands. I open it and turn the pages edged in gold leaf. The benedictions over *Shabbes* candles and prayers for weekdays and festivals await my recital. Simcha's Hassidic story about forgetting to buy a wedding ring and not being able to enter the world to come enters my mind, but I block the thought and stammer, 'Thank you, Simcha,' glimpsing the life of devotion that lies ahead.

Closing the book, I feel that my prayers have been answered. The forty-day prayer-marathon has paid off and I have merited a *zaddik*. Yet, as I extend my hand to place the prayer book back on the table, I cannot help but notice how bare my finger suddenly looks without the sparkle of a diamond ring.

6

Mazeltov!

He who marries a wife – his sins are suspended.
By entering into marriage, man and wife merit the
forgiveness of their past sins.

Talmud Yebamot: 63B

I am standing next to my mother under the awning of the synagogue building. Rain is pelting down on the London pavement. Mother, who is wearing a mink coat, clutches a brown crocodile leather handbag with one hand and keeps flipping her other hand clockwise to read her watch.

'It's not coming. We'll be late.'

'Mum, the cab will be here any moment.'

Mother takes what she thinks is a deep breath, an act she has been told by her doctor will help her relax, but in fact her inhale is no more than a shallow gulp of air. She is biting the inside of her cheek, a habit that lets me know she is on the brink of despair. Groaning softly, she turns her gold band round and round her wedding finger, which is chapped raw with psoriasis, a condition that erupts in time of stress. Every minute that passes seems like an hour. Every occupied taxi that drives by is a disappointment.

'It's no good. We'll be too late. We should have hailed a cab on the street instead of ordering one. It's all gone wrong. Oh, why didn't we just get one on the street? In this downpour we'll never get there on time. Then I won't be home to make your father's lunch. If he doesn't eat by one o'clock his hernia will act up. Oh dear God, make the taxi come!'

I want to strangle her. Her ominous forecasts affect my state of mind too and today, when we are going to the couturier to choose my wedding dress, a day I have looked forward to all my life, I want to feel calm and happy.

'Mummy, we have plenty of time. Don't worry. I'm sure it'll come any minute,' I say, and then, accessing my newly acquired skills, I pray for the taxi to arrive and put an end to the agony.

'Nothing ever goes right, does it? Well, not for me anyway.' I take her arm and can feel her slipping, collapsing into herself.

I want to shake her, tell her to get a grip, or alternatively stuff a handful of Valium down her throat. Instead, I take the role of mother and try to soothe her. Today of all days I need a strong mother, someone who can help me make decisions, someone to rely on. As much as I try to concentrate on Hilly's philosophy of fixing the soul through difficult trials, I cannot bury my childish need to be mothered and am once again trapped in the frustrating cycle of expectation and disappointment.

The taxi swerves into Mayfair, past the Dorchester Hotel and down towards St James's. I look out in wonder at the majestic solid architecture and the vast greenness of Hyde Park. It is more beautiful than I remembered. I think about the life I've left behind here: my school friends Lisa, Suzy and Vicky; the theatre and art galleries that Chris introduced me to and that I came to love; walks in Hyde park; shopping at my favourite boutiques in Primrose Hill and Marylebone High

Street; aimless strolls through Soho and Chinatown; long afternoons browsing through the stalls in Camden Lock on a Sunday; and most of all the glorious bookshops. Then I think of the sunny Jerusalem skies, the holy man I love who is waiting to build a Jewish home with me, and I am thankful for my own redemption.

Simcha has advised me to be punctilious while removed from my protected Torah world, so I open my handbag and take out my prayer book. 'Blessed art Thou, O Lord, who guides us in peace to our desired destination.' I shut my eyes tight as I recite the blessing that is meant for travellers making a journey by sea or air even though I am only going for a five-minute taxi ride.

My mother turns her coiffed head around to face me. 'After all the sacrifices we've made, the elocution lessons, exorbitant school fees, the nose job – is this our reward, having you wear that dowdy dress and mumbling prayers all the time?'

I continue with my prayer, as it is forbidden to stop in the middle.

'All that money down the drain.'

I try to concentrate on my supplication but am remembering how my mother convinced me that the tiny painless operation on my nose would make such a difference to my looks. She had raved about 'a wonderful man in Harley Street who works miracles'. Of course, I also wanted to look pretty and had hated my long nose, but my agreeing to the operation had more to do with being beautiful in my mother's eyes and gaining her appreciation than anything else. I can see myself, seventeen years old, the day the plaster was removed. It was two weeks after the plastic surgery and mother had come with me for the unveiling. She was so thrilled with the results that instead of hugging me and telling me how wonderful I looked, she threw her arms around the surgeon's neck. I never took centre stage in my mother's life, not even then, but that day I didn't care. I felt relieved and happy knowing she was proud of me at last.

'And a Hassid of all things.'

The prayer recited, I open my eyes and say, 'Mummy, really, what difference does it make if Simcha is a Hassid?'

'And not even with *frum* parents.'

'Mummy.'

'Well, it's difficult for your father.'

'Why? I thought you'd be glad I'm marrying a Jew, and a religious one at that.' This is the first time I have even hinted at the taboo subject of the Chris affair. Now the words are out, I know it's a mistake, as Mother's hand jumps to her armpit and massages the mastectomy scar that runs across her chest. It's something she does whenever she's upset and I can't stand it. The whole business still scares me, even though it happened a long time ago. I was only twelve when she was diagnosed, when my own body was developing. I felt guilty about the little buds that were sprouting on my own chest and tried to hide them under baggy shirts, as though their health and their allure might exacerbate my mother's feelings of loss.

'Reva, you are giving me a headache with all these questions. Stop it. You're pressuring me.'

I turn my gaze to the Mayfair streets, upset by my parents' reaction to my marrying a Hassid. But I shouldn't be surprised by my father's response. I know he is as allergic to the devotion of the newly religious as he is to the bad taste of the nouveau riche. For him the idea of making your whole life revolve around Jewish practice instead of weaving the practice into your life is on a par with idolatry. He isn't going to approve of Simcha looking up to his Hassidic rabbi as a guru, eating the leftovers from his *Shabbes* meal because he believes they contain sparks of holiness, or leaving his sidelocks swinging down his cheeks. My father considers Judaism a private matter. He wears his ritual fringes under his shirt in a modest fashion and tucks the tassels into his trousers rather than flaunting them for all to see.

'Anyway, I for one would be ashamed to be seen walking with a man in a long caftan and swinging sidelocks,' she says. 'In this day and age!'

'It's just clothes, Mum. It's what's going on inside a person that's important.'

'And tell me, Reva, what is so appealing about receiving a prayer book instead of a diamond ring?' Mother lets out a long-suffering sigh and caresses her own two-carat rock. 'If only you could marry that lawyer, Philip Newman, instead of this Simcha whoever he is.'

Even though I know a prayer book is the greatest treasure Simcha could have given me, I cannot deny that I would be proud to wear a diamond and I am secretly embarrassed that he hasn't bought me one. I imagine my mother is ashamed of me in front of the women at the Ladies' Guild meetings whose daughters all seem to have married well and to be spending their time skiing in St Moritz in winter and cruising the south of France in summer.

'Simcha's not materialistic. Diamonds don't mean anything to him. He's a good man, immersed in Torah and *mitzvot*.

Can't you see that's a good thing?' In my head I can hear Hilly telling me that my answering back is a sin, an affront to the fifth commandment.

'I can't believe you haven't asked after Michelle,' my mother blurts out, changing the subject, a trick she is so good at – shifting the dynamic and putting me in the wrong. 'I would have thought as a bride-to-be and a yeshiva student you would have thought to ask about your poor sister!'

Oh no. Here we go. The impossible trap. If I ask, I risk provoking an outpouring of tears. If I don't, I'm selfish. I can't win. I feel lost and alone and wish I had stayed in Jerusalem and taken Mrs Frankel's advice to borrow a wedding dress from the local charity fund.

The taxi stops at a red light and Mother's attention shifts to the Bally shoe sale display. I know she finds relief in focusing on the material. It is a welcome break from thinking about Michelle, whose thick red hair, pale blue eyes and sweet smile can never compensate for the image of the healthy child she had to let go of after the terrible day in the specialist's office.

'How's Michelle, Mummy?'

My mother sighs. I interpret this deep breath as a sign of guilt. She believes Michelle is a punishment for marrying my father, the son of a famous rabbi, when she didn't come from a religious background herself. She is not the traditional rabbi's wife with a modest dress and a cumbersome wig, nor does she give classes on family purity, and this adds to her feelings of inadequacy. But she is devoted to my father. She critiques his writings and edits his sermons and, from her hints about their sex life, I gather all is well in the bedroom too.

'Michelle is as well as she'll ever be.' Rivulets of mascara run down her Estée Lauder cheeks. I can't bear to see my mother cry. She reaches into her bag, retrieves a tissue smudged with red lipstick kisses and pats her face.

'Forgive an old woman who talks too much,' she says, her voice silky now, taking my hand in hers. 'I just don't want you to throw your life away, darling. Michelle can never marry, and I want you to be happy, I really do.' And I know that of course she does. I can feel her warmth flowing into me. I squeeze her hand in return and snuggle up to her, enjoying the comfort of her closeness and the caress of the mink against my skin. I savour every moment, as I know it cannot last for long. Growing up I felt as if I had two mothers. There was the glamorous one, wearing a beaded evening gown with her hair done and her face on, in a terrific mood. She was beautiful then, loving, promising and encouraging. Without any warning, however, her exuberance could turn suddenly to despair, and she would be transformed into an old woman wearing shabby clothes over a limp body suddenly devoid of all muscle tone, weeping and hysterical, telling me she couldn't cope. There was no telling when the melancholic phase of this cycle would end. But when it did, it disappeared as quickly as it had come, and then everything would be all right again, until the next time.

The traffic is heavy but we are creeping along Piccadilly, almost at our destination.

'Mum, try and understand. I love Simcha and everything he aspires to be. He'll be a spiritual guide who will nurture my soul,' I say, feeling secure of her love with my hand in hers.

But the moment has passed. Her hand returns to her lap, clenched. 'Really, Reva. Grow up! You need a husband to provide for you in the way that you have been accustomed, not a saint who studies all day for a pittance. Really! Anyway, it's still not too late to change your mind.'

My love turns to hate as quickly as my mother's nurturing turns to nonsense. Can she think my love for Simcha is something so transient that it can simply be forgotten? I know she has a hard time comprehending other people's feelings because she is so overwhelmed by her own, but does she really think I will cast him aside?

'I'm exhausted,' she says. There are more lines under her eyes than when I saw her last. She has had cosmetic surgery and, from afar, looks like a young woman. But now that I am up close, all her sixty-two years are apparent. She slumps into the seat. 'I didn't take my Mogadon until two o'clock in the morning. I know what you're going to say, that I've tried giving up my sleeping pills before and it never works. Anyway, I was so groggy when I woke up this morning, and I still am.'

I think of Simcha and long to hear his calm voice and see the understanding in his eyes. I can't wait to get back home to Jerusalem, far far away from my mother's craziness.

We run through the rain into the entrance of Bettie's couture house. Mum relaxes. Shopping calms her. Bettie supplies everyone who's anyone in Anglo-Jewry with bridal gowns and elegant eveningwear, of which mother has a magnificent collection, hating to be seen in the same thing twice. We enter the showroom and my mother runs ahead to greet Bettie. I know she is looking forward to seeing the latest fabrics from Paris.

Bettie's kind, smiling eyes radiate warmth. She wears fuchsia lipstick, which has smudged her two front teeth, and musky perfume, which is scenting the air around her sumptuously plump body. Her manicured hands gesticulate wildly as she speaks.

'Dolly! *Mazeltov*!' She hugs my mother and then turns to me.

'Mummy told me your wonderful news.' She takes a few steps back. 'Let me take a look at you. I haven't seen you for ages.' I have loved Bettie ever since the days when she let me wear her diamond rings during synagogue services. She looks me up and down. 'Tell me,' she asks smiling. 'Is he divine?'

'*Baruch hashem*,' I answer shyly.

Bettie is taken aback. She has never heard me bless the Lord before.

'Choose whatever you want, darling.' Bettie gestures grandly toward the rolls of white fabric.

Cream silk and satin slide over my skin like mercury and I imagine whirling down the aisle in sensuous abandon. I see myself in a sleeveless dress with my long tresses falling over my shoulders. A cluster of bridesmaids hold up my train as I take my father's arm to walk down the aisle. Mrs Frankel warned me about the spiritual danger of this trip to London, but she need not have worried because I quickly extinguish my frivolous fantasy and move on down the showroom past reels upon reels of fabric until I notice a demure velvet. 'I think this would be perfect,' I tell Bettie. 'I'll go with the velvet.'

Mother sits in an armchair as Bettie measures and drapes the fabric over me. I want the bodice of the dress to rise to a strangling neckline of appliqué flowers and the waist to fall low, taking away attention from my full breasts. I have always had to hide them, even when I didn't adhere to the Jewish modesty code. Already at thirteen they were provocative. The fashion for girls in my circle was a 'skinny', a tight ribbed sweater with a polo neck. I begged to have one and my mother bought me a sleeveless lilac skinny. But when she saw me wearing it, saw the material tight and accentuating my breasts, she exclaimed, 'It's inappropriate for your age and position as a rabbi's daughter. You look like a tart.' She made me feel so self-conscious, I never wore it again. Now that I've gone to the opposite extreme she is still disapproving.

'It's a bit *Fiddler on the Roof*ish,' she says, looking at the modest lines of the dress Bettie is pinning together. 'Are you sure you wouldn't prefer something more sophisticated?'

'No, this is perfect. I don't want to show off my body. I'm saving myself for Simcha and I shall only uncover my hair in front of him.'

'It's a phase,' Mother tells Bettie, raising her eyebrows. 'They all go through them. What can you do?'

A week later, my trousseau completed, my parents and I fly to Israel for the big event. I am overjoyed to be going home. Living with my parents again has been hard. And there were far too many reminders of the Reva I would rather forget. Passing the mezzanine floor that houses the cloakrooms in between the synagogue and our apartment brought back memories of my first sexual experiences. This floor is virtually abandoned during the week and used only by the honorary officers if they need to relieve themselves during board meetings. Thus it served as the perfect haunt for my initiation into heavy teenage petting courtesy of Mark H, who would pull out what he called 'his willie' and show me how to rub it while he buried his face in my already very large breasts. My clothes stained with come, I would sneak home, lock the bathroom door and scrub out the evidence.

Every time I walked past the brass doors leading into the synagogue, the most modern house of prayer in London with a décor of wood-panelled walls, rich carpeting and turquoise leather upholstery set against a background of stained-glass windows depicting biblical scenes, I was reminded of the night I lost my virginity; of how Aaron, my first boyfriend, a deeply spiritual boy who read auras and engaged in astral travel, slowly undressed me in the back of the men's section under the window depicting Eve being tempted by the snake. He had told me that it was not his first time, but from his inexperienced fumbling at my shirt buttons and the difficulty he had with the hooks of my bra, in retrospect, I think otherwise. Once he had released my breasts he cradled them in his young and innocent hands and let out a cry of pleasure. I snuggled up to him on the royal blue carpeted steps that lead up to the *bima*. Under the light of the *ner tamid* which hangs high above the Holy Ark and radiates a constant glow, I held onto my adolescent guru while he picked up my skirt and found his way inside me. With a single thrust and a shooting pain, I was rid of the barrier that separated me from womanhood. But, most blasphemous of all, upon seeing the bloody stain left on the royal blue carpet, I stood up naked, ascended the *bima*, faced the Holy Ark that shelters the Torah scrolls and shouted out 'Hallelujah'. Hearing footsteps I quickly squatted down to dress. It was Charles, the porter, on his nightly security check. 'Better go on home,' he had said, and I did. For months I was sure he would tell on me, but unlike my father's congregants, who reported whenever they saw me entering a non-kosher eating establishment or associating with seedy-looking characters, Charles kept quiet.

These memories belong to my past and I don't want to think of them again. I am glad to be going home, back to my Simcha and the holiness of my Jewish life, away from a past of searching. I have finally found what I was looking for.

In the arrivals lounge, I look for Simcha among the crowd of religious black-hatted men hauling heavy luggage, teenagers returning from trips to the Far East and groups of American Jewish tourists. Here he is and walking straight towards me. I run ahead of my parents and stand close to him. I stare into his eyes and he into mine. He repeats my name, 'Reva, Reva, Reva, welcome home,' and claps his hands together to keep them from touching me.

'I'm so glad to be back.'

'I'm glad to have you back.'

My parents have caught up with me. Simcha needs no introduction. My mother, dressed in a powder-blue suit, staggers towards him like a wounded animal. 'You can't imagine, Simcha, what a terrible flight we had,' she says, taking his arm as if he were an old friend. 'I think I've got food poisoning from the chicken.' She shoots him her 'at death's door' grimace and sags momentarily onto his supporting arm.

My father is wheeling the trolley loaded with matching maroon luggage and my wedding dress, covered in polythene, draped over the metal rail. His hands are arthritic and the thumb and forefinger that are holding the trolley are bent out of shape. Every time I see these deformed fingers, I feel a wave of love for him. On his small feet are black dress shoes that I know he polishes daily. Today he is sporting a bow tie, black silk with white polka dots. His midnight blue suit is well cut and he stands with his weight on one foot, hand on hip just like Grandpa's famous stance, a pose often photographed when he was speaking in public. It is easy to see the resemblance between father and son, but my father has become assimilated since his yeshiva days in Poland. He is a generation further away from the revelation at Sinai than Grandpa and this is obvious by his more modern appearance. His skullcap in black velvet is custom made and looks more elegant than Grandpa's taffeta *kippa*, which sat like a rabbinical pillbox on his head. My father doesn't wear a long morning coat that ends at the knee in the style of the great rabbis, but, instead, a hip-length suit jacket. He exudes a polish, a dapper elegance, that Grandpa, despite his silk top hat made in Jermyn Street and silver-topped walking stick, never had.

Now Father is holding out his hands to Simcha. He is a short man, only five foot four, but he fills any room with a huge presence as if he were a strapping six-footer. It is not his fine features that give him such presence – the broad forehead that accommodates his fast working brain, the elegant angular nose, the perfectly manicured beard, shaped into a half moon, not a straggly hair out of place – it is the warmth and light that emanate from him. People are drawn to this radiance and seek him out, nourished by simply being near him. I remember how the son of one of my father's congregants, on seeing him descend the *bima* in full clerical uniform of cap and gown, turned to his mother and asked her if the rabbi was God. We have often laughed over this cute titbit but, like that child,

I have often felt that my dad has the capacity to father us all. Now his mouth, a thin red strip, has burst open into a smile so warm it radiates pure godliness. I can feel Simcha bask in that love. What Simcha doesn't know is that when those thin lips stay closed and tighten into a straight line, and Father's dark brown eyes cloud over, he shuts down completely and his whole being radiates the wrath of the Lord instead of His love.

'*Shalom Aleichem*.' My father greets Simcha.

'*Mazeltov*.' Simcha embraces my father.

Seeing them hug each other seems like a promise that all will be well. Simcha tries to free his right hand to take hold of the trolley, but it has been firmly claimed by Mother, who has found a new and willing audience.

'Simcha, you know the journey's a bit much for me. It's the after-effects of not being able to fall asleep the night before a journey. I'm always waiting for the alarm to go off. I took only half a sleeping pill last night but I didn't sleep, so I'm groggy from the pill *and* the bad night . . . well . . . tell me something about yourself. Reva must have told you about her sister Michelle, terrible tragedy, ach, you can't imagine, well we're here for a wedding so let's not talk about harrowing things, how are your parents?'

I cringe and know I must be careful not to speak *loshon hora* against my mother when Simcha and I are alone. But Simcha is handling her fine. He is full of compassion and gives her support.

My father and I walk behind. I notice how my father eyes the line of turquoise threaded through Simcha's ritual fringes. He raises his eyebrows, turns to me and reports, 'Seems nice enough. Reminds me of the ritual slaughterers in Poland who wore their *tzisis* over their shirts stained with cow blood.'

I pray Simcha cannot hear my father.

'Hair is a bit long. No problem. I'll take him to the barber before the wedding.'

'Daddy! Please!' I know he is serious and remember the day I came home with the latest fashionable haircut, cropped short with a thin braid hanging down my back. Without asking my permission, my father clipped off the braid. I can feel the constriction that always grips my chest when my parents ignore my feelings. It's as though I've had the wind knocked out of me so badly I can't catch my breath. Now the anger starts to boil inside of me. I have been in this state so many times before. I must admit that I have found my father's sarcasm funny when it is not directed towards me, but now I see it is the lowest form of humour. If they notice anything, my parents choose to ignore any signs of the inner turmoil I am feeling right now. But probably they are too self-absorbed to have registered my distress.

In the taxi from the airport, my father checks his pulse and feels his forehead for signs of fever. 'I must have caught a bug on the plane with all those germs,' he mutters from the front seat.

I know my father had hoped for a heart specialist as his son-in-law and that his sudden spasm of hypochondria is due to his disappointment. He always hides his true emotions behind a physical condition, whether it is his heart or his hernia. He spends a lot of energy trying to prevent catching cold or contracting sickness. On the few times he took me to the cinema or travelled on public transport, he would move seats the moment he heard someone sniffling or coughing, fearing they were contagious. If he feels the slightest tickle in his throat, he rushes for the lozenges and gets straight into bed, wrapping himself up warm under the covers, just like he does after taking a bath. I often laugh at his ways, but his hypochondria has rubbed off on me. He has made me fragile and frightened of being ill. Every time I sense a weakness in my muscles or a congestion in my sinuses, instead of ignoring the symptoms, I worry and consider myself an invalid.

Today, I can see in Simcha what my father sees: an unsophisticated guy from a small town who is enthralled to have found his Judaism and is over-fervent in his practice. But I can see beyond that; I see what my father cannot appreciate: his gentleness, kindness and purity.

At the King David Hotel, Simcha says his goodbyes to my parents. Soon he will be saying his goodbyes to me too, for we are not allowed to see each other during the week before the wedding, as demanded by tradition. So when my parents take the elevator to their room Simcha and I sit awhile in the lobby, together for the last time till our wedding day.

'It was tough, eh?'

'Unbearable. Can't you tell?'

'They're lovely people.'

The trauma of the past week comes gushing out. 'When I said *Asher Yazar* my father stood next to me outside the bathroom imitating my mumbling the prayer. I thought he would be glad to see me finally saying the prayers, but he couldn't bear it.'

Simcha nods understandingly.

'He believes prayer is a private affair, so he hated seeing me standing in the corner of the living room reciting the afternoon *mincha* prayers. There was nothing about my keeping to the law that he appreciated. My mother kept making comments about my baggy dress and thick stockings. She made me feel downright ugly. After the fitting for the wedding dress, instead of taking me out and treating me like a bride, she regressed into one of her depressions and hobbled around in a stained dressing-gown. It's so terrible to see her like that, when her head flops loose. It's as if there are two of her: the one who is all dressed up, hair done and smiling, and the one who looks like a charwoman.'

'She does seem uptight. Could she be thinking of Michelle, who will never marry or have children?'

What a kind man he is. I feel so close to Simcha. He will never say a bad word about anybody. He's everything to me now, my strength, my confidant, and my partner.

'Maybe. It's hard for me to accept her, even though I know how much she's suffering all the time. I can't help wishing we could have gone out somewhere to celebrate, just the two of us, mother and daughter.

'I'm here,' he says, 'and in a week, we'll be together forever.'

With Simcha out of the way, my father's bug miraculously vanishes and he spends his time writing and rewriting his wedding address. My mother busies herself with the seating plan for the wedding dinner, making sure her London friends are seated near the top table. My own time is spent going to Mrs Frankel's every morning to review the laws of purity. This subject is off limits to us girls until we are engaged to be married. As it is kept secret and has to do with sex, it is the most interesting subject of all. At the yeshiva, Sally-Anne and I sneaked books out of the library and pored over them together, giggling childishly, trying to fathom the intricate laws.

I am sitting with Mrs Frankel in her home, a privilege for a new bride. A large text lays open on the table. I am eager to make sure I understand the laws. Sally-Anne and I used to hold many conversations on this topic. She had inside information from a married friend and confided that a couple can only do it half the month. Getting a period makes the woman impure and she can't touch her husband again until she's been spiritually cleansed by going to the ritual bath. It sounded exciting to me, but Sally-Anne found the idea of being unclean or impure a chauvinistic ploy to keep women in check. There are many girls at the yeshiva who have had a hard time accepting a woman's role in Judaism. Women don't have to perform time-bound *mitzvot* like praying three times a day or building and sitting in a *succah* booth on the Feast of the Tabernacles, as their time should be allocated to taking care of their husbands and their children. The rabbis in the yeshiva say that women don't participate in these or in other *mitzvot*, like wearing *tefillin* every morning and wrapping themselves in a *tallis*. Nor should they read straight from the Torah because if they are menstruating and thus impure, they shouldn't be in close proximity to the Torah scroll. But unlike the feminists, who want to be just like the men, I have no such desires. I like the segregation, sitting behind the partition in synagogue and being separate from the men. Otherwise my mind starts to wander and I cannot concentrate on God.

'Darlink, remember that before you see blood you may have what the rabbis call "a feeling in the vomb".'

'Like a first cramp or something?'

'A feeling that makes you go check in the bathroom.'

'OK.' I think I know what she means – the dull ache that I feel the day before I menstruate.

'Ven you feel this feeling, you must consider yourself a *nidda*, impure, and must separate from your husband.'

'Separate?'

'Separate the beds. You have bought twin beds, Reva, no? Ven you are permitted to each other, you put the beds together again.'

My parents have made a shipment of furniture for our new apartment as a wedding present. I'm sure they've sent twin beds.

'Ven your period is finished you must count seven blood-free days and then go to the *mikveh*.'

'I know. I'm in the middle of counting right now.'

I have only been once to a *mikveh*, with Dvorah the night before her wedding. The *mikveh* looked like a small swimming pool. Dvorah entered completely naked and immersed herself in the water seven times. I will only immerse myself three times according to the tradition in my family.

'And when you are separated, you must realise this special time is a gift from God. How do you think we sustain our marriages with the divorce rate so high now in America? By separating two weeks a month and keeping the excitement alive. It's like starting anew every time.' She smiles knowingly. I try and block out images of her and Rabbi Frankel, a scholar with a long beard and big black hat, clasped in an embrace.

'But let's talk about the wedding night itself. First of all, the room has to be completely dark.'

'Not even candlelight?'

'No. The man mustn't see his vife's body.'

I remember morning sex with Chris, still warm and dozy from sleep, teeth unbrushed, with all the smells of the night on our bodies. Lazily I would turn over, fit myself into the curve of his body spoons-style and press my ass into him, gently at first as if I was moving in my sleep and gradually with more pressure until I could feel his penis waking up. Then, still half asleep, intertwined in each other, we would begin our day with pleasure. It felt so good, exactly how a new day should begin – to fuel ourselves with love to face the challenges ahead.

'He's not allowed to see your . . . openink.'

'My opening?'

'It is forbidden.'

'So . . . there's no . . . ?'

'Reva, this is not for a nice Jewish girl. It's for the *goyim*. You vant your husband to respect you and cherish you, not put his mouth where you hev been to the toilet, feh!' she spits in the air to show her disgust.

'So . . . what is allowed?' I ask.

'The missionary position. Wear a sexy nightgown and make sure you keep slim.'

'Is it true about the sheet?' I have been dying to ask this question after hearing the girls at the yeshiva talk about the very religious who do it through a hole in a sheet.

'Only among some Hassidic sects. The voman covers her naked body mit a sheet and the man enters through the hole that the bride embroiders before the wedding.'

'But why do they do it that way?' I hope Simcha will not insist on it.

'These people are on another level. The man doesn't vant to

recall the softness of his vife's body vile he is praying, as it vould create an obstacle in connecting to God. But this is not for you, Revaleh. You and Simcha are not ready for such stringent behaviour.'

I had hoped that within the sanctity of a holy union, our sex life wouldn't be confined to strict laws. I had no idea that sexual behaviour was limited to such an extent. I doubt whether I can live like this. It will never satisfy me and I fear I'll get bored. I'm scared I'll mess up and during the heat of passion make a wrong move, slide on top or beg Simcha to talk dirty. I feel like a traitor, putting up a pious front but underneath I am the same Reva longing for wild sex, for eating while doing it, sucking a penis with a square of chocolate melting in my mouth. I know that if this marriage is to work, I need to suppress my fire, bury it so deep that I will never feel its heat again, guard my eyes from men, not watch movies or read magazines with sensual content and sweep my lusty self under the carpet forever. Maybe this is the way to repent my past, I think. I can rectify my sins by having relations with my husband according to the law, lie back like Queen Victoria and think only about God and His holy Torah and channel my lusts to a higher purpose.

'Don't look so vorried, Reva. According to the marriage contract, a man must satisfy his wife. I know Simcha is learning family purity with Rabbi Sapphire. He will learn everything he needs to know to fulfil his marital duties. Smile. You're a *Callah*. Be happy.'

The night before the wedding it is time for me to go to the *mikveh*. I beg my mother to accompany me but she tries to get out of it. She has bad memories from going to the *mikveh* in the first years of her marriage. She never liked floating in other women's bath water and cleverly appealed to my father's hypochondriac fears, complaining that she always caught cold on *mikveh* nights. Of course, he gave her permission to stop.

The Bayit Vegan *mikveh* is crowded tonight. 'All the mothers go, so I'm here too,' she tells the matron on duty.

I undress in the cubicle and enter the small pool. My mother is looking at her watch. She wants to be back safely in her hotel room. The matron needs Mother's help as she is on constant call. 'Could you take my place at reception for a few minutes?' she asks Mother.

Mother sits at the desk that is piled with towels, cotton swabs and nail varnish remover. 'I'm the *mikveh* lady!' she cries when I return from my immersion, laughing at the absurdity of her post.

My wedding day is finally here. I check into the bridal suite of the King David Hotel. I take off my shoes and lie down on the silk eiderdown covering the queen-sized bed. I count the hours till I will lie here with Simcha as his wife and we will finally be able to hold each other naked. I look around the room, amused that it is from this lavish setting with its plush sofas, soft-coloured carpets and Jacuzzi bathroom that my ascetic religious life will begin. Only the luxury of being held in Simcha's loving arms matters to me now and I wonder how it will feel to be with a man after two years of abstinence, a man I have made a commitment to. I imagine the hugging close, the whispering, the sharing of secrets and then the slow exploration of each other's bodies.

I draw the heavy brocade curtains and lay out my wedding clothes on the bed. I begin to dress. Slipping on virginal white panties, I imagine Simcha's sensitive fingers sliding them down my legs. As I hook the French push-up bra in place, hoisting my breasts into its lacy cups, I long for him to bury his face in my deep cleavage. I look at myself in the mirror and am suddenly ashamed of the provocative lingerie I have chosen. I will undress in the dark and he will not see it. I step into the modest wedding dress and fasten the delicate pearl buttons. It is heavy and weighs me down. I reach for the velvet headdress that has been custom made by milliners in Bond Street to match Bettie's wedding gown. Shaped like a shopping bag, it fans out at the bottom from a headband camouflaged by artificial white flowers. I stuff my flowing hair into the white hat. It looks awful, but now that I am about to be a married woman my hair must be covered or it will be considered 'naked'. I close my eyes, take a deep breath, and chant the mantra that is inscribed above the Holy Ark in the yeshiva synagogue: 'God stands before me at all times. God stands before me at all times.' After I have wrapped myself in His holiness again, I look at my reflection through His eyes and see that I am beautiful. Now I understand the meaning of King Solomon's famous words, 'the honour of the king's daughter lies within.'

My stomach rumbles with hunger. I am fasting, needing the atonement that only a Yom Kippur fast can bring. Mrs Frankel has explained that a wedding is like a Yom Kippur, a transition from one life to another, when one's sins are absolved. I crave a toasted cheese sandwich and a bar of chocolate, but don't want to jeopardise the fresh life that is waiting for me.

I turn the laws over in my mind, yearning for the moment when Simcha and I will leave our guests and disappear into the *cheder yichud*, the bridal room adjacent to the banqueting hall, where he will veil me before the ceremony and where we will be alone together for the first time afterwards. Even when Simcha visited me at my apartment, we left the front door wide open as it is forbidden for an unmarried couple to sit together in a private space. There we will break our fast, but I know I will only have an appetite for Simcha and will want to kiss the lips that have expounded Torah and asked me to marry him. I fantasise about doing it in the *yichud* room, my wedding dress pulled up, the lingerie pulled down. But even if we put out all the lights, I don't think this would be allowed.

There is a knock at the door. My parents have come to accompany me to the synagogue.

'You look beautiful,' my mother says and kisses the air by my cheek, not wanting to smudge me with her lipstick or crease her dress. My father places his hands on my Bo-Peep hat and, overcome with emotion himself, his rigid guard down, he intones the blessing in a trembling voice: 'May God make you like Sarah, Rivka, Rachel and Leah.'

This is the moment I have been waiting for, ever since he turned his back on me all those years ago when I left with Chris. I never imagined then that the day would come when he would include me into the family again. With his blessing, he has allowed me back in his heart. Now I want to make him proud of me and give him *nachas*.

I check myself one last time in the mirror and see Sarah, Rivka and Rachel looking back at me. The French lingerie hidden, I look like an FFB, the real McCoy, a holy Jewish bride. Taking my father's arm, I leave the room, my mother following behind.

My parents link arms with me as we enter the grand marble foyer of the ballroom.

My father scans the room filled with an ecstatic crowd of newly religious chatting and sipping cocktails. 'They look like a bunch of freaks,' he mumbles under his breath and takes out his handkerchief to wipe his forehead. 'This is the latest fad – hippies turned Hassidim. Sidelocks instead of ponytails. An embarrassment to Judaism.' Suddenly feeling ill, he coughs up a lump of phlegm into his hanky.

'Look at all the beggars over there,' my mother points to a group of tramps huddled around the hors-d'oeuvres. Simcha has taken the opportunity to emulate the ways of the Hassidic masters and invited every down-and-out in his neighbourhood to the wedding.

'Tell me, where have I gone wrong? Why has she rejected my Judaism and gone for this cultist idolising of half-wits?' my father asks my mother.

I know he could never understand that his Judaism lacked spirituality for me. There was no joy in the observance I saw at home. But my father cannot imagine there is any other way than his. For him, godliness must be expressed with decorum. He cannot take seriously either a relaxed or an over-fervent expression of Judaism.

My mother isn't paying attention. She has spotted Lady P among the crowd and waves at her, unleashing the toothy smile that she saves for VIPs.

All I can think of is being with my holy Simcha and getting away from my parents and their critical tongues. I see Simcha walking towards me with his parents. From his frown, I can tell he is also having a hard time.

Even though Simcha isn't supposed to see me before the chuppah, he's right behind his parents, who are walking towards me. This is the first time I have met the Lewinskys, who flew in last night. Patty Lewinsky, Simcha's mother, hugs me tight. I feel love from this woman dressed simply in a polyester pantsuit that she boasts she bought with margarine coupons. Matt Lewinsky is decked out in his best blue pants held up by a Native American turquoise and silver belt. The spurs of his cowboy boots click as he walks on the marble floor. Out of respect, he covers his balding head with a cowboy hat. He smiles at me, but on Simcha's instructions doesn't come too close. 'Welcome to our family,' he says and bows.

My parents are all smiles now, shaking hands and hugging their new *machatonim*. My father puts his arm around Matt like a father to a son.

'You must be exhausted after that long flight,' my mother says. 'I know we need at least two days to recover just coming from London.'

Their first time out of America, the Lewinskys look around at the religious crowd and seem bewildered.

'No problem with the flight, but things are pretty different 'round here. Takes some getting used to calling our son Simcha and not Sheldon and seeing him in that white sheet thing.'

'The *kittle*,' my father explains. 'An ancient custom.'

'Hey Sheldon, there's a black smudge on your forehead,' Matt says pointing at the ash smeared on Simcha's brow. He stamps the floor with his cowboy boot and laughs. 'Better get cleaned up before the ceremony.'

'Don't worry, Dad,' Simcha soothes. 'It's part of the law. A groom even at his happiest moment must think of the Day of Judgment. That is why I am wearing a *kittle*, as it looks like a shroud and the ash on my forehead is a symbol of mourning.'

'See what I mean?' Matt appeals to my mother.

'And Dad . . . don't call me Sheldon.'

My father leads Matt to sit at a long table with the two witnesses. He pours them both a brandy and translates the *ketuba*, the marriage contract which lies on the table in front of them, from Aramaic. 'The *ketuba* lists Simcha's obligations: To honour and provide for Reva and to fulfil her sexual needs. The sum of money pledged in case of divorce is recorded as twenty *zuzim*, which in today's market could only buy a sack of potatoes and a pound of apples.'

While the men are signing and drinking, the mothers sit on cream silk upholstered chairs in the bridal room, and my mother introduces Patty to the flow of guests. I sit on my bridal throne at the far end of the mirrored room, aware that my multiple reflections are swaying back and forth as I read silently from a long series of names. Dvorah has compiled the list, which includes all the single girls at the yeshiva looking for a match.

Bracha chana bas Leah. Rivka bas Menachem Mendel. Chana Leah bas Yittle. Leah Sarah bas Faige. Rochel bas Yonasan. Yocheved bas Moshe.

My lips move quickly, but no sound can be heard as I pray. As a bride, I have a direct line to heaven and my supplications are said to reach to the holy throne. I am so intent on my prayers that I am unaware Simcha has entered the bridal room for the *Bedeken* ceremony.

The crowd sings the melody that I have longed to hear sung for me, 'Oy yoi yoi yoi – May the bride and groom be as happy as Adam and Eve in the Garden of Eden.' Simcha is standing in front of me, bent down on one knee, looking into my eyes. He is checking to see that it is really me, a custom that evolved from Laban who tricked Jacob and switched the beautiful Rachel for her older sister Leah. Careful not to touch me, Simcha places the veil over my face, hiding me from the eyes of other men. He then speaks to me so all can hear. 'I see you, but I don't see you yet. There is still so much more to see.'

My father clutches his chest. He cannot bear the sentimentality of Simcha's love-talk, the *narishkeit* of his words, and through the mesh of white netting I watch him reach deep into the pocket of his suit jacket where he keeps his heart pills.

The fathers link their arms in Simcha's and lead him away with the unbreakable clasp of jailers leading their prisoner to the gallows, followed by an entourage of men singing, 'Oy yoi yoi yoi.' They glide across the foyer, down the red-carpeted staircase to the ballroom, and out onto the terrace, where the *chuppah* has been erected.

I rise. My veil is thick and blurs my vision. My mother in blue satin stands to my right, my mother-in-law in pink polyester to my left, each holding a candelabra with three white candles burning. We descend the regal staircase slowly, and walk towards the *chuppah*.

Simcha stands waiting under the square canopy of embroidered blue silk, which is held up by four wooden poles. The open sky recalls God's blessing to Abraham – that his seed be as numerous as the stars in the sky. Under this symbolic roof, I must circle Simcha seven times, the number of the days of creation, to create my own world with him in the centre.

I circle the first time. My veil is so thick that I need my mother and Patty to guide me. But there is little room on the podium under the *chuppah* for the three of us to circle. Patty holds onto me with the strong grasp of a competent woman, while my mother leans on me, on the verge of collapsing any moment. I know she finds this ultra-Orthodox tradition of circling seven times absurd. It is not a custom that has ever been performed in my father's synagogue. We circle the second time. I am not concentrating on the binding of my soul to Simcha's as I am worried about my mother. I can feel her panic. I pick up the pace, hoping this will soon be over so that my mother can stand next to my father and feel safe. Again and again we go round. Mother is making those sighing noises she makes when she is tired or upset. If she could speak to me, she would be giving me a minute by minute report of each and every ache and pain in her body, the sensations of nausea in her stomach, the fluctuations in her temperature. I am sure we have only circled five times when my father puts a stop to the charade. He is probably watching my mother intently and wants to prevent a scene. I dare not argue, even though I have learnt from Mrs Hillman that this custom has important spiritual reverberations in the upper spheres.

'Blessed be He that comes in the name of the Lord.' My father leads the ceremony in an operatic tenor that rings out with authority. All heads turn to him. He has a command over the audience. He asks Simcha to hold the ring and directs me to raise my left hand. Simcha gently slips on the wedding ring, a plain gold band, reciting the benediction softly, 'Behold, you are consecrated to me with this ring according to the laws of Moses and Israel.'

This is the first time Simcha has touched me, and electricity sparks inside me. I am aware of my sexy underwear. Now it is time for the seven blessings. First up is Rabbi Rabinowitz. Even though my father doesn't think much of him, I am overjoyed to have him honour me and recite the prayer. If it wasn't for him, I might not be here today. My two uncles, my father's brothers who live in Tel-Aviv, also recite a blessing each. Simcha has given the remainder of the honours to the most revered and holy rabbis, who ascend the *chuppah* in turn to recite the benedictions. Rabbi Sapphire is next. Even though I have heard the rumours circulating in the yeshiva that Rabbi Sapphire wears eighteen pairs of ritual fringes because of some deep cabbalistic symbolism, I am shocked now that I see him up close, slowly mounting the podium. His suit jacket is especially made to accommodate the bulk of the fringes, so his shoulders and chest are enormous in comparison to the rest of his body, which is frail and scrawny. He looks like a freak, so big and swollen on top that he seems deformed. Top heavy to the point that he could just topple over, he needs help to walk up to the *chuppah* and is flanked on either side by two Hassidim who support him on their arms. We shift to the right to make space for him. I can hear a gasp and the murmur of whisperings behind me in the hall. Everybody wants an explanation for the rabbi's eccentric garb.

'Looks like a quarter back,' I hear Matt Lewinsky whisper to his wife.

My father flinches. Knowing how embarrassed he must be in front of his guests who have flown from London to the Holy

Land for the wedding, I wish I had prepared him for Rabbi Sapphire's unusual appearance. Rabbi Sapphire recites the blessing in a voice like a nanny goat. Through the thick veil, I can see my father rolling his eyes at my mother.

The final blessing goes to Matt Lewinsky. The burly cowboy reads from a Hebrew transliteration that Simcha has prepared for him.

'Blessed art Thou, O Lord, who makes the groom rejoice with the bread.'

When Matt comes to the word '*callah*', meaning bride, he reads '*challah*', the braided bread eaten on the Sabbath. It is the only Jewish word he knows.

I cannot help but smile. To hide his laughter, my father is looking down at the floor. I am sure that when he gets back home, he and his brother Haim will have a good laugh about this, replay the scene and wheeze in hysterics like they do every time they get together and reminisce in Yiddish. It is time for the final part of the ceremony. Simcha smashes the ritual glass underfoot with such force that I cannot wait to feel his strength around me and inside of me. The crunch of fragmented shards incites the crowd to shout out '*Mazeltov, Mazeltov.*'

Inside the banquet hall, the women retire to their side of the *mechitza*, the divide that separates them from the men. There they dance and sing freely. The circle of crossed hands grows wider as they swirl around the parquet floor, faster and faster. On the other side, the men dance in a frenzy. My father sits with Matt, relieved the ceremony is over, and jokingly refers to the cowboy as his outlaw and not his in-law.

'Mum, dance with me, please,' I ask.

My mother rises, she takes my hand, looking back over her

shoulder at her London friends and shooting them a look that says, 'I'm trying to be a good sport, for Reva's sake, but all this Israeli dancing behind the screen is so primitive. 'Mrs Hillman pulls her into the circle. But mother's blue satin high heels, specially dyed to match her outfit, are only good for stepping in and out of a limousine. After one round, a chair is found for her next to my aunts. The effort has been too much for her and she sits looking on, biting the inside of her cheek and twirling her wedding ring around her finger. Mrs Hillman takes my hands and whirls me round and round. Her black shoes are flat, her dress loose. Her grip is strong. She allows herself to let go and have fun. I feel safe with her and let the room spin around me.

After our dance Mrs Frankel leads Simcha and me back upstairs to the *cheder yichud*. 'Remember what I taught you – not too spicy!' she whispers to me on the way. With a flourish, she throws the door wide open for us to enter.

Simcha closes the door behind us. This is it. The moment I have been waiting for has arrived. I feel shy as I turn towards my husband. He moves away from me, sits down, takes off his new hat, revealing hair plastered down with sweat, pulls a skullcap out of his pocket and plops it on his head. This is the first time I have seen him without his hat on. He looks different, younger, and not as handsome. Exhausted by the momentous day, he closes his eyes and disappears into himself. 'Give me a few minutes, Reva. I'm wiped,' he says almost inaudibly.

I feel as alone as I did during my childhood. I can feel the same pain, the same panic of being abandoned that I felt every time my father shut down and pressed those thin lips of his into a tight line, every time my mother shifted from her lively vivacious mode into one of her depressions. I sit down next to Simcha on the cream silk settee. I hope I am mistaken and he is not shutting me out. I look around the room decorated with ornate Louis XVth reproductions and walls panelled in cream silk matching the settees. I wait. Simcha's eyes are closed. I fidget and smooth my dress. Simcha's lids are twitching now with REM sleep. I reach for a glass of champagne bubbling on a tray beside me and down the golden liquid in one gulp. I can't understand what is wrong – why Simcha is not ravishing me now that I am permitted to him. Conflicting thoughts swarm in my head. Maybe he's sick, or not really attracted to me. I feel that old familiar self-doubt talking to me – 'Of course he's not in love with you. How could he be? You're worthless' – the message my parents always seemed to be sending me. Even now that I am marrying into the religious world, my father scorns my choice. Perhaps this is another of my bad decisions. Now my mother's dire predictions and dark premonitions, her sense that life is just a series of disasters waiting to happen, begin to weigh on me. Part of me wants to flee the *cheder yichud* and get on the first plane back to London. But I know I need to get control of myself and be patient. I pour another glass of champagne and sip greedily, numbing the feeling of dread that is rising from my gut. I cannot take his silence a moment longer so I plead, 'Simcha, wake up! Look at me! I'm your wife.'

Simcha opens his eyes, reaches out for my hands. Everything is going to be all right, I calm myself as he loops his fingers through mine. He stands up and pulls me up with him. But instead of holding me to him, he leads me to the door.

'Let's not keep our guests waiting,' he says in his usual quiet way, but something has changed. His tone has become forceful and I sense I dare not argue. He opens the door. I feel that familiar constriction in my chest. Again my breath is shallow. I want to scream but instead of any sound coming out of my mouth, I can hear an excruciating screeching in my head. I am disoriented but place one white and silver pump in front of the other and meekly follow Simcha downstairs like a lamb to the slaughter.

Mrs Frankel, who has been standing guard outside the room like a soldier at Buckingham Palace, gives me a quizzical look. It is unusual for the bride and groom to reappear after only ten minutes. I turn away, ashamed by my quick return.

Our guests applaud as we return to the ballroom and the band starts playing the Jewish wedding anthem, '*Simantov and Mazeltov*'.

'Everything all right?' my mother asks me. I fear that the loss of the fantasy I have played out so many times in my mind, the first moments of intimacy, the first time Simcha's lips would meet mine and our bodies would come together in an embrace, is reflected in my eyes and everyone can see it.

'Fine, fine,' I reply, but the words are stuck in my throat and I am trying not to cry.

Dinner is served and the guests take their seats. At the head table, I sit in between my father and my husband. Simcha is in a good mood. He is focusing on the *challah* breads and wants a serrated knife to cut them with. I can tell my father is getting tense with the waiting. He wants to get the show on the road and be in bed before eleven. Simcha is oblivious to my father's rising anger. He has not yet learned about my father's temper, his ability to withdraw into himself if things don't go his way. I cannot understand how Simcha can be so unaware of the shift taking place just one seat away from him. It must be because he hasn't seen what happens once my father's aura of warmth freezes over into the arctic barricade he uses to keep everyone at a distance, doesn't realise that there will be no way back then, no fathoming what has caused the change, no predicting how long the drop in the emotional temperature will last, which could be for days, even weeks. Years of suffering through these abandonments have made me hypersensitive to the signs that one is coming on. Even now I fear the sleepless nights that always follow the terror of being expelled from my father's web of love.

I know my father cannot bear the way Simcha is lifting the bread up high in the air and is whispering the blessing. He cannot stand the extravagant display of devotion, the ways of the newly repentant who have no traditions of their own, who adopt rituals at random without understanding their meaning. I try to catch his eye but he has turned away from me and is facing my mother, playing with his fish knife, swiping it back and forth across the square of white starched tablecloth in front of him. I ask the waiter for another glass of champagne.

A sexy Hassidic wedding singer is rocking out prayers to a South American beat. Under his long black coat, his muscular body ripples to the music. I can imagine him, before his repentance, in the Rio carnival, wearing tight pants and a shirt unbuttoned to the waist, with a thick gold chain sunk into a hairy chest. The champagne has gone to my head and I totter up to the stage and request a song. Mrs Frankel is coming towards me. 'Darlink, I think you've had enough now,' she says taking the glass out of my hand.

Between the starter of mushroom puff pastry and the main course of rack of lamb, the yeshiva crowd dance again. Mrs Hillman leads me to the centre of the circle and I sit on a chair. Four strong women pick me up high. I think I will topple over and I squeal. On the other side of the *mechitzah*, Simcha is also lifted up high. From different sides of the partition, we are facing each other, eye to eye. Our guests are clapping. The South American singer is belting out my favourite song '*Naa'leh* Come up to the Temple'. I am singing along. Simcha is smiling at me. He is radiating love. I am happy now. My disappointment from the *cheder yichud* is fading. All I can think about now is that the wedding night is almost here and we will soon be together. I am being bounced up and down, which makes me dizzy, but I don't take my eyes off of my husband. It is obvious that God has answered my prayers and I have merited a holy man who really is divine.

7

Pass the Salt

And her impurity will be upon him.
Leviticus 15:24

Languishing in bed under a patchwork quilt, I caress my belly and fantasise about the possible life within. Outside my bedroom window an almond tree is in full blossom and stands like a bride on the edge of spring. I look over at Simcha, who is snoring peacefully beside me. His skullcap has fallen off his head onto the pillow. Long blond lashes are fluttering in sleep. His mouth lies open, revealing the gap between his front teeth. Flowing sidelocks fall around his face like curtains. His wispy beard is rumpled and I feel a wave of affection for him.

Full of hope, I get out of bed and go to the bathroom, fill the two-handled cup with water and pour it over one hand and then the other, three times in all, washing away the impurities of the night when the soul leaves the body, bringing one-sixtieth of death. I look at my reflection in the mirror. My face is Modigliani-long and thin with high cheekbones. I have my father's soft brown eyes, protruding large and round and in need of liner and mascara to give them depth. My once aquiline nose remodelled by Dr Percy James from Harley Street is now straight. I look closer and check out my skin. Today it is glowing. There are none of the blemishes and spots that often congregate along the oily middle island of my olive complexion. I smile at myself with heart-shaped lips. They are chapped at the corners and I make a mental note to buy Vaseline. My pink flannel nightgown is buttoned up to my neck, the sleeves extend to my wrists. I wear it for Simcha, who likes me to cover my body and my hair in bed. I uncover myself only before intercourse and then I lie naked under the covers, the room darkened to allow for our virtuous love.

Simcha has only the purest thoughts even when he is inside me. He has told me that at the moment of ejaculation he says the *shema* and has advised me to think of a *passuk* to recite during the act to connect myself to God. I always pray to conceive, making my body a vehicle for God's creation.

I lock the bathroom door, whisk off my headscarf and shake my long hair over my shoulders. Lifting my nightgown over my head, I notice that my breasts seem fuller this morning. I admire my body and pout provocatively into the mirror, allowing myself for a moment to wish for the impossible: to hear Simcha shout out my name in bed instead of 'Hear, O Israel, the Lord is one'. I imagine it is his hands that are removing my underwear as I slip my panties down, but my fantasy is shattered when I see the menacing red spot on the inside of my panties. The stain is no bigger than the ruby dot that only yesterday had dribbled down my arm when taking a test at the pregnancy clinic. My period has arrived, a week late.

I sit down on the toilet and hold my head in my hands. But I cannot dwell on my disappointment, as I have to let Simcha know as soon as possible that I am a *nidda*, so I push a tampon inside of me, pull on my nightgown and go back to the bedroom. I stand next to my sleeping husband, unable to touch him now. 'Simcha, wake up,' I whisper. 'I've got my period.'

Simcha slowly opens his eyes. 'Reva, your hair is uncovered,' he says, averting his gaze.

I need him to reach out for me now, sympathise with my disappointment at not being pregnant, even break the rules and hug me to him, showing me for once that he loves me more than God, but I reach for a scarf and cover my hair, frightened to anger him again. I don't ever want to feel the humiliation I felt the first day after our marriage when, finally alone in our new apartment, I had tried to seduce Simcha. As night fell and the room darkened, I flipped off my shoes, hitched my dress up and straddled him where he was sitting on the living room couch. I tucked my arms around him and sat on him, rubbing lightly. I liked the feel of his chest under the white cotton shirt and the softness of his beard on my cheeks. 'What are you doing?' he had said, pushing me away. 'Have you lost your mind? The neighbours can see in through the window.' I looked out at the apartment across the street. The shutters were closed. The street lamps had been turned on.

'No one can see us. We're married now.'

'God can see. This is not the way a Jewish woman behaves. It's immodest.'

I swung my leg back over his lap and walked away. My cheeks were burning with shame. I saw myself through Simcha's eyes and I felt small and unworthy of his love. As embarrassed as I was, I was glad for his rebuke, as he was surely leading me towards repentance.

Simcha gets out of bed to wash his hands and I close the bedroom door so as not to arouse him while I separate the beds. Tonight we will wave goodnight to each other from opposite ends of the room like two kids at camp before lights out. I can already feel the loneliness ahead. It is not only a physical separation that comes between us at these times. Simcha turns off completely, closes himself up into his own world like a tortoise receding into its shell. Then I cannot reach him. I don't know how to switch off my need for physical love and relate to my husband on a purely domestic or intellectual plane, as he wants me to. I still need daily validation of our love, whether it be a smile, a wink or a caress. In the absence of physical attention, I feel scared. I cannot trust that the other Simcha, the one who will look fondly into my eyes or lay his hand over mine at dinner, is still there. I know of course that Simcha hasn't withdrawn his love and is just being careful not to transgress the law, but when he doesn't show affection, I feel myself regressing inexorably to my childhood when my parents' emotional instability left me with a constant ache of need and longing. Sex has always been my way of filling up the empty hole of loneliness inside me. The monthly separations open up that gaping wound and I can feel all the past flooding back.

I don't agree that these separations have a positive effect, as Mrs Frankel has taught. For me, the *nidda* laws are like a rift that interrupts the flow of our intimate life. It is impossible to build the intimacy I long for with these two-week breaks every month. When I am finally allowed to touch Simcha once again, it is not so easy to take up where we left off. At first I am shy. Then gradually we reconnect. But it takes days for me to feel fully comfortable in our togetherness again. The written law states we must separate for seven days during menstruation. The rabbis from the Talmud lengthened this time and women must now wait an additional seven clean days after bleeding has stopped to be extra careful and to guarantee that there is no blood flowing from the uterus at all. This is what the rabbis call 'a fence around the Torah', a law to protect a law. My periods are regular and I don't spot in between cycles. It would be so unlikely for me to bleed beyond the week. If we only separated for seven days it would make all the difference. There wouldn't be such a long time to wait. But I wouldn't dream of mentioning it to Simcha, as he would surely have a fit.

To calm myself, I make a mental calculation of the date when I will be able to go to the *mikveh* and try to conceive again.

I leave the room to prepare the table for breakfast dressed in my most modest dress, the long brown one with the tiny red dots and a cameo brooch pinned to the collar as a reminder to Simcha not to come close.

On my way to the dining room, I grab the fertility statue from the bookshelf, a squat figurine with the hard round breasts carved from the smooth white stone of the Island of Amorgos. It is my only relic from my old life, a gift from Chris while holidaying in Greece. I use it as another reminder of my bloody state and place it in the centre of the table. Adhering to the laws, I feel dignified and pure, close to God once again.

Breakfast is ready. I cannot pour the orange juice for Simcha or serve the food directly onto his plate, as this act of intimacy could lead to a familiarity we are not allowed, so I prepare plates of scrambled eggs and buttered toast in the kitchen and lay Simcha's plate on the table but not directly in front of him. I have learnt the rules and know that Simcha will never waver and take a lenient stance, so I am careful not to flirt with him or sound suggestive in any way lest my manner have the slightest tinge of sexuality. The first time I was a *nidda*, I teased Simcha and tried to pull him into an intimate conversation, but he wouldn't have it and set me straight. I can accept that we are not allowed to make love, but now I am already feeling the misery of being apart, even though only an hour has passed since I found blood. The way that the laws of separation prevent us from any kind of closeness, not just physical but emotional, seems inhumane to me, even cruel. All I can think about when I am suffering this much is my own immediate happiness. The knowledge that what we are doing is supposed to bring holiness to our lives only makes me feel how impossible it is to please God and please myself at the same time. But I must make His will my will as Rabbi Rabinowitz has taught.

We eat in silence until I ask, 'Simcha, could you pass the salt?' Simcha picks up the saltshaker and places it down carefully in front of the fertility statue. I understand he can't pass it directly to me as the gesture could, God forbid, lead to a touch when I am a *nidda*. There is an unspoken tension between us. It's like this every month for the first days of my period, when every action is carefully thought out and every word is censored. After a day or two, the longing wanes and I get used to life devoid of touch. But at first, the idea that I am impure always makes me feel cold, rejected and alone. Becoming pregnant will solve the problem. I will not be impure for a whole nine months. Of course this isn't the only reason I want to conceive. I want to start a Jewish family and have a baby to hold and to love.

* * *

Five lonely days later, in the bathroom, I am checking to see if my menses have ceased. Raising my leg onto the toilet seat, I wrap a white linen square around my middle finger, insert it deep inside me and twist it around the walls of my vagina. I remove the cloth and hold it up to the window to check the colour. It is clean, which means I can begin to count the seven clean days until my purification at the *mikveh*. I change into white underwear and exchange my floral bed-sheet for a white one so that if there is a stain, I can be sure of its colour. Making these preparations for my reunion with Simcha, now that the end of our separation is near, makes me feel alive again. I think Simcha feels the same way. He is also counting down and discreetly asked me this morning how the checks are proceeding and when my date for the *mikveh* night will be.

The eve of the seventh day has finally arrived, and after six days of checking the linen cloths, morning and night, and finding all of them completely clean, I make the final check. But there is a salmon coloured smudge on the cloth and I cannot decide if it is a regular discharge or if it, God forbid, belongs to the family of reddish-pink hues that secrete from the womb. I understand the wisdom of the rabbis now and their insistence on keeping seven clean days. I want Simcha close to me again and debate ignoring the stain. No one will ever know. But I cannot do this, for I, Reva, will know, and I cannot lie. I have no choice but to tell Simcha and ask him to show the stain to Rabbi Fischel, a Torah authority, for his expert opinion.

'It would be better if you could go,' Simcha implores, in a desperate tone that is hard to refuse.

'But I'm on morning shift at the hospital. I promised a new

mother who's having trouble that I'd help her breastfeed today.'

'Ask another counsellor to cover for you. It'll only take an hour, but if I miss Rabbi Sapphire's Talmud class, I'll never be able to catch up. Could you? Please?'

I have heard that one can send the linen cloth or underwear to the rabbi via his wife and receive an answer by phone, but I don't have the necessary connections, so I put the cloth into an envelope, slip it into my purse and take the bus to Mea Shearim on the other side of town. As if travelling in a time warp, I watch the tree-lined streets of Rechavia with their chic boutiques and outdoor cafés give way to a crowded run-down neighbourhood. The first things I notice are the posters hung across narrow alleyways that insist upon modesty. They proclaim that only women with long sleeves and skirts covering their knees may enter. It is dangerous for a secular woman to walk here. There is a modesty patrol and rumour has it that stones have been thrown at naked arms. The streets are bustling with men dressed in long black coats and circular fur hats, scurrying about clutching heavy books, pregnant women with matronly wigs pushing strollers, entourages of children lagging behind them. Schoolgirls walk together in twos and threes. Their hair is braided into plaits. The Hassidim have their own schools, where the Yiddish-speaking girls learn stories from the Torah and sewing. They wear checked pinafore dresses with opaque beige tights. There is no frivolity here. The bookshops offer only scholarly texts and the clothing stores stock only modest attire. Nevertheless it is lively. Music is blasting out of the loudspeakers of a stationary van. Five Breslover Hassidim are spilling out of the van. I recognise them by their white crochet skullcaps and the sidelocks that dangle down to their shoulders. They link arms and dance to the music singing the words, 'It's a *mitzva* to be happy.' Their aim is to bring joy, following Rabbi Nachman of Breslov's advice that happiness is the cornerstone for worship of God.

I get off the bus in a crowded street that resembles what Jewish life in nineteenth-century Poland must have looked like. This is how I imagine a *shtetl*. It is hard to believe that modern downtown Jerusalem is only minutes away. Along the pavements, sellers offer their wares: live chickens, kitchen utensils, sweets, fresh fish and children's clothing. The street is bright in colour and pungent in smell. I walk quickly past the colourful stalls, the stench of raw meat and sweat in my nostrils. I feel out of place. Even though I am dressed according to the law, I look different from the women here. The influence of the Western world is still apparent from my shoes, bought by my mother in the West End of London, and my long-sleeved shirt worn without a petticoat clings to my body in a way that feels suddenly slutty. I don't fit in, but with my secret in my bag, on the way to do a *mitzva*, I stride confidently up the main street. After a few minutes I realise I am lost in the labyrinths of the cobbled alleyways and stop a young man for directions.

'Excuse me. Do you know the way to Rabbi Fischel's house?'

The young man fixes his gaze on his shoes. 'First left at the corner,' he mumbles.

The words 'thank you' hardly leave my mouth before he scurries away. At the corner, the outstretched arms of a Hassid begging for charity beseech me. I delve into my purse to retrieve a few coins and hand them over. The man covers his eyes with one hand and takes the money with the other.

A line of men queue outside the rabbi's house. They stand aside, allowing me to enter.

The kitchen is dilapidated. A rickety old cupboard hangs above a sink. The fridge is humming and sounds as if it is about to conk out. The rabbi's wife is standing by the sink washing potatoes and carrots and tossing them in a steaming pot. Instead of a flat kerchief, she wears a scarf stuffed with a layer of sponge at the hairline, a fashion current among women in certain Hassidic sects. Every line on her coarse round face is witness to the fact that she has never known anything but hard work in her life. Her thick ropey fingers peel and chop. Her wedding band cuts into her flesh. Beneath her apron, a long navy blue dress of polyester covers her sturdy frame. Varicose veins protrude through brown elastic stockings and her wide feet spill over worn-out brogues. Even though everything here is old and torn, the floor unswept, the walls stained with cooking and age, the aroma of the vegetable barley soup bubbling on the stove entices me and makes me feel the wholesomeness of life here. This is the kind of religious woman I admire. Only duty occupies her mind. It is her husband and her children, their meals and their well-being that are the focus of her thoughts. Her efforts will surely be rewarded in the world to come. If only I could be like her, I would be happy. But I have not been brought up for a life of sacrifice. I am spoilt and want the luxuries of this world too.

'Eh . . . hem . . . Excuse me,' I cough to get her attention. 'I've come to see the rabbi.'

'Join the line. The rabbi hasn't begun to receive people yet,' she croaks.

I stand at the end of the line of men in black. Self-conscious at being the only woman, I rummage for my prayer book in my purse, careful not to drop the white envelope. I open to the page of morning prayers, but I cannot concentrate. The Hebrew words blur as I feel anger stir inside of me, rising from my gut, flushing my cheeks and making me clench my hands. Why isn't Simcha here instead of me? I think, embarrassed to be here among the men. This isn't modest at all. I am uncomfortable and so are they. Doesn't Simcha realise this?

But I am also angry with myself for giving in to him and not going to work. I should be there, not wasting my time here. I love my work and when I assist at a birth I feel that I am doing God's work, for I believe childbirth can be an uplifting spiritual experience. Natural birth is especially blessed because it can be the time when a woman has the greatest opportunity to feel close to God. So I try to help women have births that are as natural as possible by encouraging the use of herbs and other natural homeopathic remedies to relieve pain instead of epidurals and Demeral. That way the mother can feel what's happening during labour and be part of the creative process. I know how to administer tinctures of St John's Wort and Skullcap to aid relaxation, and Blue Cohosh to stimulate uterine contractions. If that doesn't work, I press the large intestine shiatsu point four that is nestled deep in the web between the thumb and forefinger, a point that must never be touched earlier in pregnancy as it induces labour. When the baby is about to come, I massage olive oil into the perineum to stretch the skin so that an episiotomy won't be necessary. I have helped tens of labouring mothers this year at the Misgav Ladach Maternity Hospital and am longing to get pregnant and have my own child. I think back to the way I helped a woman only yesterday; how I turned her onto all fours because her baby was in a posterior presentation and she was feeling contractions in the back. Once I got the baby off the spine and the mother was more comfortable; I massaged her lower back with aromatic oil and let her rest in Child's Pose in between pains. 'Oh that feels so good,' she had said. 'Don't stop.' I felt so valuable then in my holy work, helping her focus inwards and keeping her calm. But I feel useless here in this long line; it's going to take hours till my turn. Doubts creep into my mind that maybe my *mikveh* night is not so important to Simcha after all. Maybe he asked about the daily checks of the cloths as he would the date of Yom Kippur or another Jewish festival. Maybe he doesn't miss being close to me, but having children is a *mitzva*, so it seems out of character for him not to care. I must be mistaken.

I look around at the men in line. The Hassid behind me can't be more than twenty. A fine growth of ginger hair covers his baby cheeks. Uncomfortable that I am looking at him, he chews his nails and keeps his eyes, hidden behind thick glasses, glued to his psalm book. His black velvet hat is as large and round as a wheel, his black gabardine suit trousers are tucked into white knee-length socks and held up by braces. Ritual fringes, a cream-coloured square of material woven with black stripes, cover his grubby white shirt. Next to him stands an older man in long trousers, suit jacket and a black Stetson hat that makes him look like Humphrey Bogart. He's pulling on a cigarette. Must be a newly repentant, I think, noticing a few holes on his lobes where he has been pierced. I turn to face the front. A heavy-set man is shuffling from one foot to the other. From the back I notice his sidelocks are curled behind his ears into corkscrews and then tied up so they will not unfold. He wears a wide knit *kippa* in white with a design crocheted in blue around the diameter. I imagine it is his wife's or daughter's handiwork. Unlike the rest of the men here today, he wears jeans and a checked shirt. On his feet are Bible sandals. This is the uniform of the idealists who live in Hebron or other occupied territories, believing every inch of Israel is holy and should be inhabited. I wonder if each of the men standing here has a little cloth hidden away in his pockets and is waiting for a verdict as to the night ahead, hoping to be able to couple with his spouse. I feel jealous of those wives waiting for a phone call with the results of the checks. I imagine myself to be one of them, summoned from the labour room by an urgent call from Simcha, who tells me, 'It's kosher. Tonight you can go to the *mikveh*. I can't wait.'

Finally my turn has come and the *shammes* opens the door to the rabbi's study. I enter a large room with a domed ceiling, arched windows and a floor tiled with Arab diamond motifs. The walls are lined with hundreds of old books and the rabbi is bent over an ancient text. 'How can I help you?' He raises his eyes but does not look directly at me.

'I am supposed to go to the *mikveh* tonight, but there's a stain.' I shyly hand over the cloth.

It isn't easy showing my discharge to a stranger. This is Simcha's job, not mine, I think, as the rabbi takes the cloth to the window and examines it. I see the light shine through my stain. The coral tinge reminds me of a sundress I once owned that showed off my back and shoulders and I remember wearing it picnicking with Chris's family in the country dales.

'Not koisher!' the rabbi exclaims.

Oh no! I will have to wait yet another seven days until I can go to the *mikveh*, another seven days until I can touch Simcha. I feel so let down as I mourn the *mikveh* night I have been waiting for and the future *mikveh* nights when I know Simcha will never want what I want: to throw me on the bed and make passionate love to me. I have accepted that the room must be dark and he must lie on top, but even with these limitations, I know sex can be satisfying. Simcha will not enter a conversation about what turns me on. I know that it is his duty to satisfy me, and fear he is taking the law to extremes that go against the Torah. My disappointment allows me to admit that I don't want his soft petting of a kindly uncle any more. I want passion of the flesh as well as the spirit, biting and licking and talking dirty while doing it. I want it from behind, from on top, and I want his head down in the most forbidden place of all. I think about how Chris used to ask, 'Is this good, babe?' and then come up for air, his hair ruffled, his face flushed and him drunk with the very taste of me saying, 'Is this how you like it?'

Rabbi Fischel is again buried in his book and I know it is time to leave, but I stay. I watch him absorbed in his holy study. I see why he is considered one of the great rabbis, a pillar of Judaism. Torah is his life. I think of my grandfather. Being in the presence of a *zaddik* once again helps me access my own love of Torah and makes me centre myself and put things into perspective. I don't want to break the rules; I want to elevate myself from animal lusts. I believe Simcha will loosen up and when he feels more secure in his repentance, he will find the balance between the pleasures of this world and the next, and will satisfy me in accordance with the law. I calm down. Reconnected once again to my path, I clear the sinful thoughts from my mind and leave the study.

But I am no holy woman and walking back to the bus stop I am plagued by the memory of my wedding night, left alone in the bedroom, lighting a candle to create a romantic mood, spraying French perfume behind my ears and between my breasts and sitting shyly in the safety of the semi-darkness of the hotel suite, waiting and waiting for Simcha.

Five minutes, ten, twenty minutes pass. I throw on a robe and creep out of the bedroom to find him standing in the corner of the living area reciting from the book of Psalms communing with his true love.

'Simcha, come to me,' I plead.

'Reva, let me recite psalms so that God will bless our union with children. Then I'll come.'

Half an hour later, he comes to bed, mounts me in the darkness and with a few thrusts the deed is done. He kisses me on the cheek and falls asleep.

I was not prepared for this, even after classes with Mrs Frankel, who taught me that our lovemaking would be directed to a higher realm than our animal desires. I felt humiliated that my body had been used purely as a vessel for procreation, a fulfilment of the commandment to be fruitful and multiply; as humiliated as I had felt after one-night stands when my body was used only as a release for anonymous pleasure. I considered leaving then, getting dressed and banging on my parents' door, begging for my father to annul the marriage. But I didn't move. Paralysed by disappointment, I didn't even get out of bed. I tried to comfort myself in the darkness, listening to Simcha's gentle snores, convincing myself that he probably hadn't touched a woman for years, and that our intimate relations would improve with time when we got to know each other better and he was under less stress to perform.

Seven clean days have passed since my visit to Mea Shearim and it is evening. Immersions only take place at night, reducing the likelihood of being seen entering or leaving the *mikveh* building. I walk to the *mikveh* carrying a satchel of cleaning paraphernalia needed for the preparation. The air is clean and cool. Cherry trees are in bloom and I breathe in the blossoms' sweet smell as I stride along the pretty streets. From the outside, the *mikveh* building looks like any grey, slummy block of flats, but once inside, the atmosphere is alive with laughter and vitality. A group of women have come to accompany a bride. They are milling around offering sticky cakes to us all. One woman is shaking a tambourine, others are singing to the bride, flicking their tongues and making the tribal sound that only the Moroccan women can do.

I approach the matron in charge, sitting at the reception desk.

'Shalom. Are you ready for an immersion or do you need to prepare yourself first?' she asks.

'Prepare myself,' I reply with modesty.

The matron hands me a red plastic disc with the number seven stamped on it.

'Do you need anything?' she inquires, pointing to the tray of assorted toiletries on her desk; acetone, cotton swabs and nail files.

'Just a towel.'

Towel in hand, I am on my way to room seven, one of the ten rooms in the building, each with its own *mikveh*, a small pool containing exactly forty *sa'ah* of rainwater. I know from Hilly about the one measurement of water for each of the forty years of purification the Israelites had undergone, thirsty in the hot desert, hungry for manna from heaven, and needing the shelter of the clouds of glory, before they could enter the land of Israel.

I enter the room. There are three cubicles, each with a regular bathtub, a basin, mirror and chair. In the centre of the complex is the *mikveh*, which the three occupants share. I take the only empty booth, lock the door and put my bag down on the plastic chair. On the floor is a pair of worn blue rubber sandals. A list is pinned to the wall above the tub itemising all body parts to be cleaned. It is protected with plastic that has become grimy with time.

I draw a bath and undress. I check the list to make sure I don't forget anything.

- Soak in the bath for at least an hour.
- Use a loofah to rub off rough skin.
- If you have any dry scabs on the skin, pick them off. If the flesh under the scab has not healed completely, then the scab is considered part of the flesh. Wet pus is part of the skin but dry pus must be removed.
- Shampoo the hair and rinse well. Do not use conditioner, as it sticks to the hair.
- Remove all jewellery and false teeth and temporary fillings.
- Brush and floss teeth.
- Blow your nose.
- Clean out the ears and the belly button with cotton swabs.
- Remove varnish and cut the nails.

- Comb through all hair on the body, making sure there are no knots.

I re-check the list as I go through the preparations, washing every crease and crevice of my body so that the purifying warm *mikveh* waters will touch my skin without any barrier. I wash my ears and inside my nose, rotate a cotton swab around my belly button, digging in and taking out the dirt. I cut my nails short, remove the clear varnish and scrub them thoroughly with a brush to make doubly sure of their cleanliness. On *mikveh* days I avoid making pastry so that there's no chance of any dough being lodged beneath my nails. Since meat can get stuck between the teeth, I took the Torah advice not to eat meat today, but still brush and floss my teeth thoroughly. I comb my hair and pubic hair to smooth out any knots.

Soaking in the hot water, my body relaxes. The night I have been waiting for has finally arrived. I take my time soaping my long limbs and enjoying the steaming bath. I smile to myself, remembering the *mikveh* night back in Romeo, Simcha's small hometown in Colorado, on our honeymoon visit to meet the family members who hadn't made the trip to the wedding.

'Welcome home, kiddo,' Matt Lewinsky had greeted his son as we went out the back to the yard where he was fanning coals.

He put down a skewer of cubed raw meat and hugged Simcha. I stood back, debating if I could hug a man who was not my husband or father, but when Matt came over to me and gave me a bear hug I returned it and squeezed him tight, figuring that living with a secular family, we would have to ease up on the strictness of our Jewish practice.

'This meat is supa dupa kosher. Got it from the kosher butcher in Boulder this morning.'

Simcha glared at the skewers in his father's hand and I knew what he was thinking. 'See this skewer and the knives?' Matt said 'All new. Your mother bought plastic plates and cutlery. We're all set.'

'Dad, there's just one thing. Did you *toivel* the knives?'

'Come again, Son.'

I was mad at Simcha then for not appreciating the effort his dad was making. But Simcha didn't hold back.

'*Toivel*, make them pure, take off the *tumah*.'

'Why are you speaking a language I cannot understand?' Matt was getting angry and we had only been there five minutes.

'Purify them, Dad. Anything used for cooking or eating made by a non-Jew has to be immersed in a *mikveh*.'

'They shut the *mikveh* down last year, Son. No need for it out here. You're not in Jerusalem now, you know.'

I looked questioningly at Simcha. My *mikveh* night was in two days' time. The only possibility for our physical reunion was the ice-cold lake miles away.

After Simcha's parents had witnessed us not passing anything one to the other, Simcha sleeping on the floor of our bedroom, and my checking lettuce for bugs, I felt sure they wouldn't react strongly to my immersion in the lake, but I was wrong. When Simcha broke the news to his parents that I had to enter the freezing lake stark naked, Matt had said, 'You need your head examined. It's February – you can't possibly allow her to expose herself to that kind of cold.' And then, exasperated, he added, 'You know what, go, and take the cutlery with you while you're at it.'

I felt sorry for Simcha then, and thought about my own father with his yeshiva background, the son of a famous rabbi, who loves the Torah and the *mitzvot*, but who had been just as impatient as Matt when Simcha asked his endless questions about the *kashrut* of the dishes that had been shipped from London to Jerusalem for us. Finally, when Simcha asked my father if the dishes had been *toiveled* in a *mikveh*, my father assured him they had been meticulously dipped in the Serpentine River in Hyde Park. I couldn't imagine my father hauling crockery down to the Serpentine, and was sure he was making it up, but Simcha seemed satisfied with his answer, so I let the subject drop and hoped Simcha would too.

At the lake, I undressed in the bushes and inched my way into the arctic water. It was so freezing it took my breath away and burnt my skin. I knew I had to be completely immersed. I went under for a fraction of a second and then ran for the shore with blue lips and chattering teeth. Simcha held a towel for me, drying me and hugging me to him. I quickly dressed and Simcha wrapped me in a blanket. Then he gave me hot brandy to sip from a thermos. He looked at me with pleasure and I could tell he was filled with pride at my efforts. That night he took me with a great passion and even allowed himself to wriggle down my body and let his beard graze near the hairline of my pubic bone, before his untimely orgasm ended the only expression of his sensuality that I had known.

The bath is getting cool and I top it up with scalding water. I can hear my neighbour entering the *mikveh*. The *mikveh* lady is telling her to move into the centre of the pool. The water splashes as she plunges down. 'Kosher!' I hear the *mikveh* lady cry. Now she is pure and ready to be with her husband. My thoughts return to Simcha. It is six months since our trip to Colorado, six months since Simcha reverted to his pious ways of lovemaking. Out there in the sticks of small-town America, Simcha knew I was his only ally. The only one who could understand how hard it was for him to live in a house where the fridge was packed with ham and prawns; the only one who could sympathise at how unbearable it was to have the TV on full blast all day and deal with a family oblivious to his quest for God. Then he needed me; I was his rock, his reminder of who we are and what we are doing with our lives. I was the stronger one, descended from a lineage of rabbis and coming from a home where the TV programmes were censored, the foods were all stamped with the rabbinic seal of approval and Torah laws were the nucleus of our lives. Unlike many other mothers whose children become *chozer b'tshuva*, newly repentant, Simcha's mother didn't want to light *Shabbes* candles with me or make her kitchen kosher. She wanted nothing to do with any of it. Instead, she gave us our own two pots and we made simple vegetarian meals of rice and steamed vegetables for ourselves. Once we had finished eating, we washed our utensils under the garden hose and packed them away. Seeing Simcha so vulnerable, disconnected from his folks, unappreciated by them, I understood the alienation that he felt. Seeing him thrown off balance made me love him even more. I respected how far he had come with his repentance. When Simcha's parents ate their non-kosher meals in front of us, Simcha knew I was right there with him and I knew that my love was helping him get through the two-week ordeal.

* * *

Double-checking the list one last time, I get out of the bath. I wrap a towel around myself, slip on the plastic shoes that are two sizes too small and cut into my heels, and press the red button on the wall. I open the door of my cubicle but quickly close it as I see a young woman stepping down into the purifying waters. Her skin is white and smooth, her hair long and black. I cannot recognise her as one of the religious matrons with loose-fitting clothes I saw in the lobby when I came in.

A few minutes pass until the *mikveh* attendant knocks on my door. Her name tag, 'Fruma', is clipped to a bosom so huge that she could surely nurse the entire Jewish nation. Over her long dress, she wears an apron with a pocket in the front where she keeps her equipment.

I take off my towel and am scrutinised.

'You need to eat more. You look anorexic. Have you flossed your teeth?' Fruma asks.

I smile to myself. I look down at the extra pounds that sit around my stomach and wish I did look anorexic.

'Yes, thoroughly.'

'Belly button?'

'Clean. I've poked around and around.'

'Have you combed your hair down there too?'

I nod.

'Turn around.'

I turn so that Fruma can look for any stray hairs that have fallen down my back. She picks a few hairs off me and then feels for hangnails. My nails are smooth, but still Fruma takes a nail file out of her apron pocket and files the nail of my index finger.

'You may enter the *mikveh*.'

I step down into the purifying waters, trying to ignore the floating hair from my predecessors tonight, and stand in the centre of the pool. I take a deep breath and dunk under. With the warm waters holding me, I feel whole again. Like a foetus in God's womb, I hold myself under the water, making sure that there isn't a hair on my head floating above the surface and while I am submerged, I pray to conceive. 'Dear God,' I pray, 'give me a healthy child. I will educate him to follow Your laws.'

I come up for air and Fruma throws a kerchief on my wet head so I can recite the blessing with my hair covered.

'Blessed art Thou, O Lord, who has commanded us to immerse ourselves in the *mikveh*.'

Fruma responds 'Amen' and exclaims, 'Kosher!' and I know I am now as kosher as the salt beef sandwiches at Bloom's delicatessen – the ones made by the proprietess, an overweight balabuster with long white whiskers growing on her chin, who takes her briny hands out of a barrel of herring to cut thick slices of her famous medium rare, pink beef which she smears with Dijon mustard and serves with a sweet and sour gherkin.

I immerse myself twice more before I climb the few steps out of the *mikveh*, dry myself, and dress. I leave the room quickly so as not to look on voyeuristically at the other women who are preparing themselves.

In the communal room at the end of the corridor, I blow-dry my hair and cover it with a scarf, tied turban-style. I apply sugar pink gloss to my lips and clip on all my jewellery, except the cameo. Love is in the air as women prepare themselves for reunion with their husbands. A waif of a woman is spraying perfume behind her ears. I am amazed that this frugal-looking woman, whose drab loose-fitting clothes give her the appearance of a scarecrow, owns a bottle of perfume. Next to her at the far end of the room is a woman of about my age. She is fitting her blonde human hair wig, styled in a Farrah Fawcett layered cut, over her own shoulder-length hair. Instant transformation to a Hollywood glamour girl! Wearing an elegant beige fitted skirt and cream silk blouse, tan high-heeled Italian leather shoes and natural-coloured stockings, she is dressed according to the laws but not in the spirit of modesty, and she moves toward the door with a sensuous glide. Not all the women here are religious. *Mikveh* is a common tradition among secular Sephardic women. They may wear tight jeans and tank tops, but they are scrupulous in their adherence to the purity customs.

I walk home and in keeping with tradition I am careful not to look down at a stray cat or any other unclean animal, but keep my gaze fixed on the dark sky filled with stars. It is chilly out now and I wrap my shawl around me, taking quick steps on the cobbled pavements. I can feel the excitement churning inside me. In only a few minutes I will be able to relax with Simcha, have him close to me again.

Simcha is in his usual pose, bent over a holy book, so immersed in his study that he doesn't hear me come in. I approach the table and see that he has removed the Greek statue. He puts his book aside and looks up. Wearing a dressing-gown over blue striped pyjamas and with a kindly expression on his face, he smiles at me lovingly. Maybe this will be the night, I hope, as he holds out the chair for me to sit down. 'I have a surprise,' he says softly, his breath fluttering like a moth on my skin and I imagine him taking a slinky gold link necklace from a little box and slipping it around my neck, clasping it together at the nape.

He goes to the kitchen and I glance at the text he has been studying, open at a chapter explaining how to give pleasure to a woman during intercourse. I read the words, 'First endear her to you with foreplay and call her by name before the act.' I scorn myself for being so worried. It was just a matter of time. I must learn to be more patient.

Simcha returns with a steaming plate of kasha and steamed squash, a frugal yet substantial meal that could strengthen a survivor after years of starvation. He puts it down in front of me and I reach for the saltshaker, but Simcha is quicker and he hands it to me. I moan as the saltshaker slips from his hand to mine. This is all I want, his desire for me at last, an unbearable longing that will make him rock inside of me with the same intensity as he rocks back and forth in prayer.

After a few mouthfuls, he leads me to the bedroom, the meal forgotten.

We undress and get into bed. I am trembling with excitement. Simcha holds me close and his hand sweeps down over my thigh. 'Reva, my wife,' he whispers.

At the sound of my name, I moan and can feel myself moist. I am purring now and unable to wait any longer to feel him penetrate me. I roll over onto my back, opening my legs for him. He moves on top of me and enters my wetness. I grip his buttocks and push him in further, giggling, clasping my legs around his neck, riding him.

'*Shema Yisroel*,' Simcha shouts out. He collapses on me

with his heavy weight. A warm trickle runs down my leg.

I am still hungry for him and guide his hand between my legs. He wriggles free and climbs out of bed to wash himself, so that he can recite the nightly prayers without juices on his member. I turn to face the wall, a lump forming in my throat, a band of pain pressing on my head. How could I have been so naïve, hoping for the impossible for so long? Why didn't our wedding night tell me everything I needed to know – that Simcha is drawn much more strongly towards his prayers than to nestling in my arms? How could I not have admitted to myself that he is horny only for heaven and comes truly alive only when he is involved in performing a *mitzva*? God is his true mate and I am a mere stepping-stone to achieve holiness.

I lie alone in the bed, holding myself, arms wrapped around my chest, rocking gently from side to side seeking my own comfort. I feel alone. This is the very opposite of what I long for. I want a husband to hold me in his arms after he makes love to me, tell me he loves me, giggle and kiss. I can hear Simcha in the bathroom. Soon he will leave the house and go and immerse himself in the men's *mikveh*. Then he will say the evening prayers. He will probably go back to his study and sit at the dining table for another hour. I feel a twinge in my belly. I unlock my arms and let my right hand slide down to my lower stomach. I hold it there for a few moments and then move it in a circular motion around my stomach. I'm suddenly hungry and think about the pot of kasha in the kitchen. I pull myself up into a sitting position and pull on my robe, unaware that God has answered my prayers and instructed the angels to dispatch a blessed soul to earth.

8

Oh, Crumbs!

And you shall eat the Passover sacrifice in haste.

Exodus 12:11

I clutch my belly as I bend over to remove the plastic shelves from the inside of the fridge. A spasm of heartburn makes me stuff a few Rennies into my mouth and perspiration drips off me while I sweep an old toothbrush through the grooves of the fridge door to remove the muck wedged in the corners. After an hour of gruelling work, I stand back and admire my work. The fridge looks spanking new, just like the day it was delivered in the white polystyrene container.

I plod like a duck to the next job of cleaning out the hall cupboard, where I remove coats and jackets from their hangers, carry them to the balcony and turn out the pockets to rid them of old chocolate wrappers, snotty tissues and unidentifiable crumbs.

This is no ordinary spring-cleaning job, but preparation for the Passover holiday. Making the home free of *chometz* – cookies, pasta and bread, any food made of a grain that rises when it ferments – is a lot of work, but it's what we must do to identify with our ancestors, who had to flee Egypt so hurriedly that there was no time for their bread to rise. So, tired as I am, I continue my labours in accordance with the strict letter of the law, motivated by the knowledge that searching for *chometz* symbolises the willingness to rid ourselves of that which puffs us up and makes us big-headed in the same way that yeast swells wheat into bread. As I scour the table, I clean lustful thoughts from my mind and as I dust the furniture, I scoop up pride from my ego. Remembering the humiliation the Israelites suffered under Pharaoh's rule, I vow to behave with humility and help those less fortunate than myself.

The library is filled with hundreds of books that might hold an errant crumb wedged between the pages. I lug a few books over to the table, sit down and massage my back with the palms of my hands, wishing Simcha were around to help or at least that he would provide a cleaning lady. The past nine months have been difficult. From the first month I have felt as if my body had been invaded. I lost weight at the beginning, as I couldn't stomach food. I was unable to dwell on the blessing that my prayers had been answered and praise the Lord for His gift of life, as all I could think about was my leaden body, which was too heavy to lug around. Simcha was away all day at *kollel* and I was isolated in my bedroom, unable to leave the apartment for long. I open a volume of the Talmud and run a feather duster through the middle crease. As I turn the pages of Jewish law and commentary, I feel a basketball pushing through my stomach and I watch my belly shift to the side. Every flutter scares me, reawakening my fear of giving birth to a damaged baby. At night I play out different scenarios in my head, of babies who have Down's syndrome, or spina bifida, babies who are deformed, lacking arms or legs, or with minor afflictions like harelips or missing thumbs. I imagine the scene at the birth, my mother collapsing at the news, the hysteria, the rejection of the baby, the acceptance of the baby, giving the baby up for adoption, finding the strength to deal with the baby, the pitying looks of other mothers, the small children poking fun, and then I think of my mother and how hard it must have been for her to have Michelle at a time when mental illness was something to be ashamed of, when she was so eager to hide from the probing eyes of neighbours that she would only walk Michelle through the back streets. What must it have been like for her when she had to let go of her hopes and dreams, knowing Michelle would never be normal, never communicate, but always need to be looked after? I realise she must be anxious for the health of her grandchild, too.

As I pick up a second tractate of Talmud to dust, Simcha walks into the apartment clutching two holy books to his chest. I am glad he is back. We have become closer during the past nine months. It is so much easier to be intimate without the *niddah* separations tearing us apart every two weeks, able to cuddle and kiss and hold hands as often as we like. Simcha told me that the Talmud suggests not having intercourse during the first trimester but he didn't heed that suggestion. It is not that Simcha has fulfilled me in a sexual way. I have not had multiple orgasms or screamed out in a frenzy of passion, but we have fallen into a domestic habit of friendship, warmth and closeness. Maybe my changing body and the loss of my curvy figure and its sexual demands has taken off the pressure. But I think I look better than ever with outsized breasts and a swollen ball in front. I feel like a fertility goddess, oozing femininity. I am big. Many people think I'm carrying twins, but it is only one foetus that is floating inside of me.

'I've been at the yeshiva reviewing the laws of *Pessach* with

Rabbi Sapphire,' Simcha says, as he puts the books on the table. 'I've made sure every detail will be one hundred per cent kosher. It took forever. First we looked in one source, then in another. The two sources contradicted each other, so we had to look for a third authority.'

'It's kicking! Come and feel,' I cry, wincing as a foot-sized bump protrudes through my dress.

Simcha gently lowers his hand onto my belly. 'I had a hard time deciding which stream to follow regarding the speed of eating the matza at the *Seder*. It has to be eaten quickly, to remind us of the Israelites who left Egypt in a hurry,' he says and then, feeling a kick adds, 'Wow . . . that's a strong baby we've got there. Anyway, some rabbis say the matza has to be wolfed down within eight minutes, others say ten minutes. But I've decided on the most stringent trend of four minutes.'

'Simcha. I'm scared.'

'No worries. This doesn't apply to women about to give birth. You'll eat what you can?'

'About the baby.'

'You know God only gives tests to those who can deal with them. Everything's going to be fine.'

I am annoyed that he cannot sympathise with my fears or be sensitive enough to comfort me. 'Must we shake out every single book?' I ask. 'It'll take forever.'

'Just the ones I've studied from at the dining table,' Simcha replies. 'We can be lenient this year considering your condition.'

My condition. I must concentrate on my condition and the fact that my due date is in a week's time. Soon I will hold my baby in my arms. That will be the most joyous moment I can imagine, the start of building my dream of a Jewish home, educating the next generation. Yet the thought fills me with fear too. My devotion toward the godly path I so want to follow is being tested once again. The rabbis explain that every soul comes back to this world to fix itself, and that some must return with limited bodies and brains. But somehow I don't think that was the case with Michelle. I believe that when my sister was born, she was not made handicapped for a reason, but because God was taking an untimely break from overseeing the world.

After bringing me all the suspect books, Simcha takes the pots and pans down from the kitchen cabinets and puts them into a large cardboard box. 'I'm off to the synagogue yard. They've set up an iron cauldron of boiling water for scalding. Just think – every trace of *chometz* on these pots will be eradicated,' Simcha calls out joyfully, leaving the apartment with the box hoisted on his shoulder.

Left alone, my mind regresses to fearful thoughts about the baby and then to memories of Michelle when she was a child and still lived at home. It has been years since I have seen her, too many years, and the problem isn't because I live in Israel. I can't even ask my mother how she is. The subject is so fraught with pain, it turns my mother into a weeping mess, and brings about a sadness I cannot bear. As a child, I used to sign both our names on birthday cards for my parents, but eventually I stopped that charade. Michelle cannot sign her name and I'm not even sure she knows what a birthday is.

The baby is kicking again. I hold my belly, suddenly fearful that God will punish me for ignoring Michelle, fulfilling the 'what goes around comes around' philosophy basic to

Judaism. But surely God knows why I cannot go to see Michelle. Surely an all-knowing God would remember how hard I used to tremble after visiting Michelle in Ravenswood, how sick I always felt after seeing the other kids, so deformed and twisted. Surely God remembers how frightened I was when my best friend Sandra, who had epilepsy, would fall to the ground from her chair to the floor and lie there, her eyes rolling backwards as she foamed at the mouth. I spent my entire fifth year in primary school watching Sandra for the first signs of an epileptic fit so that I could run out of class to avoid witnessing an attack. And there were those terrible summers on Brighton beach when I would see a hunchbacked dwarf lying on the pebbles in his swimming trunks. I had to turn away from his scrunched-up body and close my eyes so that my nightmares of a tidal wave rolling up on the beach with such force that it would wipe out the entire seaside community wouldn't come true. Even today when I see handicapped people in the street, I panic. My head starts to buzz, my body tenses up and I want to get away.

My unhappy memories are interrupted as Simcha returns to the apartment with the koshered kitchenware.

'You look exhausted,' Simcha exclaims. 'Come and lie down.' He takes the feather duster out of my hand and leads me to the bedroom.

I fall into bed, hoping for a kiss and cuddle after my hours of cleaning, but Simcha tucks me in, plops a quick kiss on my forehead, strokes the enormous bulge through the bed covers and takes leave of me to finish the cleaning.

While I toss and turn, trying to find a comfortable position, Simcha scrubs the stove with bleach, covers the counter tops with silver foil and checks in every nook and cranny for any remaining *chometz*.

After a nap, I sit on the couch and watch Simcha make the final preparations. He mixes the salt water for the taste of tears and then mashes nuts, red wine and apples into a paste for the *charoset* to resemble the mortar the Jews used to cement the bricks in Pharaoh's pyramids. 'I can't wait for the first crispy bite of matza,' he admits. 'I paid a lot of money for it from the Hassidic bakery in Mea Shearim. But it's worth every shekel, as it will unite us with Jews who have risked their lives to bake matza in the ghetto and in the camps. How cool is that?'

I nod, but all I can think about is the birth and my mother's comment when I told her the good news that I was pregnant. 'Don't worry, darling,' she had said. 'You'll have an epidural.' I want the pain that she fears. I want to feel the birthing process progressing naturally. My mother was too scared to give birth naturally again and I was an elective Caesarean section to prevent the possibility of another birth accident.

'I'm going to change the living room furniture around to make a regal *Seder*. It'll be like a Roman banquet or a royal feast. We'll lie on mattresses and recline supported by cushions. You'll see. It'll be fun and I'm sure even your father will be impressed,' Simcha boasts, as he moves the dining table to the corner and pushes it up against the wall. Now that he has created an empty space, big enough for four to lie back, he helps me move to an armchair, takes the cushions off the three-seater couch and places them on the floor.

'I'm not sure my dad will go for this,' I protest, but Simcha isn't listening.

'I remember *Seder* nights back in Colorado when I asked

the *manishtana*, "Why is this night different from all other nights?"' he says. 'But I never got an answer. Only the shank bone, salt water and matza mattered to my parents. But after five years of studying in yeshiva, I know that *Pessach* is not about the food, but *Pe-sach* – literally "the mouth speaks", the telling of the exodus story, the slavery and journey to freedom is what really matters.'

When Simcha expounds the wisdom he's learnt in yeshiva, I am happy. After all the cleaning and preparations, his words put me into the spirit of the holiday.

'I had the worst *Seder* nights in London,' I say, as Simcha brings in a mattress from the spare room and nestles it next to the cushions. 'My dad always led a communal *Seder* in the King Solomon Suite, a fancy banqueting hall in the basement of the synagogue building. It was the same hall where he had set up a blood bank to donate blood for Israeli soldiers after the Yom Kippur War. That year he postponed all the lavish weddings and barmitzvahs that had been scheduled and turned the hall into a clinic, where thousands of Anglo-Jews came to give blood. My dad walked up and down the hall talking to all the donors, keeping up morale and thanking them. Afterwards, whenever we had *Seder* in that hall all I could think about was the packets of blood that were carried to the Jewish cabbies lined up outside the synagogue ready to drive them straight to the airport and it freaked me out. But I hated *Seder* in the banqueting hall anyway. My dad put on a wonderful show, but it wasn't intimate like a *Seder* should be. He had a microphone hidden in the flower arrangement and was so successful in getting everyone to sing along and follow in the *Haggadah*, that after the final blessing of "Next year in

Jerusalem" his congregants always sang out "Next year with Rabbi Mann!" But they knew nothing about coming out of bondage. They were all slaves to Ralph Lauren.'

'Reva! Guard your tongue,' Simcha reprimands me as he takes white sheets from the top shelf of the linen cupboard and spreads them over the couches. He flanks the couches with side tables so the matza and wineglasses will be at arm's reach.

Now that the living room has been transformed to look like a student pad, Simcha stops to admire his work. 'Isn't this just like a palace? Tomorrow, your father will lie on the cushions like King David, and your mother will recline like Bathsheba at his side.'

I find it hard to imagine my parents reclining like David and Bathsheba, especially now that they are calling from their hotel room and complaining about their journey from London.

'The plane was delayed and then, as if that wasn't enough, one of our bags didn't come off. They've found it, thank God. You can't imagine, my best suit and my silk dress could have been lost. Well, I was hysterical. The stress wasn't good for your father either. We haven't slept of course. Hope we'll be able to keep our eyes open for the *Seder*. So how are you? All right, I hope. We really haven't got the strength to deal with anything other than ourselves at the moment.'

'Can I talk to Daddy?' I ask, hoping for a word of encouragement now that I am at the end of my ninth month, the labour about to begin.

'He's resting at the moment.' I can tell from her tone she considers my request a selfish one.

I can sense my parents have once again constructed a front that I cannot penetrate or argue with. I cannot say, 'Oh please come over and help me with the final preparations.' I cannot explain that I need their moral support because I am scared. Instead I say what I know they want to hear.

'All right, Mum. Have a good rest.'

The feelings stirring inside of me remind me of what I always felt as a child when my parents shut down, usually because they were angry, but sometimes because they just wanted me out of the way. One of the worst times was when they found my dope stash. They called me into the living room where the evidence, a chunk of hashish, a Thai stick and a handful of sedatives, had been placed on a silver tray in the middle of the table. They grounded me and insisted I sever ties with any friends who had influenced me to take drugs. When they left the house, they took the telephone off the receiver in my father's study and locked that door so that I could not call out to anyone. There was no one to talk to. When they were in the house, they ignored me as though I didn't exist for them at all. I would sit at the dining table in silence while they spoke, never including me in their conversation, refusing to acknowledge my presence.

I often wonder who is the crazy parent and who is acting as the buffer. But they are both crazy in their own ways – Mother with her anxiety and depressions, Father, the opposite of Mother, with his rigid control over his emotions – the two of them protecting each other from the impending disasters they both expect at any time.

Again I feel the old loneliness creeping over me. Once again I am left out in the cold, my parents keeping me at a distance from the protective cocoon they inhabit to ensure I will be no trouble to them.

Oh, Crumbs!

The apartment is completely kosher for *Pessach*. Simcha wraps up ten pieces of bread in silver foil and asks me to hide them around the house. I have never heard of this tradition. When my father checks for *chometz* he does it by sweeping a few crumbs together onto a newspaper that will be burnt the following morning in the kitchen sink. I dutifully hide the silver pieces and, when Simcha switches off the light and with candle in hand sets out to find the *chometz*, I play along with him.

I nod my head as he gets warmer and then shake it as he walks closer to where I have hidden the silver balls and then further away.

After half an hour he has found nine pieces and is still searching for the tenth. I cannot help him as I have forgotten where I placed it.

Simcha continues the search. He moves the fridge away from the wall and checks behind. He pushes the cooker to the side and looks in all the kitchen cabinets.

'I couldn't have got to those places,' I say, hungry and tired, heartburn raging in my windpipe and my varicose veins throbbing, desperate for this ceremony to end.

Simcha wags his finger at me. I had forgotten that I am not allowed to talk during *bedikat chometz*. At last, Simcha finds the last silver ball, the size of an almond, under the rug.

The following evening my parents arrive at our apartment, tired out, still recovering from their journey. They step inside and look around bewildered at the living room with the mattresses on the floor. 'Didn't there used to be a couch and coffee table here?' my mother asks.

'Well, Simcha, what's all this?' My father coughs and blows his nose.

'Tonight we will dine as free men, Rabbi.'

'Very original to say the least,' my father offers, wiping beads of sweat off his forehead with his hanky.

'Thank you,' Simcha replies, chuffed by the compliment. 'Tonight we will lean back on cushions like royalty and re-enact the drama of the exodus by eating the matza and bitter herbs.'

My father politely declines the lying down option due to his severe hernia condition while my mother tries to oblige. But it is impossible. Her silk suit is too constricting for such a relaxed pose. Simcha has to bring in two high-backed chairs for my parents. Not wanting to disappoint my husband, I buckle down slowly onto the mattress, propped up with many cushions to alleviate my constant heartburn. Rennies are not kosher for *Pessach*, so I have thrown them away.

Despite his unsuccessful attempt at having a reclining quartet, Simcha is in a terrific mood. He lies, draped over the make-do throne, with goblet in hand, gazing heavenward, a king of kings.

I sit on the mattress with my legs sprawled out in front of me. My lower back is aching.

'I saw your old friend Suzy last week in the high street,' my mother says, oblivious to the fact that Simcha is anxious to begin the *Seder*. 'She married a neurologist, you know. They just got back from a cruise in the Caribbean. Lovely girl.'

'That's wonderful,' I say, trying to feel happy for my friend, but the news has made me more envious than happy. Suddenly the idea of lazing in the Caribbean seems very appealing right now.

'Will you stop that incessant blabbering for a few minutes!

Oh, Crumbs!

We are at a *Seder*.' My father throws Mother one of his black looks, the ones I'm terrified of that appear without a second's notice and for seemingly no reason at all.

Mother stops talking long enough to perform the most important commandment, the eating of the matza. She looks down at her shoes like a little girl told off by her teacher. I am glad she has been silenced, as I don't want to hear any more about luxury holidays in the Caribbean, but I feel sorry for her too. I notice the way she is playing with her wedding band and wringing her hands to keep herself in control. I am angry now with my father for upsetting her, even though I sympathise with him at how irritating she can be. I cannot bear to see him put her down this way, as I have been a victim of his sharp tongue and know how it feels. But my sympathy is something my mother would never want. Even when she is humiliated she sides with my father. And if I dared to stand up for her, she would immediately stick up for him. Whatever I might think about it, my parents' marriage is a love match. My father went against the wishes of his father and married a girl from a secular home. Her intellect attracted him, as well as her full bosom and long slender legs.

Simcha reaches for the enormous cardboard box in front of him and lovingly lifts out the first of many round, hand-baked matzas, each one the size of a large family pizza, burnt black at the edges. He hands three matzas to each of us, holds his matzas together and recites the blessing with rapture. Then he checks his stopwatch, and the countdown begins. According to the trend of the *chazon ish*, he has exactly four minutes to finish eating. He stuffs the matzas into his mouth, taking bite after bite before swallowing. Spittle accumulates in the corners of his mouth. Matza flies everywhere, spills out of his mouth and onto the floor. His beard and shirt are a mass of crumbs.

'Never seen anyone make such a pig of themselves,' my father tells my mother.

'I think I'm going to be sick. The fish I had for lunch is coming up,' says my mother, she is turning pale.

Simcha is oblivious to any talk around him and continues chewing with vigour. He has a matza beard, which makes him look like an ancient sage.

'It's an acute case of messianic fever, Dolly. He's probably hovering somewhere between ecstasy and severe indigestion. I shudder to think how my own gastric juices would react under such stress,' my father remarks.

Uncomfortably caught between my parents' mockery and my husband's piety, I suddenly feel liquid gushing out of me. My stockings are soaked and a damp patch is swelling on the carpet. My shrill cry jolts Simcha from his munching. This is it. The baby is coming on *Seder* night, and my own redemption is at hand. My mother starts to convulse and cries out, 'Oh my God! Oh my God!'

I am quick to understand that she is reliving the trauma of giving birth to my sister. Even though I need support right now, I help her lie down on the cushions and then search for the Rescue Remedy, a homeopathic tincture that helps in time of crisis. I squeeze three drops onto her tongue. As she lies down, her skirt rides up, revealing scars from her latest cosmetic surgery, the removal of her unsightly varicose veins.

And now my father's heart condition suddenly flares up as it always does in times of stress. I remember the day he visited my psychiatrist to discuss medications to alleviate my teenage depression. As soon as the subject was raised, my father's hand jumped for his heart and, instead of discussing my problems, he went into a lengthy exposition about his own health and his heart medications. Now he lies in a supine position on the cushions, holding his chest. I hold my belly with one hand and with the other search his suit jacket for his heart pills. Once he has popped a little blue pill, I lie down again, rocking my knees from side to side. My initial twinges are getting stronger and I am unable to find a comfortable position. By now my parents and I are all horizontal, just as Simcha wanted us, but the *Seder* is forgotten, each one of us focused on our pain.

'This is a *Pessach* miracle! You're all identifying with the suffering of the Jewish people,' Simcha exclaims towering above us. 'It's just like the commentary of the Maharal of Prague, who compares the exodus to a birth. We are in a tight spot, just like the Israelites in Egypt. The amniotic fluid is like the water of the Red Sea parting. Reva, your contractions are the birth pangs of a nation being born.'

'My heart!' my father gasps. 'Dolly, it is my dying wish that you tell this nincompoop to shut up!'

'My husband is dying! Shut up, for God's sake.' My mother crawls over to where my father is lying.

'Breathe with me, Simcha. I'm losing it!' I cry out.

'OK, I'm breathing with you. What is it now? Three breaths in and one breath out or one breath in and three breaths out? Breathe, Reva, breathe.'

'My back hurts,' I moan.

'Wait a minute, something with two pillows? And gravity?'

'Simcha, oh God, it hurts.'

'Rabbi Sapphire advised putting earth from the land of Israel around your neck during labour. Should I get dirt from the downstairs garden?' Simcha babbles uncontrollably. Not knowing where to turn, he walks around in circles and, realising he is unable to help, he reaches for his Psalm book and begins to pray.

I pick myself up off the mattress, waddle to the bedroom and grab my pre-packed bag. Stopping at the bathroom to relieve myself, I notice the mucous plug with bloody show has dropped from my cervix. The toilet paper is smeared with a pinky discharge and my underpants are stained. I had hoped this wouldn't happen so early on; hoped that Simcha would have at least been able to hold my hand during the first stage of labour. But now I am a *nidda* and he cannot touch me.

Simcha stuffs the psalm book into the bag along with what is left of the matza. My mother is busy attending to my father when we leave the apartment. Both of them seem relieved we are off.

'Reva,' my mother tries to get up but decides half way to stay put, 'it'll be fine; don't worry – it won't happen twice in one family.' I look at my mother. For once I can see the true person who is always hidden behind the nervous disposition. I stare at her, wanting to capture this moment and keep her with me like this always, the mother who can see beyond herself and the excruciating muddle of physical symptoms that usually occupies her, the mother I need so much. Her words soothe me.

'God bless you, darling,' my father says. 'We'll be praying for you.'

Unable to lean on Simcha or even walk close to him, I trail

behind him on the fifteen-minute walk to the hospital. I want
to feel his arm supporting me, leading me now, but I know that
even if I were to deliver right here on the street, he wouldn't
place a comforting hand on me. I am not focusing on the
extreme way Simcha behaves with the law. I am trying to get
through the contractions, which are intensifying all the time.
The streets are empty. Songs of redemption filter out of open
windows. Everyone is at *Seder*. I feel as if we are walking
through a ghost town and are the only people left in the world.
I need to stop every few minutes to breathe through the band
of pain around my lower back. I lean on a tree or sit on a
bench until the contraction passes.

We enter the hospital and take the steps up to the first floor.
This is my ward, where I work as a *doula*. But tonight there is
nothing professional about my behaviour and I am whimpering like every other labouring mother I have ever had in my
custody. Sure that after four hours of multiple contractions I
am fully dilated, I am disappointed when an internal exam
reveals that I am only three centimetres open. I press a shiatsu
point on the inside of my wrist, rock on all fours on the bed,
focus on the image of a rose opening up petal by petal, but
nothing seems to help. The sounds of the baby's heartbeat
from the monitor and of Simcha crunching matza filter into my
consciousness in between the moans and screams tearing out
of me at the peaks of pain. Simcha keeps falling asleep; the
private doctor my mother insisted I hire is taking his time
getting to the hospital on *Seder* night. Feeling completely lost
and alone, I beg for all the pain relief I can get.

Even though I am knowledgeable about the stages of
labour, the foetal presentations, the reasons for shaking and

vomiting, and I understand that the pain in my lumbar region means I am having a back labour and that I must rock my pelvis to get the baby off my back, I do nothing. The agonising labour pains are exacerbated by my fears, which have returned and are getting stronger as the labour progresses.

An epidural administered to the spine takes away the pain. I lie back, feeling a failure for having taken pain relief and fulfilling my mother's wish. I make a decision that whatever baby God sends me, I will accept it with love.

Because of the epidural I can hardly feel the pressure of the baby's head on the perineum now that the doctor is telling me to push. Simcha leaves the room for the delivery, as he is not allowed to see the baby's head crowning through my tunnel. As the head moves down, I know this is the moment of truth. I will soon see if my baby is healthy or not. The doctor injects anaesthetic into the perineum and I hear the cut of flesh. I want to throw up. Now he is using shiny chrome forceps to take the baby out. He could crush the head. 'Please,' I beg, 'be careful. Oh must you? Must you?'

It is six o'clock in the morning and my baby's head finally emerges. I stare in awe as the body, covered in white creamy vernix, slides out. The ball that has moved and kicked inside me is a healthy girl. With the umbilical cord still intact, I put her straight to my breast. Simcha creeps in, his face brimming with happiness, whispering, '*Mazeltov . . . mazeltov.*'

After a few minutes of sucking, my daughter slips off my nipple and I swaddle her tightly in a cotton blanket and offer her to Simcha. 'Ask the nurse to give her to me,' he says gently. 'We can't pass the baby till . . .'

I shift over to the right side of the hospital bed and lay my baby next to me. I don't want to let go of her but I must for the split second before Simcha can pick her up. It's OK, I tell myself, trying not to let the anger over the barbaric laws rise in me. It makes no sense that I cannot hold my husband's hand and pass the baby to him. Surely there can be no worry about the touch of a hand leading to our having relations now. Who could possibly think about having sex after giving birth, with a vagina bloody, cut and swollen, breasts oozing colostrum and a body that aches all over? Yet, I leave my arm cradling the air beneath my newborn, ready to catch her if necessary. Simcha picks her up and she holds onto the straggly hairs of his beard with all her might. He is making cooing noises to her, welcoming her to our world. She looks so tiny and fragile in his arms, the blanket white against his black jacket. 'She has my mother's chin,' Simcha reports, 'and my sister's brow – what shall we name her?'

'How about Adele?' I suggest the name of Rabbi Nachman of Breslov's daughter.

'Hello, little Adele,' he says so gently.

I lay back onto the pillow, exhausted and relieved. At this moment, I have everything I want.

My parents enter the room, which I share with three other women. Our babies lie in cradles next to us and nurse on demand. I hope that I will, at last, secure their admiration by having delivered such a perfect creature into the world.

'Darling, I know you've had a hard time, but compared to what I've been through, well, I haven't slept a wink. If only . . .'

I register and regret that the appearance of my mother's

healthy self proved so transitory. Today I want to be the focus of attention. Instead of sympathising, I proudly hand my treasure over to her, but when I see my newborn in her arms, her nails flaming red against the baby's white skin, I want to reach out and snatch her back. I don't want my baby to be contaminated by my mother. I don't want her ever to feel the ups and downs of my mother's mood swings. I want her to feel loved at all times. But then I see a softness in my mother's face as she looks at her healthy granddaughter, and I consider I may be mistaken. With a grandchild she may do a better job. A grandchild may be the very tonic that she needs. And now once again my mother emerges from the fog of her self-involvement and is talking with crystal clarity. 'She doesn't look like our family,' she says. 'That's a good thing. She'll be better off without our craziness.'

My father is overjoyed that a healthy baby has been delivered safely and plants a kiss on his granddaughter's head. '*Mazeltov*, Simcha.' He turns to his son-in-law, whom he had only yesterday thought of as the village idiot. But now that he has his first grandchild, he gives Simcha a big hug, his eyes glowing with gratitude.

Despite my oozing nipples and sore perineum, I am content. My body cries all over as I join mothers of the world in the knowledge of Eve's curse, but I look down at my beautiful baby girl and I am truly happy.

Three milky, sleep-deprived days later, I am holding my bundled treasure, standing on the threshold of the apartment that I had left in such a hurry. I survey the scene. Scraps of matza cover the carpet, the bottle of Rescue Remedy is wedged between the cushions and salt water stands stagnant in the jug. Nothing is ready for my arrival.

'Oh crumbs!' I exclaim as I enter the living room. I had hoped to bring my baby into a spotlessly clean home, the nappies piled up on the changing table, a nutritious meal bubbling on the stove.

'Where?' cries Simcha in horror, frantically scanning the floor for a forgotten crust of toast.

9

Mr Fixit Breaks Through

Thou shalt not cook a kid in its mother's milk.
Exodus 23:19

It is a beautiful Jerusalem morning. The skies are clear this October day. I walk barefoot on the cool ceramic tiled flooring of my home towards the front door. I have an appointment with a Mr Fixit who has come to survey our decrepit kitchen and make suggestions for a renovation job, a gift from my parents to celebrate Adele's birth.

I open the door to the builder. It takes a few seconds for the message that he is rugged and sexy to reach my brain, but my body has already registered the high levels of testosterone oozing out of him and has slipped back into long unfamiliar movements. My pelvis is swivelling. I stick out my Amazonian breasts, showing them off. My head tilts coquettishly to the side and my lips pout ever so slightly as I invite him inside and offer him a seat.

I take a good look at him. I notice the diamond flashing in his ear, the shaved head, muscular chest and arms, button-down jeans that hug his hips and the way his sex juts out like a mango. I pull in my postpartum flabby stomach, which now holds a new foetus, conceived two months ago despite the fact that I am still nursing Adele, who will be seven months old tomorrow.

Mr Fixit looks around at the ornate coffee table and the bureau, heavy furniture shipped from London that seems out of place in the tropical climate of the Middle East. Books that are stacked on the windowsills and on the floor are gathering dust. Adele's toys are scattered over the carpet and her Fisher Price swing stands in an alcove by the door.

'What's your real name?' I ask.

'Joe. Joe Scott at your service.'

'Joe,' I repeat. 'Joe, would you like some tea?'

'Great. Thanks.'

'Milk and sugar?'

'Two please,' Joe answers, as he checks out the dilapidated kitchen.

'You're British?'

'Born and bred.'

'Me too. London. You?'

'Buurmingum,' he says, laying it on thick.

Flustered, I spill the tea as I bring the mugs to the table.

Joe smiles at me as he helps mop up the spills with kitchen towels.

'I want to get rid of this wall.' I turn around and point to the wall separating the kitchen and dining area. 'That way it'll bring in more light.'

'No problem,' replies Joe, cocky and self-confident.

'The main thing is . . .' I hesitate, trying to focus on the plans and not on his bulge, 'I need to separate the milk dishes from the meat, as we don't eat milk and meat together and I don't want to mix them up.'

'So no fillet steak cooked in butter then?'

'What you eat affects the soul,' I explain, hating how much

I sound like a rabbi and not the femme fatale I want to be right now.

'I can separate the kitchen into two sections with a sink, countertop, and two cupboards on each side,' says Joe, cocking his head to the left. 'That way, you won't get mixed up.'

His sweat mingled with aftershave awakens in me a desire that has been long dormant. I hardly know what I am saying and though I try to keep up the conversation, I am somewhere else, already in his strong muscular arms, until Adele whimpers in her crib and brings me back to reality.

As I go to pick her up, I catch sight of myself in the bedroom mirror. I look awful. My hair is covered with a flowery scarf. My shirt is stained, my skirt is baggy and my face is bare of make-up. There are dark shadows under my eyes from the many sleepless nights.

Adele is crying when I bring her to the living room. Fixit looks up from the kitchen plans and smiles. 'Hello, little one,' he says.

I sit on the couch. If Simcha could see me unclip the cup of my nursing bra and let Adele nuzzle at my breast in front of this man he would have a fit. I don't relate to my breasts as sexual appendages any more now that they are flowing with milk. I think breastfeeding is the most natural thing in the world. Simcha has asked me to cover up while nursing, as it disturbs him to see my nudity. To please him and avoid an argument, I cover Adele with a white cotton blanket and let her suckle underneath. But she will not comply and sends out a tight fist to grab the blanket and pull it off her hot and sweating face. I laugh, delighted by this act of rebellion and feel she is my ally against Simcha's behaviour, which is getting more extreme with every passing day. Simcha doesn't find it funny and has banished me to the bedroom for feeding. Motherhood has strengthened me. After going through the pain and the ordeal of childbirth and taking care of Adele, I feel I have merited the right to make choices about how to live by the *halacha* and not simply follow Simcha's path like a lost sheep. I am a somebody now. Perhaps the result of the mix of both postpartum and pregnancy hormones has severed my desire to be with Simcha. Even though I am not a *nidda* and don't need to separate the beds, I only want to snuggle down with Adele. This has given me back my power and made me see things in a clearer light.

Adele is sucking hard and the sound of her lapping up milk is audible. 'The kitchen plan sounds great,' I say. 'Do we need to hire anyone else for the electricity or to do the tiling?'

'Nope. I do the lot myself,' he replies, flexing a bicep the size of a grapefruit as he brings the ceramic mug to his lips.

'So when do we begin?'

'How about right now? Once you've chosen the tiles and the marble tops, I'll order them and we'll start immediately.'

He's so alive, so helpful, I think; so unlike Simcha who is becoming like an old man, shuffling slowly from one room to the other. Being around Simcha's low energy makes me feel as if I'm sinking under anaesthesia. But now I feel more awake than I have in ages. 'I get a discount in a shop in Talpiot. I've got a free hour now. I could take you. Van's outside.'

'My husband wants to choose,' I hesitate, 'but he'd probably be glad not to take time off Torah study. Could you pass me the phone? It's over there on the bookshelf,' I say, pointing to the library of holy books.

Convincing myself that I am helping Simcha attain enlightenment, I dial the yeshiva pay phone.

'Hello. Light of Zion – men's division.'

'Hello. This is Reva, Simcha's wife. Could I have a quick word?' my voice is full of apology.

I hear slow footsteps and then Simcha's weak voice on the other end.

'Reva, is everything all right?'

'Yes, fine, *Baruch Hashem*. Sorry I'm disturbing you, but I've got a chance to go and choose the kitchen tiles with Mr Fixit who came this morning and is being extremely helpful.' I look round at the sexy builder. 'Will you trust my taste?'

I hear the sigh of relief. 'Go along. It's fine with me. Today is the anniversary of the death of Rabbi Nachman of Breslov, and the students are drinking a *l'chaim*. I won't be home until later in the afternoon.'

I heave Adele, who has fallen back asleep, into a sling and secure the straps around my waist. A wave of morning sickness rises in me. I stuff a salty cracker into my mouth to alleviate the nausea, grab my purse, smooth my headscarf and leave the apartment with Joe.

In the parking lot, Joe opens the truck door, and hurriedly wipes bits of tile and sandpaper off the passenger seat, which he then covers with his plaid cotton shirt for me to sit on. Out of modesty and for Adele's safety, I would have sat in the back, but since the pick-up doesn't have one, I slide in next to the driver's seat. As he starts up the engine, I notice a pale band on the forefinger of his suntanned hand.

'Are you married?'

'Recently divorced.' He winces in pain. 'I'm on my own now.'

'Do you have kids?'

'A little girl. Lives with her mum. How old is your little one then?'

'Adele, she's seven months.'

'That's a good number; seven days of creation – isn't it?'

I laugh at his attempt to speak my language. 'Are you Jewish?' I ask, sure that he isn't.

'Father is, mother not,' he says.

Not Jewish, I automatically think.

I walk with Joe into the warehouse. We are an odd-looking pair, sauntering up and down the aisles discussing colour combinations and feeling the textures of the ceramic tiles. Even though Adele is heavy in the sling and I am dressed in a long dowdy skirt, I feel freer than I have been in ages, alive again, even jubilant and my body moves like liquid along the rows. I choose a terracotta tile, instead of the plain white I had planned on. Joe deals with the business angle and gets a 20 per cent discount.

We leave the warehouse congratulating each other. In the excitement, our hands accidentally brush for a split second. I back off, as if fire has lashed its tongue at me. In that fraction of a moment, I imagine biting on his lower lip while he presses inside of me.

Giddy from the touch and the adulterous fantasy, I lean against the seat in the truck and open the window for air. Joe seems unaware of the enormity of the moment, puts the key in the ignition and drives me home in silence. I glance at his hands on the steering wheel and then look away as the sight of them makes me imagine him holding and caressing me.

'See you next week and thanks for everything,' I call, as I

step down from the van, my arms cradling Adele. I turn towards home.

Simcha comes home to find me in a frisky mood. Drunk from the many brandies honouring Rabbi Nachman, he declines my advances and goes straight to bed to nap so that he will have strength for his Thursday night get-together at Rabbi Sapphire's house.

Now that Adele is finally asleep, I begin to prepare the food for the holy *Shabbes*. Standing in the run-down kitchen, battling images of the sexy builder that have invaded my mind, I pour chopped carp into a bowl, add a raw egg, salt, pepper, sugar, a sprinkle of matzo meal and mix it together with a wooden spoon, following Rabbi Nachman's advice to serve fish on *Shabbes* as the numerical value of the Hebrew word for 'fish' adds up to seven, symbolising the seventh day of rest. Again and again I taste the mixture until it has just the right balance of sugar and salt. Wetting my hands under the tap, I roll the fish into balls and drop them into a pot of boiling water.

My stomach is cramping and my head aches. These pains are not pregnancy related but the old *Shabbes* trauma rearing its head again. They are the same psychosomatic symptoms I had as a child, anticipating the Friday nights that were always such times of tension in our family. Even though I am far away from my parents' home, no longer witness to their constant anxiety about synagogue politics and the sermon my father would have to deliver the next day, the burden of having to cook large amounts of food for *Shabbes*, allowing Simcha the luxury of emulating Abraham our forefather and inviting straggly beggars and smelly down-and-outs home from *shul* on Friday nights, weighs heavily on me. Simcha may be like

Abraham, but I am definitely no Sarah. I can't bear him giving all his attention to these disease-ridden creatures while hardly noticing my efforts or playing with Adele. Unlike the Matriarch who kneaded the love of Torah into her dough, anger and frustration have become the main ingredients in my own cooking. I feel stuck in this marriage with a second baby on the way. As I prod the potatoes to see if they're cooked, I imagine puncturing a hole in Simcha's black hat. As I tear leaves off a head of lettuce, I envision ripping pages out of his Talmud. Tonight the memory of Joe Fixit keeps me going. I keep reliving the touch of a hand that does not belong to my husband, that I would love to hold and be held by.

The onions I am frying have turned a golden brown. I add chicken pieces to the pan and cover it with a lid and scurry from one chore to another until midnight. The balls of gefilte fish sit in neat rows crowned with a slice of carrot. A pot of golden chicken soup, fat swirling on the top, is ready to be refrigerated so the fat will rise to the top and a thick layer can be removed tomorrow. Chickens roasted in wine and garlic are ready to be warmed up on the *Shabbes* hotplate. Honey cakes and a raisin pudding, burnt crisp on the edges, cool on a rack. The *cholent*, a stew of meat, barley and potatoes, is partially cooked, ready to simmer slowly on a low flame from sunset tomorrow night until served for *Shabbes* lunch. The kitchen smells of Paradise, and unable to control my cravings and wait until the *Shabbes*, I tuck into the pudding, pulling on the crusty sides with my fingers and scooping it into my mouth.

Simcha has left the house for the Cabbala club meeting. I can picture the motley crew of wannabe messiahs sitting around a heavy wooden table in the darkened living room illuminated by candlelight and the nectar of the rabbi's words. Simcha has described the scene: the rocking back and forth and twiddling of sidelocks while they study the mysteries of the Cabbala, drink brandy and munch on chickpeas until the early morning. Then, bonded by brotherhood, they march revitalised to the Western Wall for prayers. These sessions are the highlight of Simcha's week, the fuel that propels him into the holy *Shabbes*.

I get ready for bed and stretch out alone, feeling as lonely as the *Shabbes* day must have felt when God created the days of the week and paired them up: Sunday with Monday, Tuesday with Wednesday, and Thursday with Friday. But when God heard the lonely *Shabbes* weeping because she had no partner, He proposed that He, Himself, be the partner of the *Shabbes*. I hold my pillow in my arms and pretend it's Joe. I kiss the cotton pillowcase and let my hand wander down between my legs. Joe is caressing me, kissing my neck, my nipples. I'm rubbing back and forth now. He's turned me over. I prefer it this way. I'm sweating into my nightgown. He's holding my breasts, squeezing now. He's rocking back and forth inside me. 'You're so sexy,' he's telling me. 'I wanted you from the first moment I saw you.' Joe, Joe, oh my God, Joe.

When morning comes, in order to keep the daydream going, I omit the morning ritual washing of hands, not to lave the fantasy of the rough workman's touch.

Joe arrives promptly at eight this Sunday morning. Wearing cut-off jean shorts and an old T-shirt, he hauls in crates of tools and weapons of destruction and goes straight to work marking out where he will break down the wall.

Simcha, still in his pyjamas and bathrobe, shuffles off to the bathroom to relieve himself in preparation for morning prayer.

Axe in hand, Joe swings at the wall like a graceful warrior engaged in a barbaric act. His powerful limbs work in perfect unison as he hacks at the centre of the wall. I stare at his bulging muscles and manly strength. Within minutes of deafening noise and whirling dust, the wall comes crashing down. In my mind, Joe has entered me and the noise of the crash is our screaming in ecstatic pleasure.

Simcha emerges from the bathroom mumbling the prayer for after going to the toilet. 'Blessed art Thou, O Lord, who created man with openings and hollows . . . if one of them were blocked or ruptured it would be impossible to exist and stand in Your presence.' Oblivious to the fact that the house is in a state of collapse and that I am deep in sexual fantasy, my openings moist and craving, he walks up to Joe and extends his hand. '*Shalom Aleichem*,' he greets him like an honoured guest at the *Shabbes* table.

Joe rubs his grubby hand on his back pocket and the two men shake hands. Simcha looks anaemic next to the virile Mr Fixit, like milk next to meat. 'Shalom. How are you?' Joe says, staring at the Hassid in pyjamas.

'Blessed be He.' Simcha looks down at the rubble for the first time. 'This is holy work you're doing. Breaking down walls takes a lot of strength. It is the same in the spiritual world where, with study and prayer, we try to break through the obstacles separating us from God.'

'Oh, right.' Joe, who is sweating profusely, stares at Simcha's soft hands.

'Well, let us both get on with our work,' Simcha says and excuses himself to dress.

Joe goes out onto the balcony and lights up a cigarette. Adele is fussing. I take her out to the hallway, not wanting her to inhale the dust, and I rock her to and fro in my arms.

Simcha reappears fitted out in his regular black suit, white shirt, and black hat and winds a silky black *gartle* around his waist and knots it on the side to separate his lower animal self from the higher spiritual one. He goes to the study to pray.

I put Adele in the swing and crank the handle, setting it to continue for thirty minutes. She coos and smiles while I sweep up the remnants of dust and pebbles that remain on the floor, trying to make order in my home as well as in my mind. Simcha's wailing of prayers drifts out from the study.

Joe has finished his fag and is back inside feeling for rough edges in his handiwork by passing his open palms over the sides of the walls. Every time he comes near me, I can feel my longing.

His prayers offered, Simcha leaves the study.

Joe is shovelling the rubble into thick plastic bags, carrying them to the balcony over his shoulder and throwing them over the railings into the dumpster below.

Simcha walks through the hole into the kitchen and prepares his breakfast. He cracks two eggs into a glass so he can inspect them from every angle for any possible blood spot before frying them. Then he washes a few lettuce leaves and holds them up to the window. Satisfied that they are clean and insect-free, he cuts them up with a few cherry tomatoes, takes the plate of unblemished food to the table, sits down amidst the dust, blesses the source of his nourishing meal and, as he eats, lovingly turns the pages of the *Laws of Kashrut* with his lily-white hands.

Joe squats on the floor to eat his breakfast and opens the bag of provisions he has brought with him. Tearing off a chunk of bread from a loaf with his blackened hands, he dips it into a container of cottage cheese and licks his lips in satisfaction, grabs a handful of olives, tosses them into his hungry mouth, and spits the pits into the bin.

I am sweeping up and watching the two men. I feel split between their worlds. I know I don't belong with either of them but wish I could have them both; explore my sensuality with Joe while Simcha opens up the heavens for me to see God. I want to merge them into one entity to satisfy my unquenchable thirst for this world and the next. The synthesis so impossible and my longing overwhelming, I lean the broom against the wall and announce, 'I'm going to the store.'

I flee the dusty apartment, leaving Adele in her swing, and dash down three flights of stairs into the fresh Jerusalem air.

I walk gloomily down the street, leaving a trail of dusty footprints behind me. I pass outdoor cafés where couples sit happily in the sun sipping iced coffees and I wish I were like them. I wish I had another life with another partner. I know I cannot ignore my passions any longer or deny the life force that is the essence of who I am. I can no longer separate the two sides of myself like the milk and meat dishes in the cupboard. Without love and intimacy from Simcha, my drive to build a holy Jewish family is gone. The desperate quest for holiness seems less important to me now that I have a daughter who wakes up through the night and another baby on the way. I feel my milk coming and know that Adele wants to feed. I quickly turn towards home and run back the way I came. Ascending the stairs, I take note of how quickly the walls of *tshuva* have come tumbling down. In a last attempt to clutch at the straws of my disappearing faith, I try to recall the Rambam's famous words – words I had once loved and repeated religiously. 'When one falls into the depths of impurity . . .' I open the door to my home and remember the next line. 'There is only one way out . . .' But as soon as I see Joe Fixit bending over the kitchen counter, scraping the old tiles off the wall, I cannot, for the life of me, remember the end of that quote.

10

The Golden Scissors

*The first fruits of thy ground thou shalt bring
unto the house of the Eternal.*

Exodus 23:19

Adele is standing, facing east, bowing and rocking, imitating her father as she carefully pronounces the *Shema* from her leather-bound prayer book where her name is engraved in gold leaf at the bottom right hand corner and a blue silk tongue marks the page of the morning prayer.

She seems young, just four years old, to be so punctilious in the performance of the *mitzvot*, especially the modesty laws, dressing and undressing in the bathroom or under the bedclothes, covering up her little body until only her hands and face are visible. I think it is her way of ensuring her father's love and attention. She has become a serious and pious child.

Yankele, her brother, is riding his plastic car up and down the hall, making the sound of screeching brakes as he turns the corner into the living room. He wears different hats for each variation of this game, which keeps him occupied for hours; sometimes he's a taxi driver with a wad of Monopoly money in his pocket, sometimes a paramedic with an injured teddy bear on board in need of urgent medical care. With golden locks that fall like a sheet of sunshine down his back, he is my hippie child, and reminds me of the seventies – an era, I remember, of peace and love.

The fears I had in my pregnancy with Adele came back again with Yankele. Even though my body had produced a healthy child, I couldn't trust it to do so a second time. I feared that as God had answered my prayers with Adele, I didn't deserve to ask for another perfect creation. There had been a moment during the final stages of his birth when I could tell that the midwife was panicking and I looked at the baby monitor and saw the altered tachycardia pattern, an indication of the abnormally rapid beating of the heart that can cause low blood flow and blood pressure and damage the baby in the way Michelle was damaged. But the moment passed and Yankele was born, strong and perfect, with no hair on his head, my Buddha child.

When I saw Yankele for the first time, I understood why having a male child is preferred. It is not that I loved him more than his sister, but producing a boy from my womb filled me with pride. A son. I felt more worthy now that a penis had been formed inside of me.

I am baking a cake for his third birthday. This is a milestone that I don't welcome, for from now on he must don ritual fringes and a skullcap and go to *cheder* and learn to read Torah from an old rabbi with a cane and I am fearful I will lose him. By the time he's thirteen he'll live in the yeshiva and come home only twice a month for *Shabbes*. Once he's gone, I'm afraid I will no longer be able to cope with the lack of love and affection in my marriage. My son soothes my loneliness, and comforts me when Simcha cleaves solely to the divine, leaving us earthbound creatures to turn to each other. Neither of us can live up to the expectations Simcha has of us, and we are bonded not only as mother and son, but also as victims of Simcha's fervour. He is much stricter with his son than with his daughter. He wants Yankele to follow in his path, to become the man he wishes he were, untainted by a secular upbringing. At the age of three, he expects Yankele to behave like a little rabbi and frowns upon his natural desire to spend hours playing, a pastime that Simcha considers wasteful. Simcha wants Yankele to spend his time reading from the prayer book and accompanying him to the synagogue. But I can already tell that his immense yearning for his son to be a Torah giant is pushing Yankele away.

With his spiritual ambitions and his lack of attention to me in the bedroom, Simcha is pushing me away too. I know the Torah doesn't want to produce sexual frustration. The opposite is true. The laws are specific as to satisfying the woman. I have met women who have confided the romance and lovemaking of their *mikveh* nights and I have come to understand that Simcha has sexual inhibitions that he conceals under a guise of piety. He is so afraid of himself and his lusts that he has found asylum cowering under his prayer shawl. The Torah has become the perfect hiding place for issues he doesn't want to deal with. I too am guilty of using religion to hide my skeletons. I couldn't cope with the infidelities of the secular world, never trusting a man to be only mine. The purity code in the *frum* world, the guarding of eyes and prohibition against even a handshake between the sexes, made me feel safe. I wanted a sexual sanctuary, where my marriage would be protected from cheating and where I would never have to look over my shoulder at a younger or prettier girl who had caught my husband's eye. I often wonder at the irony of ending up with Simcha, who doesn't even notice me, think I'm pretty or want to have sex. God must have a terrific sense of humour as He matched up two people with opposite fears: Simcha with his inability to overcome inhibitions, and me with an inability to put on the brakes.

The need to escape from sexual freedom was not the only thing that led me here. The warm Torah community served as surrogate family for me. I thought I had found the acceptance I never felt from my parents. And as long as I keep to the laws I will be accepted, but now I know that if ever I stray from the path, they will cast me out. Already I am on dangerous ground, not nearly strict enough in my observances for them.

Simcha and I have grown further apart. I no longer wait anxiously for my *mikveh* night, and now merely suffer through the sex act. The longing for Joe Fixit is in the past too. I'm only interested in a good night's sleep and getting to work on time. I love the work I do in the labour ward and feel that I am doing something truly meaningful by helping couples have a natural birth. But sometimes, when I see a husband helping his wife in labour, obviously in love, or when a loving couple kiss or hold hands after the birth, I feel a pang of loneliness and I wish I could have had what they have. Then I quickly occupy myself with the business of birthing to move past the pain inside.

Watching Yankele play as I sift flour into a bowl and spoon in beaten eggs, I imagine him on stage with an electric guitar in his hands, shaking his blond curls for the audience at a Hyde Park concert, like the one I went to when Mick Jagger released hundreds of butterflies as a freedom gesture to a crowd of freaks preaching love not war. Yankele will never know of such things, his blond sidelocks will sway only over the religious text he'll soon be studying. I'm not ready for him to move away from me to the men's side of the synagogue partition. It is too soon for me to sacrifice him to the yeshiva world.

I decorate Yankele's birthday cake to look like a football pitch, using green icing for the grass, liquorice to mark out the field and a Lego man for goalie. I hope Simcha won't mind that I have deviated from the tradition of baking cakes in the shape of a Torah scroll for the *upsharin*, the third birthday ceremony in which, according to Hassidic custom, Simcha will shave off his son's long hair, which has not been cut since birth, leaving only golden sidelocks to dangle down his baby cheeks and identify him as a Jewish boy. Simcha has bought Yankele a navy polyester suit and a white shirt to wear for the *upsharin*, also a blue velvet *yarmulke* that will stick to the fine bristles of his hair like Velcro once his head is shaved.

I know that Yankele is looking forward to one of his birthday gifts, the shiny red train set he has seen in the window of Cohen's toy store, but not to the pair of fringes and prayer book Simcha has told him will soon be his. Last night he cried and confided in me that he is afraid once his hair is cut he'll lose his strength like Samson and won't be able to fight Dovid in the stairwell for his marbles.

I take Yankele to his room to dress him in his synthetic suit. 'It hurts!' he cries, pulling at the constricting fringes from under his starched white shirt.

'Yankele, you must wear your suit and fringes,' I plead half-heartedly. 'Today you will have your hair cut and you will look like *Abba*.' But I don't want Yankele to be like Simcha. I want him to be in touch with his sensuality, to taste the delights that God has offered us and not to abstain from the pleasures of this world. Yankele must hear the quiver in my voice and starts to cry. Simcha comes in to see what is happening. 'You'll be dressed like all the other boys,' he says forcefully. 'Today is an important day for you.'

Yankele obeys. He stuffs the fringes into his trousers, then lets his arms fall passively to his sides. Probably the memory of having his ears boxed the previous Friday night, when he had spoken during *kiddush*, is still raw. I had been terrified that Simcha had done damage to Yankele's hearing or to his brain and was appalled that he could hit our son so violently for speaking during prayers. Seeing his violence supported my theory that Simcha is perverting the religion, twisting holiness into a dogma that has no place in Judaism. His behaviour reminds me of the depraved Esau, brother to Jacob, who was so excessive in his religious practice he asked his father how to tithe salt. There is no law to tithe salt, unlike the laws of tithing fruit and vegetables. Simcha too wants to be more religious than the greatest rabbis and, like Esau, he is capable of cruelty.

We leave the apartment and climb the hill to the yeshiva, where I have often waited for Simcha after *shul*. I haven't felt as nervous since Yankele's circumcision, when he had whimpered through sucks on cotton wool soaked in red wine while my father held his legs firm during the slice. Simcha had been happy then, bringing his son into the covenant of Abraham, getting rid of his foreskin, a barrier to closeness with God. I had also been proud that my son was now considered a Jew and I changed the bandages on his little penis hourly and sprinkled the yellow healing powder on his wound.

I had hoped that giving birth to a son would redeem me in Simcha's eyes, especially as in giving birth to a child of each sex, I had succeeded in performing the *mitzva* of 'be fruitful and multiply'.

But today, as we enter the yeshiva building, I want to cling to Yankele and not let him cruise into Simcha's world.

We stand in the foyer among men dressed in long black coats and fur *shtreimels* who shmooze in Yiddish. Some carry towels, wet from a morning dunk in the *mikveh* and the mouldy smell of damp towelling fills the air. It is immodest for me to linger among the men, so I leave Yankele in Simcha's custody.

'I'll be watching you every minute from upstairs,' I comfort my son. 'Don't worry, my darling boy. You'll be fine.' I walk away with a feeling of dread in my bones.

Yankele, one of five boys who will receive the honour of Rabbi Sapphire's blessing and the symbolic first snip, grips his father's hand as they walk into the synagogue.

Adele, in a maroon coat with a velvet collar and black patent shoes, her dark braided hair held neatly in a black satin bow, has a smug expression on her face, probably secretly satisfied that her brother's crown of glory is soon to be diminished. We climb up the four flights to the women's gallery where we join the Hassidic women wearing lace squares pinned on top of their human-hair wigs and fancy aprons over dresses that stand stiff over their shapeless bodies. They turn to scrutinise us as we enter the gallery. I can feel them staring at the gold anklet protruding through the thick denier of my beige stockings and at my satin fuchsia shirt, which shines like a strobe light in the dingy light of the gallery. I know they want to keep a distance from me, as in their eyes I represent the outside world and all the temptations they try to ignore. They will not allow their teenagers to babysit for me, for fear the atmosphere in my home could have a negative influence on their girls. I can never fit in here. Simcha has chosen to belong to the most severe religious Hassidic sect. The men have a camaraderie born of their love and reverence for Rabbi Sapphire and the prayers that they join together to say. But for women it is different. Their friendship revolves around the family, the matriarchal society that works together as one unified body, the traditions handed down from generation to generation along with the gefilte fish recipes. I have my own traditions, from my father and my grandfather, but in this world they are meaningless. There is one woman here, the rabbi's daughter-in-law, who grew up in America and with whom I can exchange niceties. Sometimes I bump into her in the street and we stop to say hello. But when I see her among her peers in *shul*, she nods politely and continues talking with them in Yiddish, the language that was spoken by my parents to exclude me because I didn't understand it. I still don't.

The singing begins. I hold Adele so she can peep through the egg-sized hole in the lattice partition. Down below, we see the *bima* laden with pyramids of pastel pink and lemon iced cupcakes, chocolate chip cookies, sugared almonds, and an array of sweets, a feast meant to instil the sweetness of Torah in the boys. The aroma of butter and freshly baked cakes wafts up to the top of the building where we are sitting. I hear the *shammes* calling Yankele's name first and watch Simcha usher him to the altar like Abraham leading Isaac to the slaughter. Yankele hangs his head as Simcha encourages him along. His chubby limbs are heavy. His ethereal blond hair whispers down his back.

The congregation stands as Rabbi Sapphire walks from his seat next to the Ark, down the aisle to the *bima*. The rabbi picks up a plate of cookies soaked in honey and baked in the shape of the letters of the Hebrew alphabet. He stretches out his hand, which emerges from the mammoth jacket sleeve like a miniature doll's hand, and offers the sweets to Yankele.

I realise then that Yankele has never seen the rabbi up close and must be terrified by the strange sight of this man dressed as always in a jacket huge enough to cover the eighteen fringes he wears. I can understand why Yankele is reaching for an *aleph* with such a shaky little hand and bringing it straight to his mouth, forgetting to say the blessing. Rabbi Sapphire prompts him: 'Blessed art Thou, O Lord . . .'

I feel sorry for my little boy, who must have stage fright and has forgotten the blessings he knows by rote, and for Simcha too, who must be cringing, hearing his son muttering the blessing as if it were in a foreign language.

Rabbi Sapphire takes a pair of golden scissors out of a purple velvet pouch lying on the *bima*. Towering over the boy's head, he slips a shining lock in between the arthritic fingers of his left hand and snips it off. Yankele watches the curl float downwards. As it comes to rest on the dark carpet below, it resembles the letter *bet* and I'm sure my poor Yankele is already imagining his prized marble collection in Dovid's grubby hands.

Tens of Hassidim clamber up to the *bima* and loom over Yankele. I lose sight of my son as each one cuts off a curl, their body language showing clearly, even from up here in the gods, how eager they are to compete for the *mitzva*. A ripple of black swallows up my Yankele. A wave of nausea rises in me and I feel as if I am about to faint. They are taking their time, now moving like vultures descending on their prey. This is the moment when they begin moulding my little Yankele into one of their own. I've made a huge mistake. This isn't what I want at all.

The next few minutes seem like an eternity until Yankele emerges like a shorn sheep. His hair has been cut at random, each piece a different length. Simcha reaches into his bag, pulls out a shaver and buzzes off the wisps that remain, careful not to touch the sidelocks. The next toddler mounts the *bima*, stepping on the remnants of Yankele's precious blond hair. Yankele doesn't move. His severed curls lie around him on the carpet like a fallen halo. Any connection I had held to my flower child past has been severed now that my son looks like a skinhead.

A blood-curdling cry rises from my stomach. Without my permission, it escapes the confines of my fragile body, shoots out of my quivering mouth and shakes the entire hall. 'Noooooooooooo!'

Years of denial buried deep inside me have surfaced. Perspiration breaks out in droplets on my forehead and I can feel my hair damp under my headscarf. I sense the world fragmenting around me like a mirror shattering into hundreds of shards. I'm disoriented. I don't know what is happening or what I've done. This is not the first time I have shouted out in a holy place. The memory of screaming out 'Hallelujah' when I lost my virginity in my father's synagogue comes back to me.

'Mummy?' Yankele cries, looking up for me.

Even from way up here, I can see Simcha's face is black and closed. He stuffs the shaver nervously back into his bag, and without making eye contact with Rabbi Sapphire or the other Hassidim, picks up a bewildered Yankele and storms out of the synagogue, ignoring the weak *Mazeltovs* offered in consolation.

Adele makes a run for it out of the women's gallery away from me and away from the horrified glares of the Hassidic matrons.

Rabbi Sapphire and his Hassidim join hands and dance in a circle around the *bima*, singing loudly to drown out the echo of my scream which is still reverberating around the domed roof of the yeshiva synagogue.

I don't want to move. Sitting here is like staying in a moment of truth. I feel a great relief and take my time arranging my headscarf before I pick up my handbag and rise from my seat. Standing tall, I glide past the Hassidic women. I don't feel humbled in front of them any more. They keep their eyes glued to their prayer books and ignore me. They sing quietly along with the men who are swirling faster and faster around the *bima*.

Downstairs in the foyer, I find Yankele standing next to a stone-faced Simcha. I hug my son close. 'You're still my beautiful boy,' I whisper, stroking his head. 'Don't worry. Everything's going to be all right.'

'Mummy, what happened to you? Why did you scream?' Yankele asks me in earnest.

I hug Yankele even closer to me. 'I felt a pain . . . a terrible pain. But I'm fine now.'

Yankele puts his pudgy arms around me and relaxes. We

walk home from the yeshiva with his plump hand secure in my palm.

Adele walks on the side of the kerb, kicking a stone angrily in front of her.

Simcha walks on ahead, gripping his prayer book so tightly that his knuckles have turned white. Adele catches up with her father and slides her hand into the crook of his arm. Now she feels safe, I think, fearing I have frightened my daughter with my outburst and alienated her from me.

Ever since Yankele's birth, Adele has only wanted her father. She feels I have deserted her by loving her brother and has never forgiven me. I can tell she doesn't trust my religious practice and always checks with Simcha, not me, as to the prayers she should say and how long she should wait between consuming milk after meat. She is only a child and I feel she can be lenient until she reaches the age of twelve, her *batmitzva*, but she wants to keep the laws as if she were an adult.

We reach home and Simcha closes himself in his study. The atmosphere in the house is thick with reproach. I feel a deep shame at having embarrassed my family and myself in front of the entire Sapphire congregation. I rationalise the horror of it by speculating that I must have been overtaken by a *dybbuk*, which entered my body and spoke through me. But I know that I have finally expressed how I really feel about the religious life. It is not my way. I don't want my son to belong to the world his father cleaves to, and there is no going back now, no way to retract those words and thoughts and pretend they don't exist.

Simcha comes out of his study to take a plate of cold cuts from the fridge. He looks straight through me as if I'm invisible and returns to his isolation. Adele spends the afternoon brushing her long hair and sticking pictures of the holy temple in a new journal that Simcha bought her in Mea Shearim when he went shopping for Yankele's synthetic suit. Yankele stays close to me, holding on to my apron strings, while I cut two slices of birthday cake. I don't light the candles or sing happy birthday. We eat in silence.

Now the children are asleep, I knock on the study door. There is no answer and the door is locked. I knock again softly, fearful of Simcha's anger, but I have to talk to him and explain. He opens up.

'How could you scream like that?' he shouts before I can speak. 'What has gotten into you?' Simcha stands on the threshold of the study barring my entry.

'This life is too harsh for me. I want different things. I want to be free,' I beg from the hallway.

'Free? . . . Free? . . . Only one who keeps the Torah is free. You are a slave to your desires and your rose-tinted memories.'

'Simcha . . . I . . .'

'Don't you realise what kept us Jews from assimilating? Never forgetting who we are, guarding our Jewish names and traditions – and you scream about your son looking like a Jew. Go and repent, woman. I hope God will hear your prayers, for all our sakes.'

I stretch out my hand and touch Simcha's arm, trying to appease him. It is only when I see the furious look on his face that I remember I am *nidda*. The blood has drained from his face, which is so distorted with anger that I do not recognise him as my husband. He pushes me away from him. I lose my balance and smack into the wall behind me. The study door slams shut.

'Simcha!' I cry out. 'Simcha!'

I pound on the closed door. I have to make him understand. I have to make him forgive me. Silence. He is not opening up. I pound again but I know it's no use. He is probably reading a holy text, shutting me out of his consciousness.

I hobble to our bedroom and crawl into bed. I pull the blankets over my head and massage the back of my shoulder, purring softly, trying to comfort myself in the darkness.

I fall asleep and dream. It is *Shabbes*. Adele is two years old and Yankele one. They are both whining. I am standing at the top of the hill above the yeshiva, gripping the handles of the double stroller tightly, waiting for Simcha. The Hassidic women ignore me as they walk past. Simcha is the last man out and leisurely strolls towards me, taking his time, enlightened by the liturgy he has recited with undisturbed devotion, smiling the satisfied smile of a man whose soul has been nourished. He starts to climb the hill towards us. When I see that smile, I want to crush it. I let go of my tight grasp and release the stroller. Yankele's white cardigan flaps like a flag in surrender, the nappy bag swings madly on the handles, clapping against Adele's back, and the children's shouts of 'wheeeeeeeeeeeee' turn to shrieks of fear as the stroller picks up speed and rolls towards Simcha in defiance.

11

Beyond the Mask

We are commanded to get drunk on Purim ad delo yada, *until we cannot tell the difference between good and evil. The theme of Purim is a turn around of events. In keeping with that theme, if you turn around the letters of* ad delo yada *you get* adi yeled de'ah, *which means you should drink until a new idea is born.*

Rabbi Yitzchak Ginsberg

There it is, the rising and falling wail of a siren in the distance. I must hurry, for after the sound of the siren there are only seven minutes to prepare for the landing of a Scud missile that could kill us with its poisonous gas. I take a moment to make sure the sound I've heard is not the toilet flushing or the kettle boiling, noises that in the week since America's invasion of Iraq have made me jump more than once.

'Simcha!' I cry. 'Is this it?'

'This is it! Do the door.'

'Oh my God!'

Only a month has passed since Yankele's *upsharin*. Now that the Gulf War has begun, the 'no' I screamed out to my marriage and my husband's religion has morphed into an urgent 'yes', to life, to family and to God. I realise that without my faith I have nothing. Only God can help us now. I find solace in the prayers and the *mitzvot* once again. Simcha has been a great comfort. Immediately, on hearing about the threat of chemical warfare, he cut through the icy wall that had formed between us like a *mechitzah* and told me he would stay by my side and we would be safe together. Like many other Israelis we were bound by our fear and by our desperate quest for survival. For the first time since our marriage, Simcha took time off from yeshiva to stay at home. He sealed a room, covering the windows with thick plastic sheeting insulated with masking tape. He stocked the room with staples – cans of tuna and sweetcorn, biscuits, crackers and bottles of mineral water – and he bought batteries for the torch and radio in case the electricity blows. Seeing him busy himself with these tasks makes me love him again. Finally we talk more about the mundane than about lofty philosophical ideals. I have what I always wanted: Simcha here at home, not married to the yeshiva but to me, the two of us together in domestic day-to-day life. I know it isn't easy for him to stay home and deal with these chores, especially since his peers are studying. Their wives must have more faith than I do. They don't need their husbands to babysit them in case of an attack. But I cannot cope with getting the kids into the sealed room by myself. Simcha hasn't made me feel weak or stupid at all. He has made me feel safe and secure. I know I can trust that he is with me through this ordeal.

'The door!' Simcha screams.

It is two in the morning. I rush to unlock the door so the Red Cross can enter in case of casualties. The children wake as

I carry them into the sealed room and lay them down on the double bed. 'It'll be OK,' I say. 'We're all together.'

I wish I felt as hopeful as I sound. My legs are jelly. I taste bile. The tapping of quick footsteps is audible from the flat above. The people upstairs are running to a sealed room too. Five minutes to go.

We are used to sirens. In Jerusalem a siren-like signal sounds every week to announce the commencement of the Sabbath. Every year on Holocaust Remembrance Day, a siren begins the minute of silence when we stand to attention and remember our dead. I like to be out on the streets at that time and see how traffic comes to a complete standstill, drivers stand by their cars, pedestrians freeze, shoppers focus inwards and the whole nation stands in solidarity with our ancestors who died torturous deaths. In the yeshiva world, the rabbis preach that reciting psalms or learning Torah is preferable to standing in silence. In their minds, standing up for a siren is a non-Jewish way of mourning. They believe that through the merit of learning Torah, we can elevate the souls of the dead to a higher place. My father abhors this way of thinking, as did my grandfather before him. He believes that standing together at the sound of the siren, even if it is just for one minute, is of paramount importance to the bonding of the Zionist nation. But tonight this bleating alarm brings us together, religious and secular alike, not in mourning but in fear. Everyone is rushing for cover, hurrying to their sealed rooms.

Simcha is in the sealed room taking down the brown cardboard gas mask boxes from the cupboard. The boxes come with shiny black shoulder straps so we can carry them around with us everywhere we go. Decorating the boxes has become a fashion. Teenagers paint colourful designs over the brown coating. Simcha has just written our individual names on the flaps, as we all have different sizes. Yankele's mask is brightly coloured with a red and yellow hood that fits loosely over his head and upper body. The new blond bristles on his head push up against the plastic. He holds his baby blanket, a transitional object with a silken border, which he folds and caresses. His little fingers work quickly, making pleats with the silk.

It is stuffy in here and smells dank. The window has been taped up for a week and there is no other flow of air. Inside this twenty-square-metre space that we use as storage is a double bed, a cupboard and an armchair. The walls are bare. It is neither cosy nor inviting. Rolls of black plastic garbage bags are piled on the floor. We will have to wear them over our clothes if our area becomes contaminated. I imagine tearing holes in the bags for our heads and others for our arms and plodding outside into a destroyed world. In the wardrobe are toys I will use as bribes to get the children to co-operate.

Three minutes left. I pass a bath towel under the tap in the bathroom to dampen it. Then I roll it lengthwise and jam it into the one-inch crack under the door to prevent gas from leaking in. My stomach is heaving. Simcha switches on the radio. Nachman Shai, spokesman for the army, is addressing the nation in a calm voice. 'Don't panic,' he soothes. 'Put on your masks and stay in the sealed room. I'll play some music for you now and keep you posted.' The announcement is repeated in English, Russian, Arabic and, due to the recent Aliya from Ethiopia, in Amharic. The sound of the alien language makes us burst out laughing in a kind of hysteria. Simcha is doubled over.

I have never seen him giggle like this, shaking all over at the gibberish sound, sidelocks swinging as he wheezes. His laughter is contagious and I am laughing too, laughing and crying.

I rush for the bathroom and empty my bowels. We're lucky we have a bathroom adjoining our sealed room, or I'd be doing my business, like so many other Israelis, into a bucket. Fear has induced a spasm of diarrhoea just as it did when the Drug Squad entered the apartment I shared with Itai and busted us for ten kilos of hashish. I ran for the toilet then, too, and a burly policeman insisted on staying in the bathroom with me to make sure I wasn't throwing drugs down the bowl.

One minute to go. Simcha slits open the gas mask boxes with a knife. I remove the anti-chemical injection kit that comes with each mask and put it on the shelf. Just holding the syringes puts me on edge. I know I won't be able to use them.

I put on my mask before helping Adele with hers, according to instruction. The rubber around my face is thick and smells of glue. It presses on my head. The straps are too tight. I'll deal with it later. Now I must help Adele.

Adele is whimpering. Her mask is uncomfortable and hot. I try to speak to my children through my mask, but my words are muffled. I sound as if I am speaking underwater. We use sign language, making jerky movements with our hands.

Men with beards have been advised to shave because the hair on their faces will prevent the masks from being air-tight. I move over to Simcha and pull on his beard to remind him.

He shakes his head no. I know it is hard for him. His beard is a symbol of his Jewishness, but I am scared and make insisting sounds. I bang on his chest.

He goes into the bathroom and shuts the door. I feel guilty

now I can hear the snipping. And then there's a silence. Simcha must be looking at his reflection in the mirror. Seeing himself without his beard, grown long for as many years as his repentance, years he worked so hard to mould himself to the religious world, must be hard. He is doing this for me, I think; only for my sake.

'A Scud has hit,' Nachman Shai announces after we have been sitting for forty minutes in the sealed room listening to Hebrew songs from previous wars, 'fifteen kilometres north of Tel Aviv. No one is seriously hurt. There are no chemicals. Three people have been taken to hospital for concussion. Jerusalemites may remove your masks but do not leave the room till further notice.'

In the dimmed light, we take off our masks. My face is wet. There is a thick wedge indented on my forehead. I help Adele, careful not to pull on her hair. I can see she has been crying. Simcha releases Yankele from his hooded mask. His cotton pyjamas are soaked. He has wet himself.

'You were so brave,' I praise the children, 'like little soldiers.' I reach for two presents from the pile in the cupboard. Adele opens a puzzle and Yankele a wind-up car. They sit on the floor playing happily now that the adventure is over. I look over at Simcha. Patches of hair have been cut off his beard. Spikes and coils stick out over his face. Now that we are safe, I fear I have made a mistake insisting he shave, putting more belief in the Israeli Army than in God.

It is four in the morning and we have been told we can leave the room. I pad to the kitchen, feeling like an explorer discovering my home for the first time. Everything is in place. We have been spared. I mutter thanks to my creator under my breath as I walk with trepidation to the front door and lock it for the remainder of the night. Simcha is preparing a makeshift bed on the floor of the bedroom with blankets and sleeping bags for the children. We want them near us in case there is another siren later.

In the double bed, Simcha and I lie curled up like kittens with ears pricked open listening for trouble. I am happily scooped up in his arms. The children are fast asleep on the floor below. The struggles of the past months, culminating in Simcha's violent outburst and my synagogue scream, do not even enter my mind. Worries about his extreme religious practice seem unimportant now. Fear of death has put me in touch with my most primal and primitive desires. I want to feel life. I want to feel another baby grow inside me. 'Make me pregnant, Simcha,' I whisper, snuggling up to his warm body. 'I want to live.'

Simcha kisses me and lifts up my nightgown. As his hands sweep up my bare legs, it is me, this time, who is praying to the Almighty. I pray to conceive.

This is the first time in our marriage that Simcha isn't running off to the *mikveh* to cleanse himself after the sex act and he cuddles me close to him. He won't leave me here alone now in case of another attack. Warm and satisfied from our closeness, I doze off.

I awake to find Simcha sprawled on the couch watching the news. Until last week the television my parents gave us as part of my trousseau was kept in storage. Simcha never wanted the outside influence of the television in our home, the immodest advertisements and children's programmes that could lead our two angels astray. I listen to the latest scoop.

Over two hundred Ethiopians have injected themselves by mistake and are being treated in hospital. There were many robberies last night. Unlocked doors proved to be a looters' paradise.

Now that I can see my husband clearly in the light, I hardly recognise him. His chin is just a dimple in the crater under his bottom lip. Where is the sensitive man I married with the long flowing beard that gave him such a saintly look? I have been fooled. Without the straggly weave covering his face, he looks ugly to me. The face that I once thought was angular is really as round as an orange and the skin as rough as the pith. It is not Simcha I see, but Sheldon, the boy from Colorado, the one who wore checked shirts and jeans, who lazed around glued to the television without a holy thought in his head.

Simcha doesn't get up to pray or study; he cannot take his eyes off the screen. Even though I know he is staying home for my benefit, it doesn't please me. I have to admit that I want the old Simcha back, the one who looks pious and is absorbed by his holy work.

Eight weeks have passed since the beginning of the war and we have entered the month of Adar. This is a time of happiness and joy, when we celebrate the festival of Purim commemorating the victory of the Jews of Persia who, instead of being annihilated by the wicked Hamman, lived to see the villain hung on his own gallows. Our pleasure is two-fold, as Nachman Shai has just announced the blissful news that we may tear down the plastic sheeting from our sealed rooms. The threat of chemical warfare is over.

'It is no coincidence that the war ended today and our triumph coincides with Purim,' Simcha tells me. 'History repeats itself. Saddam Hussein is a modern-day Hamman and we are victorious like our ancestors.'

I am glad he has reverted from being a couch potato to a scholar but, without his long rabbinic beard, Simcha has lost a certain dignity of demeanour and his words don't carry the same weight with me.

While Simcha strips down the plastic sheeting from the spare room, I am painting a black moustache on Yankele's upper lip. Like many other boys this Purim, he has chosen to dress up as Saddam Hussein for the kindergarten Purim costume party. He finds it hard to stand still. 'You're tickling me,' he says.

Adele is dressed as Queen Esther. She wears a long white lace dress and a diamante crown on her head. In her hand she carries a silver sceptre. Her young and innocent face, long with high cheekbones, is precociously beautiful today with the help of blue eye shadow, blusher and pink lipstick. Afraid her lipstick will smudge if she moves her mouth, Adele is talking like a ventriloquist.

Purim is my favourite of all the festivals, the one day a year when we can let go, when it is a *mitzva* to get inebriated until we cannot tell the difference between blessed Mordecai and the wicked Hamman. Everyone is in costume. Simcha explains that the masks we wear are symbolic of God's glory, showing us that there is something below the surface, beyond what the eye can see.

As I tilt a beret over Yankele's spiky hair in the style of the dictator, my gaze is drawn to a smattering of spots on his neck. They look like beads of water. I undo his camouflage army shirt to get a better look. His chest is spotted with the rash.

'Do you feel all right?' I ask Yankele, and place my palm on his forehead, which feels warm to my touch.

'My tummy hurts. But I still want to go to the party.'

Simcha enters the bedroom and takes a look. 'Could be measles or chicken pox. All kids get them.'

I call the doctor, even though I consider he may already be too drunk for a consultation.

'Chicken pox outbreak,' he says soberly. 'Nothing to worry about. A few days in bed, liquids, and just don't let him scratch. It could leave marks.'

'Can he leave the house?'

'Better not. You've had it, I presume, when you were a kid?'

'I've had measles, I remember that, but I don't think I've had the pox.'

'Nothing to worry about unless you're pregnant.'

I feel dread trickle into me slowly like medication from an intravenous drip. It is at this moment that I realise my period is a few days' late and my breasts are sore to the touch.

'I could be right at the beginning,' I stutter. 'But I'm not sure.'

'Take a pregnancy test immediately. If you are pregnant, you'll need a blood transfusion to give you antibodies against the pox. Can Simcha take care of the kids while you leave the house? Go to a friend till the kids' spots have dried up and they aren't contagious any more. If you contract the pox when you're in the first trimester, your baby could be damaged.'

'Damaged?'

'Physically and mentally. There's a test you can take in the sixth month to see what the damage is, but it'll be too late then to do anything about it. Think clearly. You must get away.'

My mouth is dry. I need water. I always knew this time would come. Oh my God. I always knew I would have to face my worst nightmare.

Yankele is in bed, running a fever. Simcha is dabbing calamine lotion on his itchy spots.

'I don't want to play nursemaid any more,' he says impatiently. 'I've had enough of this. The war is over. I'm going back to study.'

I need the changed Simcha now but fear he has returned to his pre-war behaviour. I am about to tell him of our predicament and relay the doctor's advice when I notice a water blister on my forearm. It's too late for the transfusion. It's too late for antibodies. There is no point now in going away. My baby is in danger. It could be damaged like Michelle. I think about my sister, how I have denied and run away from the knowledge of her, not visited her for years, blocking her existence from consciousness. Now she is fully in my mind and I can think of little else.

I lie in a darkened room. The pox has spread all over my chest, arms and legs. I feel as if cacti thorns are pushing out all over my skin. Pregnancy nausea adds to the unpleasant cocktail of maladies. I lie in bed trying to decide whether to terminate this pregnancy. I think about the advice I have been given in the past few days.

'You must seriously consider aborting,' the doctor told me.

'Reva, listen to me,' my mother commanded. 'When it comes to having a handicapped child, I know what I am talking about. I pray that you will never have to go through what I went through.'

'You can't run away from *tszores*,' said Mrs Hillman. 'It will only come back in another way. That is how the world works. God gives you a trial and if you cannot withstand it, He'll give it to you again in another form.'

Simcha says little. He knows this subject is emotionally charged for me. But abortion is a forbidden act. 'I think that Rabbi Sapphire may judge this case leniently considering your history. You should trust a Torah giant. That's the way we do things. We don't take matters into our own hands.'

I dare not consult the rabbi. If he says to carry the pregnancy to term, I will be obliged to take his advice.

'Rabbi Sapphire doesn't know you personally,' my father argues on a transatlantic call. His voice is calm but adamant. 'Does he know how you shook and trembled after visits to Ravenswood? Does he know you had to sip brandy in the middle of the night? Will he be taking care of this child or will you?' I know he is talking sense and I am listening to him carefully. 'Look to your own family. Your grandfather ruled that an unwanted foetus that endangers the mother is defined in Jewish law as "a pursuer" just like an assassin who is running after you with an intention to kill. In both cases you may kill the pursuer in self-defence. See for yourself – look it up in Grandpa's book.' I think about my grandfather and the special bond I had with him. Having him behind me is a comfort. 'You are facing a similar danger. A handicapped child would ruin your life. Emotionally you might not be able to cope. Then what? It is a *mitzva* to save your own life.' My father pauses and then continues in a more professional tone. 'I, as your father, take full responsibility for this action. Reva, get rid of it today.'

I am relieved that my father is taking control. He has always told me what to do and I have rejected his advice, wanted to do things my own way. But now, I am ready to surrender to his rabbinical expertise and rely on his authority. I know he's right. I also know that if he is taking responsibility for aborting a foetus, he is well aware of what he is doing. After all, he is a learned rabbi and is well aware of the Judgment Day that awaits us all.

As I lie here in my bedroom with the shutters closed, I consider how I will evolve if I accept my fate and keep the baby. I will have conquered my fears. I will be a stronger person, one who doesn't need her husband to stay home in a war, one who isn't frightened by deformity. But I know I will abort. I am not strong enough to go ahead with the pregnancy and face my fate. I know I cannot deal with a handicapped child. I will not leave this in God's hands. I must take control.

Six weeks after the abortion, I find myself pregnant once again. My interpretation is that a unique soul is determined to descend into this world. This makes me feel that I am not guilty for killing a life, that God has understood my dilemma, has granted me a pardon and another chance. I think Simcha feels this way too.

Since I came back from the hospital with my belly empty and my heart drained, Simcha has been treating me with care. My rejecting his advice and accepting my father's counsel has deposed him from his position of head of the household. He can tell that it is not only the endangered foetus I have aborted, but also the stringent orthodoxy he preaches. Simcha never comments that I am becoming lax with the laws, allowing my scarf to slip back an inch from my brow and revealing a line of hair and even letting my ponytail hang down loose. He doesn't show any disapproval of my shirtsleeves rolled up way above my elbows or my wearing baggy maternity pants that provide the comfort I need since I have already put on weight. He has surrendered. His silence is nevertheless out of character – so unlike the era when I kept strictly to the modesty laws and he was repulsed by any show of skin. It was only a year ago that he looked at me as if I was a leper when my dress accidentally rode up and an inch of leg was exposed. Then, feeling his revulsion, I covered up my leg in shame.

Adele says nothing about the recent exposure of my flesh, but I can sense she is not pleased. When Yankele saw my bare arms for the first time, he cried out, 'I can see your *Yetzer Hora*, Mum.' I didn't rebuke him for equating my bare arm with the evil inclination, as he was only regurgitating dogma he had heard from the rabbi in *cheder*.

Both children are delighted with my news. They are focusing on the baby instead of my lack of modesty. They stroke my growing belly and talk to their new sibling. In their games, they play mother with Adele's dolls and take turns burping and bathing their babies.

This time around I am not taking any chances and have undergone amniocentesis. The results of the invasive test have put me at ease. I no longer imagine deformities or lie awake at night dreading the moment of truth when I give birth. Now that I am assured that my growing daughter is healthy, I am trying to enjoy the rest of the gestation.

Babysitters have been arranged for when I go into labour. I have bought a video player and a selection of Disney movies to entertain the children while I am in hospital and for the weeks after birth. Simcha is not challenging me any more. He is silent. Brightly coloured animated films flash on the screen and bring technicolour to our monochrome lives. The children huddle in front of the TV, watching in awe. I feel that we are a family now, enjoying the normal joys of life. But I am aware that this action will cause a shift in my children's consciousness. I am opening our home to the outside world, to Hollywood, to all its brilliance and creativity, but also to less desirable influences that will inevitably filter through.

I sort through Adele and Yankele's baby clothes to get ready for the newborn. Among the religious, preparing for a baby is considered bad luck and an invitation to the evil eye. But I am confident this time that all is well and allow my nesting instincts to express themselves. As I fold up the miniature sleepers and cloth nappies, I feel a painful contraction in my back. And now another. The baby must be coming. I call Simcha and leave a message for him, then call a fellow *doula*, a colleague, who will accompany me throughout the birth. I know the advantages of having a labour coach to support women in labour and want the same luxury for myself.

In the labour room, the birth is proceeding fast. The midwife tells me that I am almost fully dilated and will deliver soon. Where is Simcha? I fret. I need him here with me now. I cannot birth our baby alone. The *doula* is helpful, but I need Simcha, the father of this child. In between primal screams and animal growls, I instruct her to call my husband once again and beg him to come.

The contractions are getting stronger and I feel the urge to push. Simcha is not here. He has not come. The *doula* holds me from behind. She supports me underneath my arms. I can feel the strength of her as I bear down. She is encouraging me. It is almost time.

My daughter has a head of black hair. She is pale skinned and beautiful now, wrapped in a cotton blanket and lying in my arms. I am happy and content. I know she is my last child. There won't be any more. Simcha walks in. Smiling meekly, he approaches the bed. He hasn't realised that by taking his time to get here, he has finally released me from any illusions that I may still have about needing him. He has released me from hiding behind a mask of weakness. I do not bear a grudge. I do not ask him where he has been or why he is late. Instead, I smile the smile of a satisfied and strong woman. I feel independent and sure of myself, and I say, '*Mazeltov*, Simcha. Meet your new daughter, Leah.'

12

Breaking of the Vessels

Shvirat Hakelim – *when the husk is broken
the sparks of truth are released.*
Hassidic concept

I can hear Simcha's key click in the front door lock. It is my cue
to retreat to the bedroom. In the past few months, we have
become like shift workers. I take care of the kids in the day
while Simcha is studying but, once home, he takes over the
evening chores of bathing and preparing dinner. I am unable to
bear being in the same space as him. The walls press in on me
when he is near and there is a clashing sound inside my head.
Since his absence at Leah's birth, I have lost my respect for him
completely and in the process found a new respect for myself.
I feel empowered. The children have become quiet and sullen.
Adele is biting her nails till her cuticles bleed. Yankele is
daydreaming at school. On Friday nights I make the effort to
come to the table for *kiddush*, but once I have served the
Shabbes meal, I excuse myself and return to my sanctuary. I
have not been to the *mikveh* for months and Simcha doesn't
sleep in his single *nidda* bed. He has taken to sprawling out on
the living room couch.

I lie on my bed and try to make sense of the emotional
maelstrom in which we live, knowing it can't go on much
longer. I think about the past two years, the delight we felt at

having a new baby in the house, which brought a sense of calm and well-being to our family. Leah, who has grown into a lively and healthy two-year-old, was colicky at first, and Simcha and I had to team up in the evening hours to calm her down. Our nightly ritual of bouncing and rocking her bonded us for a while. But with no crises to bind us together, the old problems soon returned to the foreground and with them all our anger and resentments.

The more estranged I feel from my husband, the more aware I am becoming of my inner feelings and desires. I enjoy making my own decisions on what to wear and what to eat. But as I gain independence I remember how the rabbis warned that one good deed leads to another and one sin leads to hell. With each step I take away from Torah practice, I can feel the downward slide and fall from grace. My God consciousness is fading. I have grown apart from Him. I understand now why the laws are so strict, to keep the creator at the foremost of one's thoughts and deeds, bringing Him into every aspect of life. But I am becoming desensitised to holiness and sanctity. The blue jeans I wear feel like a second skin. Letting my hair cascade over my shoulders feels natural. I cannot live in denial of earthly pleasures any longer. If I do, I will go mad. That is why I have decided to go ahead with my plan to meet Joe Fixit tonight.

It was a week ago that I bumped into Joe at an outdoor café. I was sitting alone, drinking cappuccino, when I noticed him at another table. I smiled and waved. After a moment, there was a shock of recognition in his eyes. The last time he had seen me I was a pious matron. I felt his eyes all over me, taking in the transformation: the sexy clothes, the loose hair and the come-on in my eyes. As he watched me, I could feel my body, pore by pore, coming to life with desire. He asked about my metamorphosis. I invited him to sit with me and he listened ardently to my tale. When I had finished, he said, 'You're beautiful.' These were words that I had been starving to hear for years from my husband. Joe invited me to dinner, but I couldn't accept, couldn't be seen with another man. Even sitting together in the café was enough to arouse the neighbourhood's wagging tongues. He left me his phone number in case I changed my mind. I carried his card around in my purse for three days. During that time, I would take out the rectangular tag and slide my finger over his name. Just touching the print raised on the card like Braille induced my neglected female equipment to stir back to life. I spent three days obsessed by the phone number that I didn't dare call. I knew the digits by heart. I added and subtracted them, hopeful the sum total would bear a sign in favour of my calling. Then, suddenly, I couldn't contain myself any longer; I dialled.

I know the children will not ask where I am going and Simcha will not pick his head up from his book when the revving of a motorbike beckons me from downstairs and I go to meet the man waiting for me there in the shadows. I know that once we are together there will be no time for sweet talk or foreplay and we will devour each other at first chance. Even though I am aware of the seriousness of infidelity, I cannot stop myself from keeping this illicit appointment. I decide that my grandfather would decree that having my vitality squelched and my femininity repressed for years has put me in emotional danger, so that meeting Joe tonight is an act of *pikuach nefesh*.

I exit my bedroom in a haze of perfume, pushing all feelings of doubt and hesitation into the recesses of my mind. Instead, I focus on how Joe will give me back my life and make a woman out of me again.

The hum of the bike downstairs serves as the musical score for my dramatic exit. Adele is stacking blocks for Leah, who is demolishing the plastic towers faster than her elder sister can construct them. Yankele is doodling on the cover of his history textbook, pressing his biro down so hard that he has made a hole in the map of Israel. Simcha slowly turns over a page of Talmud. He looks like a great rabbi, stroking his growing beard to the rhythm of his rocking. A part of me cannot bear to leave my precious children this way, to let them see me dressed for seduction, but I cannot help myself. I need Joe. I need him to rehabilitate me.

'See you later,' I call out to no one and everyone.

Leah waves goodbye. She seems to be the only one sorry to see me go.

I straddle the throbbing bike and slip my arms around Joe's muscular body, which is now enveloped in black leather. As we drive away into the night, I push my already pulsating triangle into the small of his back. The cool Jerusalem air is a light caress on my bare arms and legs. I have never felt so free as the bike twists in and out of the narrow side streets into the open space of the Haas Promenade. The panoramic view of Jerusalem is visible here. The gold-domed mosque glitters in the night. A glimpse of the old city walls, and the knowledge that the holy of holies nestles within them, triggers uncomfortable feelings of guilt. I pray for forgiveness for what I am about to do and hope the light wind will carry my message to the source.

Joe rips open my shirt before I even step over the threshold of his apartment.

I try to slow him down, as I want to savour every moment. 'I have fantasised about this for so long,' I moan, unable to believe how good he feels on me. His body is now writhing over mine. 'Did you know I wanted you all the time you were working in the kitchen? Did you realise I was so crazed I could have mauled you?'

'Maul me now, baby,' Joe purrs as his hands greedily paw at me and his mouth ravenously covers mine. It has been a decade since I felt my body liquid like this. I let go of years of frustration and longing and melt into his arms.

Joe's unshaven cheek chaffs my soft one as he waltzes me to the bedroom. He pulls me down onto his unmade bed. Moving my hands over his bare chest and inhaling his woody scent, I become aware of just how forbidden he is to me. Joe tears off my jeans and panties and within seconds he is inside me. I scream out at the thrust of him. I am like a virgin, experiencing coitus for the first time. Joe pounds into me with the same intensity as he hacked at the concrete wall. My head is banging rhythmically against the headboard. I don't even try to move away because I am aware that I deserve to be punished.

Now that our biting and clawing and greedy penetrating of orifices has come to an end and our animal passion is quenched, the enormity of what I have done hits me. Lying next to a panting Joe, I realise I do not love this man. I have sinned for only a transient moment of pleasure. Suddenly I am fearful of the chastisement of *koret*, excommunication from the divine forever. In his treatise, the Rambam lists the sins for which there is no repentance. I try to remember if adultery is one of them. I imagine my soul floating in the dark of space, lonely, abandoned, unable to attach itself to God's light forever, and I tremble in the darkness. I need to know if I have truly been cut off. I say a prayer under my breath '*Shema Yisroel . . .*', to test if I can still connect to the divine. I am relieved to find that I can still conjure up an image of God in heaven and of myself as His servant below.

It is past midnight now. Filled with shame, I quietly unlock the door to my Torah home, hoping Simcha will be fast asleep. I don't want him to see me. I know I must stink of Joe's come. My body is smudged with the transparent matter.

Simcha is still slumped over at the dining table with a heavy book. A cup of tea and the remnants of a slice of apple strudel lie in front of him. He looks angelic to me now after experiencing Joe. I am jealous of his ability to study the holy books into the night while I have been trashing the very values written there. The children are tucked up safely in bed. I check on them and kiss them in their sleep. Seeing how innocent they are makes me feel even dirtier.

It is the morning after my night with Joe and my head is throbbing as I drag myself out of bed. I have hardly slept. I re-ran the hours with Joe again and again in my mind. Now that I have broken my marriage vows, all I want is to feel him thumping into me again so I can forget my terrible transgression. The loveless, lusty sex that I share with Joe in the weeks that follow helps me ignore the heartbreak that surely lies ahead with the inevitable termination of my marriage.

The children are at school when Simcha returns from morning prayers. I am about to retreat into my room when he calls me. 'Reva,' he says, 'we need to talk.' His voice is soft and gentle.

I cannot escape the conversation which I both long for and dread. Sheepishly, I sit down on the couch and fold my hands in my lap like a good girl. Simcha is standing in front of the library of holy books.

'According to Jewish law,' Simcha begins, 'a man cannot live under the same roof as an unfaithful wife.'

I freeze. How could I have been so stupid as to think my sinful actions went unnoticed? I imagine Simcha must have confided his suspicions to Rabbi Sapphire after prayer services earlier this morning.

'I know the law,' I say. I am scared Simcha will take the kids away from me. I have heard rumours about the rabbis at the Rabbinical Court who give custody to the more religious party. If they think I am committing adultery, I don't stand a chance. I say nothing, even though I am dying to shout that it is his fault I took a lover, that he has neglected me and channelled all his love to God. I want to blame him and make him suffer, but for once I am smart enough to keep my mouth tight shut.

'I want to move out as soon as possible.' There is no anger in his voice, no reproach. As usual he is focusing solely on following the law.

I never thought this stage of our separation could go so smoothly. I feel tension releasing from my body. Simcha is smiling at me. He is relieved too.

'In Hassidic literature,' he says, 'there's an idea that everything in this world is covered with a husk. That is what causes spiritual darkness.' He picks up an apple from the fruit bowl. 'See this apple,' he says. 'It also has a husk surrounding it, but once I say the blessing before eating the fruit, I will break that shell open and release holy sparks that will influence our universe for good.'

I'm listening intently. This is the Simcha that I loved, the one who taught me about the secrets of creation.

'Our marriage is a bit like that.' I can see tears gather in the corner, of Simcha's blue eyes. 'Reva, now that we are breaking up, I hope God's radiance will be released. May it illuminate the path to a better future for both of us.'

'Amen,' I say. A lump is forming in my throat. I don't want Simcha to see me cry.

We are sitting together in the living room as a family for the first time in months. The children are aware we are about to discuss something of great importance. They somehow know their hearts, which are already torn apart, are about to break.

'*Abba* and I want to tell you something.' Three wide pairs of eyes are staring at me. I say it; there is no other way. 'We are going to separate.'

I know Adele finds the polarity in our different ways imposs- ible and it will be easier for her to deal with us separately. Yet, her face is blank. It is impossible for me to be sure what she is thinking, as she keeps everything inside. I can almost hear the fear and anger grinding inside her, but she will not let on.

'It's not your fault . . . I don't want you to think that this has anything to do with any of you.' I have done my psycho- logical homework and know that kids blame themselves for divorce, but now that I hear myself articulate these time-worn truisms, they sound so fake and trite that I wish I hadn't said them.

Yankele takes the news hard. His delicate features seem to dissolve into one another as he tries to keep from crying. I can see that his worst fears are materialising. For the first time in his life, he pushes my consoling hand away and retreats to the comfort of his room.

Leah may not understand what I am saying, but she is inching closer to me and has crawled into my lap. I smell the milky sweetness of her hair and touch the downy skin on her chubby arms. Images of the wholesome family I held onto for so long, all of us seated at the *Shabbes* table singing *zmiros* together, with the light emanating from the *Shabbes* candles and uniting us in its glow, are gone. In the cold reality of the here and now, there is only separateness and fragmentation. I still harbour doubts that I will be able to cope alone with the children. The old habit of self-degradation is rearing its ugly head. I look over at Simcha, hoping to find a thread of possibility to hang on to. But he is smiling that stupid smile of his, the one that tells me he knows someone is in emotional pain, but has no idea how to respond. He reminds me of my father and for the first time I realise that once again I have been longing for the impossible, replaying an old scenario of desiring emotional honesty from a man who is too blocked to give it. But as I think about Simcha's limitations, he surprises me once again.

'We both love you so much,' he tells the children, who have checked out and are staring at the carpet. 'My little darlings, I know it will be hard at first, but we will get used to it. I am going to look for a place of my own close by. You can visit and stay with me whenever you want. There will always be a loving home for you with your *Abba*.' Simcha says this with so much tenderness and sincerity that tears begin to fall down Adele's stoic little face, and I too succumb. Whopping tears the size of raindrops fall down my face, defeating my attempt to hide my sadness. I am finally witnessing Simcha's capacity for loving which has been shut down for years. It has come too late.

13

Get a Life

When a couple get divorced, heaven weeps.
Rav Eliazar

I hold the summons for the divorce hearing in my hands. It is December and winter is in full force. The white Jerusalem stone is streaked with rivulets of rain. I sit indoors in the warmth and glance back at the writ and see it is called for next Tuesday, a day doubly blessed in Genesis as a very, very good day.

I note the date of the hearing at the Rabbinical Court in my diary. I fear the rabbis, whose bias always favours men, especially men whose wives have become lax in religious observance. I am anxious about the trial. Simcha and I have discussed joint custody of the children, but I do not trust him and fear that once in court, he will fight for full supervision on religious grounds. I cannot bear to think what I will do if the rabbis rule against me.

This is a world where my father has influence, but he doesn't want to be involved, doesn't want his name stained by my actions. Divorce was considered a disgrace in the world that he comes from, and this mentality still lives within my father. I know he will not tell the news of my break-up to anyone but will continue the charade that I am happily married any time a congregant or friend asks after me. He isn't thinking of my future, of the possibility of my remarrying, only of the front he needs to keep up at all costs. I wish he would help me now, as he has helped me often in the past. Even when Itai and I were busted for possession of ten kilos of hashish he didn't hesitate. He instantly went into professional mode, accessing the Rolodex in his mind and making phone calls until he found the number of the lawyer Chaim Cohen, his study partner from Mir Yeshiva, who represented me in court. Of course, he probably dreaded the thought of the 'Children from Good Families' headlines which would inevitably have appeared to trumpet the titillating news about the son of a famous lawyer and the granddaughter of a well-known rabbi being arrested on drug charges. Whatever his reasons, he did everything he could for me and even my mother had been kind and encouraging that day I was released. I went directly from the prison cell I'd shared with ten Arab women to my parents' room at the Plaza Hotel. There I recovered from the nightmare of sitting on a filthy mattress under the yellow light of a bare bulb that burnt all night long and having to relieve myself in public in a toilet in the centre of the cell. I told my mother how terrified I'd been that the Palestinian women who were my cellmates would harm me and she soothed my fears, tucked me up in her luxurious bed, gave me her silk nightgown to wear and ordered room service. But now there's no support coming from either of my parents and I feel very alone.

I arrive at the Rabbinical Court in Havatzelet Street, a dusty side road. The court building, a concrete four-storey block, is sandwiched in between an office supplies shop, where swivel chairs and computer tables are displayed on the pavement, and a typical Israeli kiosk selling pumpkin seeds and freshly squeezed orange juice, produce that constitutes the only flash of colour in this grey Jerusalem alley. I am wearing a skirt and a long-sleeved shirt in an attempt at modesty, but I don't feel comfortable and miss the ease of my jeans.

I climb the open stairwell to the third floor where Simcha is waiting in a hot and noisy hall. The place is as run down and shabby as the apartment blocks in religious neighbourhoods. Why is it that the religious have no sense of aesthetics? I wonder, as I look around. Sephardim, Ashkenazim, Ethiopians, Russians, religious and secular alike, are all waiting to see the rabbis. They have come for rabbinic rulings on marriage, divorce, monetary squabbles, adoption, and conversion. The rabbis rush about, mopping their sweaty brows and delivering their chauvinistic decrees. Many different languages merge into a Babel of confusion.

Threading my way through the crowd I find Simcha and sit next to him on the pew. I feel surprisingly calm. Simcha fits in here with his long straggly beard and religious attire: black suit, white shirt, black hat. He nods hello to other men wearing the same uniform. I make eye contact with some of the women. Opposite me sits a tarty looking woman. Make-up is caked onto her face, her blouse is pulling at the buttons and her lacy bra is visible. In an attempt to be modest, she wears a skirt, but the slit up the side reveals a tanned thigh. Feet with chipped red lacquered nails are squished into open-toed stilettos. Every finger is ringed. Gold hoops hang from her ears and gold chains around her neck glisten in the light. We smile at each other knowingly. She looks confident and, I imagine, pleased to get rid of the creep sitting next to her. The man is grossly overweight. A roll of blubbery fat hangs over the waist of his jeans. I notice the heavy, gold link bracelet sunk into a dense forest of hairs on his muscular arm as he turns the page of the newspaper he is reading. I cringe at the sight of the nail on his pinky, which is grown long like a talon. A well-known status symbol in the underground world of petty thieves, it's called a *ziporen hygena*, a hygienic nail used to pick noses and clean ears. To my right sits a modern religious couple. They look too young even to be married, let alone divorced. The woman is crying. She wears a simple cotton kerchief on her head and baggy pants covered by a tunic. The original bottle-green colour has faded and is turning grey in patches. Her husband's freckled skin is tanned. His blond hair falls down his neck. He is thin and lanky and leans his Uzi machine gun against his undeveloped torso as he sits.

A clerk, his right arm withered and a line of spittle drooling down his chin, emerges from the courtroom calling the next name on his list – 'Lewinsky'. At the announcement of our name, I look at Simcha and notice that his shirt cuffs are fraying, his sandals are worn out and his big toe is poking through a hole in his sock. A wave of tenderness washes over me. I want to darn the sock and take care of him. I watch how he is quiet within himself. I like that. He looks up at me and his lips break into a half smile. I feel close to him once again now our marriage is about to be annulled.

This closeness between us has been present since we told the children and made arrangements for Simcha to move out. The hurt and the anger subsided and an intimacy formed between us.

I follow the clerk into the large courtroom, where three rabbis sit at a bench on an elevated stage. An olive-skinned

Moroccan rabbi sits in the middle. His small frame is swamped by a heavy black frock coat. A black hat that is too large hides his face. I can only see his goatee nodding up and down as he mutters something to the older rabbi on his right, a heavy man who is smoothing his white beard with long rhythmical strokes. The third rabbi gets to his feet. He looks severe and swollen with power. His sidelocks are tightly corkscrewed behind his ears and the tails of his frock coat flap like bat wings as he moves down from the podium into the space before our bench. I feel afraid. The rabbis' decisions will be final. I think about the children and the nightmare of possibly losing them and then about the pain in their little faces when I told them we were going to separate.

Simcha stands alone on the left-hand side of the courtroom. I stand on the right next to Moshe Cohen, my lawyer, a clean-shaven man who wears his velvet skullcap at an angle falling over his left ear, talks with a thick Brooklyn accent and fidgets, making the tassels of his fringes tremble against his trousers. I am nervous but think about what he told me last week in his office: 'Look, we are holding a trump card, Mrs Lewinsky. If things get dicey, we'll play it for all or nothing. Wait till those judges realise who they're dealing with. Your grandfather, Rabbi Mann, awarded those judges their rabbinical degrees. Without him, they'd be nobodies. They owe him . . . get it?'

The courtroom door opens and Mrs Frankel enters. She stands next to Simcha and shoots an icy look in my direction. I had no idea she was coming. Simcha hadn't told me. My jaw drops open. My heart thumps. I fear Simcha has told her of his suspicions that I have been unfaithful. I watch her unbutton her coat and I wonder if she knows about Joe.

'It's going to be AOK,' Moshe Cohen whispers in my ear.

One of the rabbis stands up, descends the bench and addresses Mrs Frankel. 'Can you verify this man is Jewish?' he asks, pointing to Simcha.

'He's Jewish. I made the match. I met his parents, and I hev seen their birth certificates. This vun,' she pauses as she points to me, 'this vun doesn't behave like a Jewish, *oy gevalt*! Vat vill happen to the *kinderlach* with such a mother!'

The rabbis at the bench write in their ledger. The standing rabbi turns to me. 'Is your father Jewish? Who is your witness?'

'OK, here we go,' Moshe Cohen mumbles under his breath. 'I'm her witness. I know the family,' he says with confidence. 'Her father's a rabbi.'

'By what name?'

'Mann,' I answer softly.

'Mann. Which Mann?' The rabbi twirls around to make sure the rabbis at the bench are taking note.

'Rabbi Yechezkiel Mann was my grandfather, my father's father,' I say, envisaging my grandfather's kindly blue eyes, his wispy white beard, modest sidelocks tucked behind his ears, top hat and cane. I remember the way he set a sugar cube on his tongue and then sipped lemon tea through it.

The rabbi raises his thick eyebrows, which are joined at the bridge of his nose. I can tell he is surprised.

Rain drizzles outside the courtroom window and I know God is weeping for us, as He does every time a Jewish couple divorces.

'I knew your grandfather well,' the standing rabbi addresses me, 'and I am sure he would have been ashamed to see his granddaughter standing in public without a head covering.'

What did he just say to me? Anger and fear churn together in my stomach. I am stunned and disgraced. I hate the ultra-Orthodox. I want to lash back and say that he has obviously learnt nothing from my grandfather, who would never embarrass anyone, but I don't. I stand rooted to the spot and look down at my shoes. I am so humiliated that I don't react when the rabbi announces, 'The *Beit Din* grants a divorce.' All I can think is how my grandfather was a true *zaddik* and if a woman would offer her hand, ignorant that a great rabbi doesn't touch women apart from his wife, he would give his hand and shake hers lest he embarrass her for her mistake.

'The *get* will be written shortly,' the rabbi announces, 'by the resident scribe.'

'What about custody of the children?' Mrs Frankel pipes up.

'In the name of Torah from Sinai, children stay with their mother. When the boy reaches the age of barmitzvah, we will review the situation.'

'Am I right or am I right?' Moshe Cohen jabs me in the side, but I don't react. I am dreaming about sitting on my grandfather's knee, his favourite grandchild. 'Revaleh,' he is saying, 'Revaleh, how is school? What are you studying?' This was often the extent of his conversation with me. But our bond went far beyond words. I worshipped him, and just holding his hand or kissing his beard, even though I knew my father didn't approve, filled me up with love.

The scribe is summoned and provided with our full names for the *get*. The rabbi hands Simcha a chicken feather and the parchment. 'These implements now belong to you. You must give them to the scribe and ask him to write the *get* for you.'

Simcha looks lovingly at the quill, an instrument of *mitzva*. He takes his time examining the sharpness of the chicken feather and the smoothness of the parchment before handing them over, making sure that he is taking an active part in the ceremony. 'Take my implements and write the *get* for me,' he says in a serious tone.

The scribe takes the tools and starts to work with Simcha, checking and double-checking that everything is one hundred per cent kosher.

I wait alone in the stuffy hall while the *halachic* umbilical cord still connecting my soul to Simcha's is being severed. I think back to the moment when we were bound together, when I stood demurely under the *chuppah* dressed in my modest gown and Simcha slid the plain gold band on my finger. I had reached out my hand to him to walk together as man and wife to the *cheder yichud*, the little room where we would be alone for the first time, but Simcha, behaving with utmost modesty, had walked on ahead, rejecting any public display of intimacy, and I had tagged after him like a lost puppy, humiliated. My thoughts wander to the very first day of my marriage when I tied a scarf over my head so that not a single hair showed. It didn't suit me. My long thick tresses had always been my best feature. I spent hours in front of the mirror, tying and retying triangles of material around my head, but whether I used scarves I'd bought in London for my trousseau or batik-printed sarongs I found in a bazaar, I couldn't get it right and looked like anything from an African tribeswoman to E.T.

The scribe is taking his time. Simcha stands over him,

gazing with pleasure at the drawing of the beautiful holy letters. This is the same look Simcha had on his face at the first of our *sheva brachot*, the seven dinner parties in our honour following the wedding. I watched him standing there, peering through his bifocals at the sexy women who'd gathered at the home of Ilanit, my girlfriend from the Childbirth Association. It had been hard for me to show up in my new headgear, such a contrast with my old friends dressed in their provocative clothes and looking gorgeous. I felt ugly. I was surprised that Simcha had agreed to go and even more astonished that he seemed to have such an enjoyable time, chit chatting away with all the women and playing teacher. It occurred to me then that marrying into the religious world didn't necessarily provide a safe haven from infidelity.

The court door creaks open and jolts me back to the present. The *get* is ready. Inside, the rabbi instructs me to stand opposite Simcha and cup my hands together to catch the scroll when Simcha drops it into my hands. I look down at the love line that stretches from my wrist across my palm and recall a fortune-teller telling me that I would be lucky in love.

'Drop the *get* into her hands,' the rabbi orders.

Simcha lets go of the scroll of parchment.

'Tuck the document under your arm and walk up and down the room to show you own it,' the rabbi orders me.

I stride up and down the room owning the scroll. All eyes are upon me as I walk.

'Now return the *get* to Simcha.'

I am no longer his wife. Six years of marriage have just ended with the passing back of the scroll. I have thought about this instant, how I will avoid looking directly at Simcha, but I look straight into his blue eyes. He looks back at me with the compassion that I have been afraid to see – my Simcha, a pure soul who has hidden himself from me for years. I remember the things that made me fall in love with him, the way he delighted me by weaving Hassidic commentaries on the Torah together with lines by Yeats, the way he arranged food in artistic patterns on the plate.

'I'll make sure everything will be kosher with the kids,' I whisper, and I am sincere.

Simcha nods. He is too choked up to speak.

'You are free to marry immediately,' the rabbi announces to Simcha.

I am shocked and realise that I am already replaceable. It will be easy for Simcha to find a new mate. The matchmakers will be onto his case immediately. Mrs Frankel probably has a line of girls much younger than me waiting. I envisage Simcha married to a pious woman. He could have other children. They will be sisters and brothers to Adele, Yankele and Leah. He will build a happy family with a woman who will not need and desire what I need, who will be happy with her lot. My children will enjoy the family feeling at their father's house. They will feel more at home there with new brothers and sisters, and they will end up calling Simcha's new wife 'Mama'.

'Only after ninety-two days can a pregnancy be determined and then you will be permitted to marry,' the rabbi announces to me.

I touch my belly, remembering that last time I was with Joe we hadn't used protection.

I walk away from the law courts towards home a free woman. I cannot walk quickly, even though the rain is pelting down. My limbs feel heavy and I push one leg in front of the other. I have no umbrella and am getting soaked. My hair is dripping and my socks are wet. But with each step, I can feel the change. I am walking faster now. There is a hint of a spring in my walk. The ancient rituals must have taken effect. The circles I spiralled round Simcha under the *chuppah* are slowly unwinding, allowing me to pirouette into my new life.

14

Tikkun

*Judging is done in heaven, but fixing takes place
in this world. A soul that needs fixing has to come
back into the world so that it can eventually
find its resting place in heaven.*

Rabbi Shlomo Carlebach

I draw a bath, pour in liquid bubbles and drops of perfumed oil that stain the water pink, and sink luxuriously under the foam, using my toes to adjust the hot-water tap. Tension slowly eases out of my neck muscles, tension that's been held there since this morning's shift in the labour ward, when I helped a young American woman give birth. She pushed for hours until the midwife cut her fleshy perineum and the nasty smell of faeces infiltrated the room. Her newborn slid through the birth canal into the world, his tongue long, hanging loose, and his eyes Asiatic. The features of a Down's syndrome baby were immediately recognisable. After the midwife handed the baby to the mother and delivered the placenta and we had made sure the woman was not losing too much blood, I left. The sight of the shock and pain on the new mother's face was too much for me. I walked quickly down the hall, skipped down the flight of stairs to the lobby and, still wearing my white working coat, ran out of the hospital premises as fast as I could. I had always imagined that if I were to witness the birth of a less than perfect baby, I would have the tools to help the mother, the sympathy to support her and the knowledge to encourage her. But my first such experience has shown me otherwise. My job could be at risk should the department head get wind of my cowardice. I lie back into the hot water and feel my muscles slowly relaxing. I let out a sigh as the sadness leaves me.

Wrapped in a terrycloth robe, I rummage through my wardrobe for the perfect outfit for my evening out. I have planned this night for weeks, but after my stressful day, all I want to do is hibernate in bed with a cup of cocoa and a good book. There is a knock on the door. It is Tali, the babysitter. I press my forefinger to my lips to indicate that the children are finally asleep. Now that she is here, it seems crazy not to go. I slide on my tight-fitting blue jeans, button up the white cotton shirt that gives me a carefree look, tie my long hair into a ponytail and examine my reflection in the mirror. Yes. I look good enough to embark on my night out.

The Chakra Bar is within walking distance. I passed it often in my old life, when it was out of bounds. On the awning over the doorway, next to a neon-orange sign written in both English and Sanskrit, is a diagram of the *chakras*, the openings through which life energy flows in and out of the aura. My own life energy is pumping through my veins. It has been a long time since I felt so free. Statues of Krishna and Vishnu stand at the entrance, enticing customers, beckoning with multiple arms, but I avert my gaze as I enter, remembering it is forbidden to look at idols. Inside, Indian cotton wall hangings cover the walls. A polished wooden bar circles the far right corner and small tables lit by the glow of candles crowd the floor. Sickly sweet incense permeates the smoky air as I thread my way through the bodies and climb onto the only vacant stool. The bargirl takes my order for a glass of chilled Chardonnay.

Waitresses dressed in flowing skirts and minuscule tops undulate their flat midriffs to the background beat of Ravi Shankar. As I slide my fingers up and down the stem of my glass, I imagine Simcha living in an ashram and consider how well the life of a swami, with its negation of bodily pleasures, would suit him. A lean young man seated to my right is guffawing with the bargirl as she mixes his drink. Their laughter makes me feel foolish sitting there on my own. I avoid looking at them and sip my wine. Go home, Reva, I tell myself. This is not for you. You can't regress into your adolescent ways.

I think about the last six months, the barren patch of time I've spent adjusting to our new lives. The children live with me, but every other Friday night they go to Simcha's and stay there through *Shabbes*. It hasn't been easy for them; they have had to learn to balance between two worlds: Simcha's strictly Orthodox home and my much more loosely religious one. Now that he is alone, Simcha has focused on tightening up his religious practice even more. I am trying to keep a kosher kitchen, but have become lax and sometimes mix up the milk and meat knives and spoons. Even though I found *Shabbes* with Simcha unbearable towards the end of our marriage, now I realise that he instilled the day with importance. For me, *Shabbes* is just a day I dread, and keeping the day of rest with no one to help with the children is challenging. At first I invited guests to join us when the children were with me and I worked hard, cooking and cleaning to make ready for company, just to avoid the pain of the four of us sitting alone and broken at the Friday night table. I was trying to cover the void, something I have always been good at. But no matter how hard I tried I knew this was only a temporary measure and that in the end there would be no hiding from the pain. Lately I have stopped inviting company and our Friday nights have been quiet ones. Yankele recites the *kiddush* and breaks bread, taking his father's role. On Saturday mornings, the children don't want to go to *shul*, and even if we did go, Yankele would not be able to manage alone on the men's side of the partition, so I make a game out of morning prayers at home. I give Yankele the duty of leading the prayers, wrapping him in a *tallis*, and Adele, Leah and I follow his lead. This worked for a week or two, but the novelty is wearing off. The children are sad. Adele speaks to me with anger. Whatever I do is wrong and she blames me for her split life. Yankele is quiet at home and, according to his teachers, not concentrating at school; instead of studying he is looking dreamily out of the window.

It always chokes me up when Simcha picks up the children, who look like three little refugees dragging their bags of toys and clothes and wearing troubled looks on their faces. In the first few weeks after the divorce, I stayed by myself when they left, with nothing to fill the emptiness. I was lonely like only a mother separated from her kids can be. But I want to change all that and meet someone special to share my time with. Go home, Reva, I tell myself again. This is not the way.

'I'm Sam,' says the man next to me, the one who'd been laughing with the bargirl. He raises his glass to me, his penetrating green eyes giving me the once over. 'But everybody calls me Flash.'

'Reva. Reva Mann.' I say, using my maiden name.

'Mann? Wasn't there a Rabbi Mann or something?' he asks.

'Yes, my grandfather . . . I can't believe you know about rabbis,' I say, taking in his bare head, washed-out T-shirt that is now the colour of clay, and khakis – all emblems, in my mind, of the secular.

'There was a case years ago. My mother was involved in a demonstration, something to do with abortion.'

'That's right! My grandfather was the only rabbi to rule in favour of abortion. He thought that an unwanted child could place the mother's life in a kind of psychological jeopardy and he compared abortion to the act of self-defence.' I think about how I used this ruling for my own abortion and I feel sad.

'Whatever. They're all corrupt. The only thing I know is that I pay half my fuckin' salary in taxes to feed those religious families.'

'Hold on a minute. That's my grandpa you're insulting!' I say, getting angry.

Sam smiles a sexy rugged smile, obviously turned on by my little outburst.

'So you come from rabbis?'

'Yes I do,' I say, proud and on the defensive.

'How about a drink? Tequila?'

I haven't had tequila for years, but I answer, 'Thanks.' He has that heroin chic look about him that I have always been attracted to. The hungry look in the eyes, the sallow complexion, the raw sexuality. 'So why are you nicknamed Flash?'

'I'm a Flash of light to my father!' he grins cheekily. 'I light up his darkness.' His lips stretch into a lazy smile that boasts of mastery in loving, a promise that he won't leave any crevice of my body untouched.

'His darkness?'

'Bergen-Belsen.' His playboy exterior falls aside moment-arily, revealing a vulnerability that makes me want to soothe away his pain. 'He's haunted by his memories and at night he howls like a wolf in his sleep.' Sam sucks in his lower lip, gulping air. I sense he is not used to opening up so fast and notice how he compensates by looking away, scanning the tanned belly of the bargirl as she slides the drinks, the salt and the lemon wedges across the counter.

I pick up my shot of tequila, wary of him, and bring it to my lips. I say nothing.

'*L'chaim*, to a hard life.' We clink glasses. 'So what do you do apart from bar hop?' he asks.

'Bar hop? This is the first bar I've been to for years. I'm a birth counsellor and a *doula* . . . I help women in delivery.' I feel a pang of guilt remembering the fiasco of today's shift and wonder if I still deserve that title.

'Aach . . . You mean you see inside pussy all day?' Sam extracts a cigarette directly from the pack with his teeth. He lights it, pulling on the nicotine. 'What a great job.'

'Oh yeah . . . all that blood and amniotic fluid are such a turn on! Look, my sister was damaged at birth, so it's a *tikkun* for me to do this work – I feel that maybe I can fix something that went wrong with my sister if I can help babies to be born healthy.' I remember Mrs Frankel telling me not to mention Michelle to men, but there is something about this Sam that makes me feel I can tell him anything.

'A *tikkun*! You don't believe in all that shit?' He drags long and hard on his cigarette.

I don't know what I believe any more. I spout dogma without thinking, still programmed to a world I've left behind, but I do believe that one can fix things in this world. All I know right now is that I feel more alive than I have for ages from the challenge this Sam is giving me.

'So what happened to your sister?' He sucks on a lemon wedge, tearing the fruit from the pith with his amber-stained teeth.

'Lack of oxygen at birth. She can't talk; she makes weird grunting noises like . . . '

'Like a wolf howling?' Sam tilts his head to the ceiling. 'Aaaooooooooo.' He lets out a growl, bends forward, and playfully bites me on my neck.

'You're crazy,' I laugh and rub my skin, enjoying the way he pushes the limits. This is the first time I have ever been able to laugh about Michelle. 'Just tonight I thought about my sister. It's been ages since I've seen her.'

'Ages?' Sam takes a long drag on his cigarette, the orange glow eaten up by ash. 'Tut tut . . . bad girl,' he flirts. 'Better fix things and do the *tikkun* fast.'

'I'll fix you in a minute! Give me your arm and I'll give you a fix of faith.' I grab his arm and pretend to look for a vein. His skin feels soft to my touch and my heart beats fast.

'I'd love a fix.' The playfulness in his tone is gone and I recognise the mix of despair and need in his voice and remember my own attempts to numb myself with drugs, which began when I was fifteen, taking diet pills my mother procured from our family doctor. The buzz took me away from the stifling atmosphere at home and I was hooked. Then I started smoking dope, lots of it. Thai sticks were my favourite, and the sticky Paki black hash. Realising the potential for oblivion, I soon moved onto heavier stuff. The gang at Compagne Gardens supplied me with acid, but the acid trips were too scary. I couldn't handle the hallucinations, which usually turned bad: cockroaches crawling out of mouths, walls blowing in the wind. I would go home and see tinsel flying off my father's perfectly manicured beard. Finally I discovered heroin. Once I had vomited and emptied the contents of my stomach and the illusion of wholeness was on the way, I knew I had reached heaven. The effects made everything feel 'just right'. I smoked the heroin but not enough to become dependent on it. I was only addicted to not having to deal with pain. Any temporary high would do. But I think God was looking out for me because before I could become a certified addict, I contracted hepatitis B and had to stay two months at the Royal Free Hospital. The humiliation of the constant probing of student doctors and social workers about how exactly I had contracted the disease made me wake up to the fact that I was endangering my life. My body had both let me down and saved me. After I was released I still smoked dope and snorted the occasional line of coke, but didn't use heavy drugs again. Since starting my childbirth studies, which have made me responsible for the women under my care, I have given up the dope too.

After years of abstinence, the dormant craving for an altered reality is flickering to life. I ignore the danger signs and focus on Sam, who is blowing smoke rings in my face. Perfectly round thick circles that look like lifebelts float towards me. I reach out my hand to grab them, hoping Sam can rescue me from years of disappointment. Sam looks into my eyes and with the recognition of one junkie to another, he knows I have understood him.

Sam takes my hand in his, but then suddenly turns his head to check out the young blonde who has just entered the bar. I feel abandoned and play with the salt. A minute ago, I had felt Sam close to me like a twin, just as Rabbi Rabinowitz had taught that all Jewish souls stem from soul roots and are connected at the source. Now I'm not so sure. 'So, Sam, what do you do?' I ask, trying to get his attention back.

'Who, me?' Sam slurs absentmindedly, taking a last look at the girl. 'I write for TV. Right now I'm writing a documentary about my father's family in Berlin. They were all wiped out. My father is the only survivor. They were rich, well known, owned factories. All gone. Musicians too. Played piano and violin. What a waste. I grew up without any extended family. Just my brother and me.'

'And your parents, what do they do?'

'My father's a doctor, internal medicine. My mother is into women's rights, politics, feminism, you know.'

'I don't actually.'

'Yeah, I guess you don't since you come from the religious, who treat women like shit, putting them behind the barrier in synagogue and saying a prayer every morning of "Thank God for not making me a woman!" ' He laughs out loud.

Before I can defend the Torah view of women, explain that women are thought of highly in the religious world, that they have *bina*, a wisdom that is born from intuition and that is a far deeper knowledge than the cerebral intelligence acquired by men, Sam takes my hand in his, spills salt on the triangle between my thumb and forefinger, sticks out his tongue and licks the salt off my hand, grain by grain, before tossing the tequila down his throat. 'Let's go to my place,' he tempts. Grains of salt stick to his upper lip.

'I have a babysitter at home,' I whisper, still feeling the lick of his tongue on my hand.

'You have a baby?'

'Kids – but the sitter probably crashed on the couch.' I hesitate for only a moment, before consenting. 'OK. Let's go.'

'Kids?'

'Three.'

'You married?'

'Divorced.'

'I don't do married.'

We walk the ten blocks to Sam's place, hand in hand. I feel like a teenager. It is almost two a.m. The fact that the kids will wake up in a few hours and I have to be at work at eight is irrelevant to me. Only the touch of his thumb caressing my hand matters to me now.

Sam's apartment is a mess. With the Chinese paper lantern hanging over a light bulb and the Indian patterned cloth covering the threadbare couch, it reminds me of Compagne Gardens. Cigarette stubs litter the floor and mouldy teacups lie forgotten on the table. I have to move a pile of newspapers to make room to sit down. The windows are shut and the air is thick with a smell of mould and stale tobacco. So unlike the order in my own home, the toys neatly shelved, the washing-up draining by the sink, it makes me feel young and carefree again.

Sam slides a Rizla out of the slit in the orange packet lying on the coffee table and spreads it out on a newspaper, fills it with grass, tears off a sliver of cardboard from the flap of a Marlboro box, uses his thumbnail to make a filter, rolls it up and hands me the joint.

'Not for me. I haven't had a joint in years.'

'Come on. It's going to feel sooooo good with the tequila.' He pushes the roach onto my lips.

One joint isn't going to hurt, I tell myself, part my lips and inhale. I am high after one puff. I giggle and nestle into the familiar sensation that holds me, which is like meeting an old friend after a long absence.

Gently kissing, our tongues dance in each other's mouths and our bodies fit together perfectly as if this is where they have always belonged. I'm on fire. Every pore in my body is alive and singing as I lift my hands to cup his face.

'I've got my period,' I warn as Sam unzips my jeans and slides his hand inside.

He yanks the jeans off me and pulls on the white string peeping out of me. 'Yummy!' He licks his lips and dangles the bloody tampon above his mouth like a succulent delicacy. He is more outrageous than I have ever been and I adore him for it.

When I pull off his T-shirt, I find a tattoo of a cross with a loop over the top. 'What's that?' I ask, delighted by the forbidden symbol.

'An ankh. Ancient Egyptian symbol. Union of male and female – something like this,' he says, pulling me closer and enveloping me in his arms. I can feel so much warmth emanating from him. He holds me like a father holds a small child. There is a generosity to his touch. This man knows how to give. It is just what I need. I sense he can heal me.

Sam takes my hand and pulls it down to feel him hard. I undo his belt and open his fly, then feel for him through the slit in his Y-fronts and cup his balls in the palm of my hand. He is big. God loves me, I think, as I feel him swelling even more. He has not forsaken me after all.

I slide down and slip him into my mouth, savouring the salty taste of cock. He is getting harder. I don't want him to come, as I can't wait to feel him penetrating me. I take away my lips. Sam senses my hunger and sits up, teasing me, hands me a bottle of mineral water to irrigate my sticky mouth and rolls another spliff. I suck greedily at the joint, my thighs trembling, and lie back on the couch, floating high, the laughter bubbling out of me.

Sam lifts my legs onto his shoulders and flicks his tongue inside me. I can smell the blood of my period now that he is biting my inner thigh. He's not playing any more but hurting me. I feel tears gather. I want to get him off of me. 'Sam! That hurts!' I shout but now he's deep inside me and the pain is forgotten as I feel the pleasure of his urgent penetration. I dig my nails into his buttocks to pull him even closer, and he screams. I think he is shouting from pleasure and do not know that I have punctured his lily-white skin and branded him until we fall back on the bed exhausted from our fucking. I am stunned to see that our hands are streaked with each other's blood. I cannot help but remember how shocked Simcha had been the time I bled during intercourse. Appalled by the impurity of the first show of pinky menses streaked on his leg, he had jumped out of bed, washed himself in the bathroom and run to the *mikveh* to purify himself.

Sam revels in the mess we have made. The couch is stained and the wall above us is smudged with my period. He is laughing and wiping his bloody hands on my legs. I start laughing too at the idea that I have made a *tikkun* in reverse.

15

End of an Era

And Jacob went out from Be'ersheva,
and went towards Haran.

Genesis 28:10

Rashi explains that the Torah's depiction of Jacob's exit from B'eersheva shows us the glory and the splendour that are lost upon the departure of a righteous person from a city.

The entrance hall of the private hospital resembles the lobby of a five-star hotel. The seats are plush and the carpeting thick. It seems inconceivable to me that, on the upper floor, my father is lying in a hospital bed, sick and on the verge of death. I had raced to the airport as soon as Mother called, not even taking the time to change my clothes, but my flight to London was delayed by an electric storm that made me fear I would get here too late. I rush to the lift, hoping I will have time to say goodbye.

Looking in from the hallway, I see my mother slumped in an armchair in the dimly lit room and my father lying unconscious in the bed. His face is wizened and his pallor yellow. He is breathing noisily, wheezing like an asthmatic. He looks a hundred years old. This is the first time I have seen my father unkempt. His beard is now straggly. Tufts of greying hair stick up clown-like from his scalp. The buttons of his pyjama jacket are open, revealing his ageing naked chest.

'Thank God you've arrived,' my mother says as she pulls herself up. She hugs me to her and holds me in her arms.

'Mummy.' I hug her with true affection, the two of us united in our grief.

'What's that weird noise Daddy's making?' I ask, moving over to my father's bedside.

'The doctor calls it the death rattle,' my mother tells me. 'Speak to him. Nurse told me the last sense to go is hearing.'

Now that my father is unable to control my life, disapprove of my every move, poke his finger between my shoulder blades to remind me of correct deportment, I realise how much I will miss him when he is gone. I take his hand in mine and whisper, 'Daddy, I'm here now.'

His lips are parched. I take a piece of cotton wool, wet it under the tap and gently run it over his mouth. Seeing my father so weak makes me think back to his heyday. With his beard and black velvet *kippa*, he commanded attention. Walking with him to Hyde Park for his daily constitutional, I would watch how people lifted their caps to greet him. Sometimes a gang of ruffians would swear at him and he would raise his walking stick and give them one of his terrifying black looks, which invariably made them run away.

Mother has been sitting in this room for days, waiting for my father to die. Now that I am here, I insist she go home to rest. My father impatiently tosses off the tightly tucked bedclothes, revealing an emaciated leg and withered torso. I cover him loosely with a sheet to protect his modesty. As a girl, I always craved an audience with him but he had so little time.

When he did invite me into his study, it was to read together from the weekly Torah portion. I tried to pay attention, but he preached rather than taught. I would begin to yawn and Father would get insulted and dismiss me. I curl up on the armchair across from his bed, finally alone with him, and listen to his breathing. Tired from the red-eye flight, my lids slowly close and I let myself remember.

Even though he was strict about dress and decorum, my father had an original way of interpreting the law and was a sensitive interpreter of *Halacha*. He understood it is a dynamic living organism that changes with the times and with individual circumstances. Once, when we were on a summer visit with my parents in Hove, Adele was obsessed with her computerised toy, an automated cocker spaniel which was programmed to ask for food every hour on the hour, waking her (and me) all through the night. I wanted to throw the damned thing away. I'd spent years being woken by crying babies and I didn't want my sleep interrupted any more. As the Friday afternoon sun was setting, I reminded my daughter that she must switch off her toy pet, as using any battery-operated or electrical appliance is forbidden on the Sabbath. I was also eager to have a break from its incessant beeping. Her maternal instincts in high gear, Adele threw herself on the bed crying, which was out of character for a child who was so punctilious in her observance of the *mitzvot*. My father, in an authoritarian voice, proclaimed, 'She must continue to take care of the pet, as we know that if she doesn't care for it for twenty-four hours it will die. The law states that one can desecrate the Sabbath in order to save lives.'

'But, Dad,' I argued, desperate for an uninterrupted night's sleep and doubting his grasp of programmed toys, 'it isn't real!'

'It is to her,' he replied.

No other rabbi that I know of would have allowed a child to bring the toy into Sabbath services. I remember hearing it beep, the signal for needing food. Adele stood up and walked out of the ladies' gallery in order to nourish her pet. My father looked up and winked. I doubt this could have taken place in his London synagogue. But in Hove, in another rabbi's domain, my father's little secret with Adele must have served as a timely distraction from the unfortunate rendering of the Prayer for the Queen and the Royal Family, recited by the local rabbi in a guttural Germanic accent, making the hilarious mispronunciation of 'God shave the Queen'.

Now my father's body is heaving with the effort to draw breath. I want to soothe him so I hum a tune, a favourite *Shabbes* melody: '*Vetehar libenu l'avdecha b'emet*' – purify our hearts to truly do Your will'. There is no response, not a flicker of recognition of the song he used to sing every Friday night while my mother served the roast chicken and *lokshen* pudding. I fall back to dozing and another memory surfaces.

My father is asked to say a few words at a fundraiser for the handicapped in the synagogue hall. Very few of his congregants know about Michelle. He stands up and all eyes are upon him. But instead of delivering an erudite speech on the importance of charity, he breaks down and flees the hall. That was the only time I ever saw my father's rigid exterior crack and his true feelings revealed for all to see.

* * *

My father is moving. I must call the nurse. Could he be regaining consciousness? I may have a second chance to know and love him. He is rising up from the bedcovers and raising his head. His eyes open wide in awe and he stares heavenward. His lips part and form a trembling hole. He is trying to speak, but no words come. I jump up. 'Daddy,' I cry, 'what is it?' Fear crosses over his face like a shadow. I rush over to see what he sees. There is nothing there but cracks in the ceiling. His expression tells me he is seeing an apparition that fills him with awe. Could it be that the Angel of Death has come to guide him to the next world? The fear in him is dissipating now and his dry lips break into a smile. I am relieved. Maybe Grandpa has come to lead him by the hand. I can feel another presence in the room. I shiver. My father takes a gasp of air, and then another, and finally, like a deep-sea diver plunging into the big blue, he surrenders this world for the next. As he falls back onto the pillow, I see he is now just a waxen body, the vessel that has carried his soul for eighty years.

'Nurse,' I cry, and then louder, 'Nurse!'

A Pakistani nurse rushes in and walks around to the far side of the bed.

'What's happening?' I scream.

'He's going,' she tells me. 'He's going now.'

I close his lids and pull the sheet over his face in keeping with tradition, so as not to shame the soulless body. I am used to seeing life brought into the world. This is the first death I have witnessed. It is beautiful. I had always considered death to be a sad event, but now I realise it is just another journey. I am filled with God consciousness, high on awareness, just like the time I saw the fairy lights on the cafeteria ceiling and understood God is everywhere. Suddenly I understand my own fragility and how my every breath is a gift. I feel sorry my mother has missed seeing him go. '*Shema Yisroel* – Hear, O Israel . . . God is One.' I recite the *Shema*, the prayer my father used to whisper when he tucked me into bed, surrounding me with protective angels to ensure my welfare through the night, the prayer inscribed in the *mezuzah* on the doorposts of our house, which he taught me to kiss every time I came and went. Now I say it for him, '*Shema Yisroel*,' declaring the unity of a God I hope will judge him lovingly when he stands before His throne of glory.

My mother's nap has been interrupted by the nurse's call. The porter walks with her the five blocks back to the hospital and leaves her at the entrance to the room. She has aged years in only a few hours.

'It was beautiful,' I tell her, 'how he went. It was incredible. I think Grandpa came for him.'

Mother is not interested in the details of his passing, only that her husband of fifty years is gone. She doesn't want to hear and she doesn't want to know. I pull down the corner of the sheet for her to see how peaceful Father looks and to say good-bye, but she cannot bear to look, and I cover him again. She reaches under the sheet, undoes his watch and straps it around my wrist. The inside of the strap feels warm against my skin.

The hospital is suddenly a hubbub of discussion. Distinguished rabbis and leaders of the community have gathered outside my father's room to pay their respects and discuss the funeral arrangements. I am sitting on a chair next to my father and holding onto his arm through the bed sheets. I can hear the rabbis arguing the finer points of laws as to when the funeral should take place.

'If the funeral takes place before sunset, then the mourning period will be shortened by a day, but it will be a rush,' one rabbi explains.

'We can wait till tomorrow,' another rabbi answers.

They are disturbing me. I don't want to leave my father's side. I feel once again I am protecting him, as I did in *shul* when I tried to use my magical powers to silence any interruptions to his sermons. Nurses are walking in and out, removing catheters and drips from his body. I don't want them to touch him. This is a holy time, a time of quiet, introspection and prayer. My mother is busying herself with packing his things. She opens the drawers noisily and sighs and huffs as she crams pyjamas and books into an overnight bag. I am listening to the rabbis, forming my own opinion about the time of the funeral, remembering how my father always tried to bury the dead immediately. He would want to ease the burden of the mourning period for my mother at all costs.

Wearing skin-tight blue jeans and a revealing shirt, the clothes I was wearing when I got the call from my mother, I leave my father's side, stand by the entrance to the room, and face the black-garbed rabbis. I feel confident. Something has changed within me. I am the daughter of a man who has just died and I have witnessed his death. I command respect. I feel my father's authority has been passed down to me as the crown is passed from king to prince. There is so much of my father buried deep inside of me that I have denied for so long. Now that he has passed away, I refuse to let him die. He must live on through me.

I stand tall, as my father always encouraged, and I speak as his heir.

'The burial must take place as soon as possible – before sunset. This is the way my father would have interpreted the law.' I am strong, so unlike the trembling mess I had been in the presence of the divorce rabbis, so unlike the naïve girl awestruck by the yeshiva rabbis whose word I considered as sacred as the word of God.

The rabbis nod in consent. I resume my seat at my father's bedside and hold his hand under the sheet. This is the first time since my yeshiva days that I feel confident in my Jewishness. I am a woman wearing what the Orthodox would call immodest attire, yet my mind is focused on *halachic* guidelines concerning the funeral. At my father's deathbed I feel I am coming into my own, discovering that I do not have to choose which side of the *halachic* fence to live on. I am suddenly aware that I can weave all the strands of my life together, creating my own expression of Judaism, my own connection to God, even if I am not obeying all the rules the way I used to. I think of Sam. I want to call and tell him how I feel. But this is not the time. I will have to wait.

Men in black suits arrive from the burial society. They ask me to leave the room. My mother has finished packing and is standing in the hallway holding the overnight bag, ready to leave. I don't want to go. I want to continue holding my father's hand for a little while longer, but the men are opening up a large black plastic bag that looks like a giant dustbin liner. They are in a hurry to put his body inside. Even though they assure me that my father will be washed and clothed with modesty, they seem so rough. Now I am crying, despairing that my father will soon be disposed of, wrapped up and discarded. I have no choice but to take my mother's arm and walk out of the room, leaving Father in the care of the undertakers.

Back at my parents' flat, I glide from room to room with a lightness of being I have never felt here before. Still, I am looking over my shoulder, making sure Father isn't swivelling around in his green leather chair ready to catch me doing something wrong.

Even in her distress, my mother is focusing on what to wear. She demands I not do anything to shame her now, and makes me wear her long black crêpe de chine skirt and an Ascot hat that presses down like a pudding basin on my head. Considering the circumstances, I do not argue. Mother dresses in a smart pin-stripe suit and a velvet beret, a perfect widow outfit. I fear that when the funeral and week of mourning is over, she will collapse.

The funeral home is filled with the members of my father's synagogue, all the people from whom I hid as a teenager, so that they wouldn't see my unruly behaviour and report back to my parents. I greet them now as an adult, connected to them by their love for my father. There is dear Bettie, pressing a cotton handkerchief to her eyes, and the Kleins, how they've aged, and the chief rabbi and other rabbis coming towards me offering condolences. I am glad to see them all. And here is another familiar face: Ian Isaacs. I can't believe he came. As he walks towards me, I remember the disco benefit I organised in aid of Israeli orphans, the well-known DJ setting up his equipment in the *kiddush* hall in the exact spot where my father raised his chalice, the dimmed lighting, 'Je t'aime moi non plus' playing on the sound system, creating just the right vibe for kids to smooch while they slow danced and made out in the corners. At midnight, the kissing competition began. Mr Gland, entrepreneur and synagogue member, who was on first name terms with Andrew Lloyd Webber, had donated the prize: two tickets to the sell-out show, *Jesus Christ Superstar*. Like my father, he probably imagined I'd set up a Bible knowledge contest. But I was far too cool for anything like that. Four couples competed for this incredible award. They took centre stage and the DJ explained the rules into the microphone. 'The couple who can kiss for the longest time, without coming up for a breath of air or separating their lips, even for a second, are the winners!' He played Mary Magdalene's song 'I don't know how to love him' as incentive. Ian was my partner. He scooped me up in his arms and we began. In the limelight, I went off into a trance where the only thing that existed for me were Ian's full lips and the mystery of his mouth, the probing of his tongue and the hardness of his sex against me. I was unaware that the other contestants had fallen away giggling after only a few minutes, that the entire crowd was clapping and egging us on, and that my father had decided to make an appearance at just that moment to thank us youngsters for our good work.

It is twenty years later, yet I redden with shame at the memory of my father grabbing me by the arm and pressing his index finger into my scapula as he pushed me out of the *kiddush* hall, into the lift, and upstairs to my room where he ordered me straight to bed.

'I'm so sorry for your loss,' Ian says. He hasn't changed at all, I think, as I search for a tissue in my bag. His gesture has touched me deeply and made me cry.

Pallbearers are lifting the shiny black coffin off its stand. My mother and I walk behind them. My legs feel like rubber and I can hardly stand up. I cannot bear that my father is lying in the rectangular box with its lid shut. I don't want him to be buried under the earth. I think about Michelle and wish my sister could be here, wish she were able to share and ease the grief. Mother grabs me under my arm and supports me. I am surprised by her physical strength. For the first time in my life, I lean on her.

Earth is shovelled over the coffin and I watch until the last inch of glossy black wood disappears. Prayers begging the creator to have mercy on my father in his journey to the next world touch me deep in my soul and I too pray for his salvation.

'Goodbye, Daddy-Pa,' I say under my breath. Then I add, 'I'm so sorry. Please forgive me.'

As I walk away from the grave, I realise I will never again be able to experience my father's unique interpretation of Jewish law. It has been buried with him. He is the last of a generation of thinkers who were not afraid to mould the law to respond to the needs of an ever-changing reality. Younger rabbis feel the need to cling tightly to the written word in order to counteract what they call the global descent into impurity. Simcha is like that too, with his rigid practice and closed mind. The loss is great. But of course I have also lost a father, a man I loved even during the angriest moments of my rebellion against him. My mother is standing alone, gazing at the mound of earth. I move towards her and take her arm. We walk away from the grave. It is just the two of us now.

16

The Hidden Light

And God said 'Let there be light' and there was light.
'Light', the twenty-fifth word in Genesis, hints at
Chanukah, *the Festival of Lights, which falls on the*
twenty-fifth day of the month of Kislev.
The Ben Ish Chai. Laws of Chanukah

Today, the first day of *Chanukah*, I am about to leave for a fantasy week with Sam, a whole seven days together travelling south from Jerusalem towards Sinai with no children to feed, no laundry to wash, just Sam and me, lying on the sandy beaches and bedding down in hotel rooms as closely intertwined with one another as Christmas and *Chanukah*, which overlap this year. Standing near the door, holding my bag packed with menorah and candles, sexy underwear and a Christmas pudding, an annual gift from a London friend, I bend down to kiss the children goodbye.

Tali the babysitter is already here, arranging the *Chanukah* doughnuts on a plate and filling the menorah with candles. Adele is scowling. I want to comfort her, but nothing will deter me from my precious holiday. I know that she can't bear Sam. She has told me that his pockmarked skin and shabby clothes disgust her and she can't stomach him prancing around the apartment in his Y-fronts when he stays over for the weekend. She has never seen her own father in his underwear. Even when he walks from the bedroom to the bathroom, Simcha wears his bathrobe. She doesn't realise that for Sam, who feels completely uninhibited in his skin, even wearing underwear is his way of making an effort for her because he is used to walking around naked whenever he feels like it. Sam has told me he grew up with nudity, that he and his brother and their parents were all comfortable being naked in front of each other. Adele's aversion to Sam is my fault, for I have been careless. Whenever he's around, which isn't often but is too often as far as they're concerned, the children sense that I want to escape into an intimate bubble of smoke and sex with Sam and they cling to me even more. I must admit I have taken Sam into my bed and loved him in earshot of my children. I have moaned and groaned in pleasure and ignored their worried calls of 'Mummy' when the sounds of our sex must have been as frightening to them as two tigers stalking. When Adele banged on the thin wall of her bedroom adjoining mine, I resented her interrupting us and ignored her demands for quiet, pulling Sam deeper into me, fearful he would leave.

If Yankele minds my leaving, he doesn't say, but from the way his head is cocked to the side and he is standing close to Tali, I can tell he feels lost. Leah is easily distracted with a jelly treat. I am not a bad mother, I tell myself, trying to assuage my feelings of guilt. I just need fuel to keep me going. But deep down I know that the new strength I thought I had achieved at my father's funeral, the ability to merge the holy and the not-so-holy parts of myself, is not being realised and that I have lost my balance once again. I concentrate on thinking about how loving Simcha is as a father and how glad he is to be with the kids for a few days and have a chance to counteract their exposure to impurity. In his house, they'll pray each morning, recite Grace after Meals, and study Torah. On *Shabbes*, they'll probably eat at Rabbi Sapphire's house, where Adele will play hopscotch with Faige, the rabbi's daughter. They will get a good dose of Torah and I will grab at all the intimacy I can get.

Cold, I wrap my fake fur tightly around my body as I drive to Sam's. Rain splatters on the windshield in heavy drops and the wipers move back and forth, revealing the dull Jerusalem morning. The ground is wet and strewn with leaves. Rivulets of rain stream down the roads. I am as excited as a schoolgirl on her first date. I park outside Sam's building but he is not waiting downstairs as we had planned. I dial his number on my mobile phone. My fingers are pressing down the number keys in frustration. Where is he? I wonder. Why doesn't he pick up? Agitated, I call again. A voice groans on the other end, 'Whaa . . . What do you want?'

'Shit!' I curse as I clamber out of the car and slam the door behind me. I run up the stairs and let myself into Sam's apartment, determined to wake him.

He is sprawled out on the living room couch fast asleep. The coffee table is covered with empty whisky bottles, glasses, mugs, overflowing ashtrays, mess. The air smells of mould. 'Sam, come on, get up,' I kiss him on the cheek, then on the lips. He wipes off my kiss as if disturbed by a mosquito.

'I only got to sleep at six in the morning,' he drones.

I debate leaving him to sleep, going back home and making *Chanukah* with the kids. I know this is the right thing to do, but I cannot bear the thought of giving up my precious holiday. I kiss him again and shake him lightly.

Sam opens his eyes and slowly pulls himself up, reaches for a cigarette, lights up and inhales deeply, coughing and spluttering. He looks awful, older than his twenty-eight years. The nightly abuse of drugs and drink is showing. He yawns and I can see his nicotine-stained teeth rooted crookedly in his mouth. His brow is heavily lined, and his eyes are ringed with black.

Listening to Sam spit up phlegm into the toilet bowl, not at all the way I had pictured this holiday beginning, I reach for the box of grass and roll. I hadn't planned on lighting a joint at nine o'clock in the morning, but to bond with Sam, I am joining him in self-destruction. This isn't all that different from what I used to do with my husband. To commune with Simcha, I had to have a threesome with God, bringing Him into every aspect of my life, nullifying my own needs. I am sick of myself always running to extremes. I hesitate for a brief moment before lighting the joint and see how I am again using the numbing effects of drugs to abate my loneliness. I will never find what I need to nourish my soul this way, I think. But the thought is fleeting and I inhale deeply to alleviate the disappointment I felt when Sam didn't come out to greet me with a beaming smile, shaved, ready, willing, and eager. What a fool I am. All my efforts to be on time – kids organised, refrigerator full, laundry done – are wasted, unnoticed by Sam, unappreciated by anyone else.

Sam lopes about, throwing a few faded T-shirts into a duffel bag. Still half asleep, he stumbles over books and shoes strewn over the floor. He pats the dope supply to make sure it is safely in his pocket and yawns his way into the car.

Laying his heavy unshaven cheek on my shoulder, Sam falls

back to sleep. Even though he has checked out, I am relaxed, having taken off the edge with the pot.

The rain has ceased and we travel out of Jerusalem, past the Hebrew University on Mount Scopus and into the Judean desert through rolling hills that look like bodies reclining in the hot sun, past golden dunes that rise and fall like heaving breasts under clear blue skies. Three hundred metres below sea level, the first glimpse of the Dead Sea is a breathtaking strip of silent turquoise water. It stretches to a horizon of pink Jordanian mountains only fifteen kilometres away. Away from the demands of the children at home and the cries of labouring mothers at work, I allow myself to relax in the desert heat. I take off my fake fur and roll up my sleeves. Sam is waking up. I take the turning to Sodom at the Dead Sea, where tourists and natives alike dip their afflicted limbs into its viscous waters and miraculously heal. I glance at Sam and think he is in need of healing too. I know that from the moment he wakes up in the late afternoon, he is doing drugs, using joints and booze to relax, cocaine for a speedy rush. When that isn't enough to reach total oblivion, I fear he turns to crack.

Along the coastal road of Sodom, we pass blocks of salt that rise like glaciers in the oily water. 'Which pillar of salt do you think is Lot's wife?' I ask Sam.

'Don't tell me you believe people turn into salt,' he says as we drive past fields of date palms and banana groves.

There is a nastiness to his tone that pisses me off. The fantasy weekend already feels like an anti-climax and we haven't even reached our first stop yet. I feel small and stupid. Like Lot's wife, I want to turn back. But I continue on, waiting for the Sam that I love and that I so desperately need, the loving man who understands the depth of my soul, to surface.

In the hotel room, Sam's mood changes. Now that his hangover has lifted, he rolls a bunch of spliffs to prepare for the next state of bliss and to anaesthetise us through the weekend. We smoke and collapse in each other's arms, drift, float and merge into one body and one soul. We are lost in each other in the queen-sized bed made up with white linens that accentuate Sam's cocaine-white skin. This is all I want: to have him hold me with no disturbance. I think about the children and hope they are having a good time with their father.

'Let's go down to the spa,' Sam suggests after the dope has peaked. He is in a good mood now, alive and flirtatious, the Sam I love.

We don the terrycloth robes that hang in the marble bathroom and take the lift down to the second floor admiring our reflection in the lift's mirror and kissing Hollywood-style for an ever-changing audience of staring hotel guests.

A stench of sulphur hits us as we enter the spa and inch our way into the hot pools. I wrap my legs around Sam and he slips inside me as we float along, giggling at our daring. The sulphur starts to sting and we head for the Turkish bath and huddle together on the marble bench, caressing each other's sweaty bodies. Sam moves over to the raised platform in the centre of the chamber. I follow him and soap him from head to toe. He is like a king and I his servant, filling up an earthenware cup and rinsing him with water.

'You remind me of the Santa Claus in Selfridges department store my mum took me to when I was little,' I say, pointing to a beard of lather on his chin.

'Your mother took you to see Santa?' The white bubbles on Sam's chin are already dissolving.

'Yeah. I really wanted to go and she didn't have the strength to say no. She also wanted time to look through the designer labels. I climbed onto Santa's knee and he looked just like my dad and all the other rabbis I knew.' I scoop up what is left of Sam's beard, stick it onto my chin and hold my belly. 'Ho ho ho! Have you been a good little girl?' I imitate.

'You were never a good little girl,' says Sam, as he picks up a bar of soap and begins to lather my body. I relax to his touch. 'You had a hard time when you were a kid, huh?' he says.

'Very hard . . . what makes you ask?'

'Things you've said. And I can feel you. You want to be held all the time like a child. Every time I hold you, I feel how starved you are for love, how much you need it.'

'I know. I just hoped it wasn't that obvious.' I try and make a joke of it, but I turn away as I am crying. No one has ever got this close to my pain before.

Down at the deserted beach, we take lounge chairs splattered with dry mud and encrusted with salt, drag them down to the water and relax in the desert sun. Even in December the sun burns at my skin so I enter the oily waters to cool off. Jelly sandals on my feet, I try and balance on the slippery stones until I plummet down and push off with my hands, floating in liquid that has the same consistency as my mother's *Shabbes* chicken soup. I rub the sea's natural oil onto my skin, lie back on the water, buoyant, as if I were still lounging on my chair. Sam digs down into the seabed and grabs a handful of black mud and draws mud tattoos on me. It spreads like butter. I smear mud all over Sam, turning him into a Zulu.

We giggle, relaxed in our bodies and with each other and, washed clean of the mud, walk back to the room. Pulling the white covers up over us, we snuggle up in bed.

'We should go to visit your sister sometime,' Sam says, stroking my face. 'What do you think?'

'What do I think?' I sit up. 'That's the kindest thing anyone has ever said to me.' Even though I try not to tell Sam how much I love him any more, as he has never once reciprocated the endearment, the words seem to have a life of their own and I hear myself saying once again, 'I love you so much, Sam.'

'Don't love me.' He is looking me straight in the eye. I can see he is serious but I cannot for the life of me understand why.

My stomach rumbles from hunger and I get up, rummage through my bag and take out the Christmas pudding. I call room service and hand the pudding over to be nuked. It is returned hot and gooey, spilling over its plastic container. I open the lid and inhale the aroma of sweet sultanas cooked in brandy, which takes me back to Christmas Days of old. I remember Christmas with Chris, attending Midnight Mass and wanting to take Communion, how his mother pulled me back as I stuck out my tongue to receive the Eucharist. She knew one day I would regret accepting the body and blood of Christ into my body. I dig my spoon deep into the pudding and feed Sam and then myself. We lick our sticky fingers and melt, once again, into each other's warmth, with the taste of our supper on our lips.

The time has come to light the first *Chanukah* candles and I place the menorah on a table near the balcony in accordance with the tradition to advertise the miracle, displaying it where others can see it. Outside, the desert sky is black, lit up by millions of stars. I light the candle and make the blessing. 'Blessed are You, O Lord, King of the universe, who performed miracles for our fathers, in days past.' I think about my father, how he used to give me chocolate coins on *Chanukah*, and I miss him.

I stare into the flickering candle while Sam moves towards the menorah with an unlit spliff. 'You can't light the joint from a *Chanukah* candle,' I shout at him. 'It's forbidden to use the flame for anything but to appreciate its light.'

Sam doesn't argue. He can hear from my tone that I am resolute. I remember Rabbi Rabinowitz teaching that the *Chanukah* light was the original light created on the third day of creation. It was too radiant for the ordinary man to contain so it was saved for the righteous in the world to come. Only on *Chanukah* can we tap into its purity and connect to our higher selves. I need to bask in this light and I know Sam needs it too.

I want to stay in the safety of the health spa but Sam wants some action and is ready to move on south. I hope once we reach Eilat, the Vegas of Israel, I won't have to go to another go-go club and watch Sam moon over dancers covered only by slivers of Lurex, or to a sex shop and witness him slurping over porno pin ups and salivating over an open pussy. I know the Sinai beaches will be full of naked Scandinavian girls and I can already feel fear shift deep in my body. Muscles are tensing up in preparation for the challenging days ahead when Sam will ogle every pubescent curve with longing. I feel aged and flawed. When did my young and enviable body change so dramatically? It seems that it happened without my noticing. The elasticity and tone are gone and now when I look at my arm, it looks like my mother's arm. But it is Sam who has made me aware of the sack of skin that has dropped from my triceps, my inner thigh that spreads as I sit, and my wobbly neck that he loves to jiggle. It seems so unfair that this is what has happened to me during the loveless years with Simcha. It was not only my heart that withered away, but also my body. I feel I have lost something precious, a feminine power.

For the first time I understand my mother's obsession with fixing up her body – a tuck here, a cut there. In fact it was not Sam but my mother who was the first to make me feel insecure about my body. My mother always looked at me with a critical eye. When I developed at the early age of ten, I proudly stuck out my chest to my father to show him the tiny mounds visible under my dressing-gown. My mother pulled me away, reprimanding me that it was inappropriate behaviour to show myself to my father, a rabbi, and an upholder of modesty. That was the first time I felt shame about my body and it has never abated. I always felt my breasts were too big and my belly too fat. I was only happy with my long slender legs. I know men find me sexy and attractive, but I prefer to undress in candle-light and not let them examine me too closely. I felt safe in the darkened room prescribed by Jewish law, but Sam won't have any of that. He likes to look at every crease and crevice, every orifice, every pore and blemish. There is no hiding anything from him. I wish I were young and beautiful and could give him enough pleasure that his eyes wouldn't constantly wander off. I take a deep breath and tell myself to hold on tight. Even though it is *Chanukah*, I can feel the special light dissipating as we approach Eilat. Sam feels the constriction in me and my fears create greater distance between us.

* * *

The border crossing from Eilat to Sinai is always fraught with tension. We cannot get used to having Egyptian officials check our passports. We stand and wait in line. The bureaucracy is slow. I think about the good old days when Sinai was ours and Egged buses ran from Eilat down to Nuweiba and further to Sharm el Sheik. I shoot Sam a reassuring look now that it is almost our turn, letting him know the ordeal is nearly over. With his rucksack at his side, he looks like a teenager going away to sleepover camp. Soon he will cheer up, I think, when we get to the other side and he can stock up on booze at the duty free. I slide the passports over the counter. The customs official, in a starched white colonial uniform with shiny gold buttons, takes his time. I imagine he is having trouble recognising me as the pious matron in the laminated square.

In the Bedouin taxi, Sam is caressing my leg. I know the other passengers are looking at us and I both love and hate the exhibitionism of it. I had always longed for Simcha to take my hand in the street or put his arm around me on a park bench, but my indecent requests had angered him. 'I'm not your boyfriend,' he constantly reproached. 'Behave like a married Jewish woman already.' I look out of the grimy window. The Bedouins still squat at the side of the road, revealing gold teeth when they smile. Women covered by black burkahs that expose only kohl-lined eyes, sell the same old trinkets and beaded bracelets as before. The purple mountains, still loom majestic around me and the water is still a glittering aquamarine. But much has changed. The sand dunes have been flattened into a coastline dotted by an endless strip of hotels.

Sam is slipping his hand up my mini-skirt. There is a young

Israeli man sitting next to me in the back seat and I am embarrassed when I feel Sam's finger creeping into my panties. He is singing our favourite Frank Zappa song, 'Dinah-Moe Hum', 'apply rotation on her sugar plum', and then whispers, 'Can you come like this?' swivelling his finger inside me. I push his hand away but soon regret it as he is now lazily eyeing the two girls in the front seat and fixating on the blonde. I notice that his hand is creeping inside his trousers, deep into his most private of places. He opens the top button and reveals the tip of his magnificent lollypop. 'Get the girl's attention,' he croaks. 'Ask her the time or something.'

I feel humiliated and don't know how to react. I turn away, feeling abandoned, so easily replaceable, and find myself longing for the comfort of the familiar world of Torah modesty, where the strict laws of right and wrong are set out, where the body is covered, where sexual relations outside marriage are forbidden and where men avert their eyes from women. Words of wisdom from *Ethics of the Fathers* come to mind: 'The more women, the more witchcraft. The more Torah, the more life.' I think about the children and regret having left them for the holidays. I think about myself and wish I could give up my addiction to Sam and meet someone else. But I need him. Only he can penetrate as deep into my soul as he does into my body.

'What's wrong now?' Sam asks, as I pull the hem of my mini-skirt down, suddenly ashamed of my bare legs. He buttons himself up, angry now that I won't play his game. I stare out of the window, ignoring him, gazing at the endless yellow desert, angry with myself for being so needy of his loving side that I put up with his sleazy side. I try to focus on the landscape, a vast expanse of nothingness, searching for the exact spot where Moshav Neviot used to stand. There is no sign of the kiosk or the guesthouse where I spent happier times. A cluster of sandy hillocks reminds me of the first time I travelled down here as a teenager, sent by my father for a year to work on a kibbutz in Israel. But I had soon left the rigorous labour of picking oranges under the relentless sun, seven days a week, and followed the hippie trail down to Sinai, the place where the Jews received the Torah and where manna fell from heaven. My money soon ran out and so I took a job as a chambermaid in exchange for mattress, shower, food and pocket money.

I can see myself wheeling a trolley laden with linens and cleaning materials through the crazy-paved paths to the guest rooms and passing a group of Thalidomide adolescents newly arrived from Germany, each one with a different deformity. Some had hands growing from their shoulders and smoked by placing a cigarette in between their toes and bringing it to their lips. Others, unable to use their legs, glided along in wheelchairs, and most distressing of all were those with hands joined to elbows, playing ping-pong. I hoped their rooms had not been designated to my shift, but as soon as I entered the first room on my list and saw the rubber sheets laid down on the beds, I knew it was my destiny to be close to the handicapped. There was no running away from reminders of Michelle or my parents' sadness. I return my attention to Sam.

'So what is it?' he repeats.

'Nothing,' I say, and then add, 'Nothing at all, Flash,' using his fitting nickname.

* * *

Two hours of travelling and we have reached Dahab. The heavy atmosphere between us is slowly dissipating. We make up in the hotel room and Sam takes me gently in his arms and hugs me tight. This is all I really want: for him to hold me like this and cradle me. In the protected intimacy of our hotel room, I can be sure that Sam is completely with me. But I know that as soon as we venture out to the white sandy beach, he will switch from caring lover to public playboy.

We lay our towels next to the water's edge where the sea is as clear as spring water. Dahab is a diver's paradise with unspoiled coral reefs close to shore. I relax for a moment as Sam slides the bikini straps down off my shoulders and rubs coconut oil into my arms and back. The relaxation ends when I sense that he is scanning the sands for yet another set of tits and ass. He rubs oil on himself and lies back on his towel.

The beach is packed with nymphets, tanning, snoozing, reading, and smearing on lotion. Some wear thongs, others minuscule bikini bottoms and some nothing at all. Most are topless. The girl closest to us is lying face down on her towel. She is long and skinny. Her skin is golden brown. Her platinum white hair falls like a sheet of sunshine across her face. I notice her muscular back and the hint of the curve of her breast. Sand is stuck to the fine blonde hairs on the back of her legs. She wears pale blue bikini bottoms that have slipped inside the crack of her perfectly round ass. Next to her sits another girl completely naked. She is equally blonde and bronzed and intently reading a paperback. Her nipples are soft and pink like candyfloss. Her pubes are a weave of golden spun silk that runs like rivulets down the lips of her sex. These lovelies flock here on cheap package deals, escaping the freezing Christmas weather in Europe. Most are twenty years my junior. Their stomachs have never stretched to accommodate a pregnancy, the skin on their legs is smooth with no trace of varicose veins and their ripe young breasts sit up high, nipples pointing heavenward.

'You know what I'd really love?' Sam needles me.

I already know.

'I'd love to line these girls up, bend them over, and just fuck them from behind, one after the other. I don't even need to see their faces.'

I am sickened by his bawdy fantasy, yet I am unable to take my own eyes off the sheer beauty of them all, and since Sam is always drawing my attention to a perfect curve he wants to touch or a shapely bum he wants to bite, I cannot help but imagine these girls separating their legs for him. It is as if Sam has ripped a blindfold off my eyes and now I see all these women as sexual objects for him to fuck.

Sam picks up his snorkel and goes for a swim. I watch his supple physique, covered only by tiny Speedos, splash through the water. My ageing body, skin sagging at the buttocks, and breasts that have lost their shape nursing the children, slumps as I watch Sam swim back to the shoreline and sit watching a group of girls stretched out on floating lilos. By the way Sam is rocking back and forth on his arms in the water, I understand he is erect. Feeling like an old maid, a has-been, floppy, scarred and marked by life, I long to retire from this roller-coaster ride. I don't want to try and be younger than I am any more. I've had enough of pulling in my stomach whenever he touches me, and squeezing into size 28 jeans that leave welt marks on my skin. I'm going to age gracefully. I look at my watch and make a mental note that we are leaving Sinai in seventy-two hours. I miss the children and want to feel them close. It calms me to count down the hours until I can go home and end this cruel affair.

I smooth lotion over the reddening skin on my legs and my chest. I feel something aching under my arm. It is like a foreign body resident in my armpit. My probing fingers touch on a lump the size of a hazelnut. I hold them there and gently rub them back and forth. The lump is hard. I feel the other armpit to compare. No lump. I have played out this scenario so many times in my head since my mother's cancer, but never imagined it would come to pass. The bump is real and tender and I am terrified I am touching death. I shiver in the bright sunny day. I reach for my wrap and tie it around my shoulders. It is hard to breathe. The extremities of my toes and fingers are turning numb and I feel dizzy. I am afraid I will have another panic attack like the one that overtook me one *Shabbes* day before the divorce, when I felt that my body could no longer hold the sadness in me or withstand the lie of my marriage. I had pulled myself out of bed that morning and inhaled the musty aroma of *cholent* filling the apartment and felt as though I was suffocating. I told Simcha I didn't feel well. He offered to stay home instead of attending services but I could tell his offer was half hearted and assured him I would be fine. But I wasn't. After Simcha left, the panic crept slowly over my entire body while my breathing got shorter and shorter and a band of pressure sat tightly over my brow. By the time Simcha returned from *shul*, I could only whisper through gasping breaths, 'Call a doctor.' As it was *Shabbes*, he had rummaged through the holy books until he found *Laws Pertaining to the Sabbath* and the chapter on 'How to use the telephone during an emergency'. I somehow managed to run to a neighbour for help and once she saw my jaw locked into a grotesque grimace and my hands atrophied into a claw she called the emergency services. An intravenous injection of Valium calmed me. I realised then that I could never trust Simcha again, that his religious observance was bordering on the insane.

I cup my hands over my mouth and take long breaths. I will not lose control. Now I am exhaling into the fleshy vessel of my palms, determined not to hyperventilate. Slowly, the symptoms leave me and I relax. Sam throws his snorkel onto the sand and kneels down beside me. 'What is it?' he asks, concerned. I feel a rush of love coming from him. I look deep into his green eyes and I see that he is here for me. The other girls don't exist and only I matter. I want to tell him how scared I am. I want to tell him what I have found. But the only words that come are, 'Sam, do you believe in *Chanukah* miracles?'

17

Where is God?

Ayeh M'kom K'vodo – Where is the seat of His glory?
from the Shabbat Mussaf Kedushah

I sit outside the surgeon's consulting room anxiously awaiting the results of the biopsies taken from the lump under my arm and the pea-sized bump in my breast and ask myself, Where is God? Is He looking out for me now as I fidget in my chair, blindly leafing through a tattered copy of *National Geographic*, staring at the closed door, waiting for the very second the handle will turn and the door will open just a crack, when the doctor will call my name and I will stand up on wobbly legs and cross the threshold into my future?

Sam is sitting next to me. Today he is not salivating over the pretty nurses but focused on me, worried. In our hotel room in Dahab, he had checked and double-checked the bump under my arm and it was he who found another in my breast. At night when I couldn't sleep he held me close and I felt him with me then, knowing I wouldn't have to face the possibility of bad news alone. Upon our return to Jerusalem, he stayed with me during the biopsy procedure despite the doctor's warning that he might faint. I needed him there when the long thick needle punctured my breast and suctioned liquid and tissue for a microscopic check.

The handle turns. Anxiety makes my innards feel as if they

are collapsing like a house of cards. 'Mann?' the doctor calls my name. I stand and ask myself as I walk in to hear the results, Is God with me now, even though I have been lax with His commandments and have not adhered to His laws?

I sit down in an armchair and Sam sits next to me. I look up at the doctor, willing him to tell me I'm healthy.

'I'm afraid I don't have good news.' The surgeon hands me my test results. I read the headline 'High Grade In Situ Ductal Carcinoma' and realise I have received my mother's unfortunate inheritance.

I cannot absorb the outpouring of information, the pile of printouts for tests I need to have in the next few days: CT, bone scan, gynaecological exam, ultrasound of the ovaries and stomach and MRI. Even in my state of shock I can tell the surgeon is blabbing endlessly to cover up his discomfort at having to give me bad news.

'Wh-what about my breast?' I stammer, unable to bear the thought of having my body mutilated. Even though I am sure I have used up my prayer merit, my supplications answered and my children born healthy, under my breath I pray to God to help me just one more time.

'During surgery I'll be able to tell if the cancer has spread deep into the breast.' Seeing a look of panic cross my face and knowing my family history and my dread of losing a breast as my mother had done, he adds, 'Medicine has advanced so much since your mother's cancer. Today, a breast can be reconstructed with an implant filled with silicone gel or saline solution. An areola and nipple are tattooed onto the tip. Results are good.'

Sam perks up, as though excited by the thought that I will

have a new set of tits, the kind he ogles on the *Playboy* centrefold.

I entertain the idea of having a butterfly or a rose tattooed along with the nipple, or even the words 'Flash Was Here'.

'We need to establish if you are a carrier.'

'A carrier . . . ?'

'A carrier of the cancer gene. With your history you might well be and then you'll be at risk for other types of cancer.'

'And if I am a carrier?'

'Then it would be safest to whip out your ovaries.'

'Not my ovaries,' I say, horrified at how swiftly I am being dismembered.

'It's no big deal.'

No big deal! 'I won't want to have sex any more,' I say.

'Reva, get real.' Sam winks at me, knowing that there isn't a minute of the day I don't want to feel him penetrating me.

As we leave the doctor's surgery, Sam holds me close. 'You know I'm here,' he whispers. It may not be 'I love you' but it's close enough to the words that I have been dying for Sam to articulate that I am comforted, even though I'm paying a very hefty price to hear them.

Sam is with me when I walk into Hadassah Hospital the night before surgery. We walk in through Emergency, the unit that receives the wounded after terrorist attacks. I cover my eyes, not wanting to see anything that will bring me to tears in my already fragile state. It is quiet here in the Emergency waiting room tonight, and I am aware only of the bright fluorescent lights, the buzz of the coffee machine, the hum of prayers from patients and their families and the reproduction lithographs of Miro and Matisse adding a splash of colour to the long white corridors. The waiting room is filled with Palestinians. The women wear long *jallabias* over pants and cover their hair and most of their faces with a headscarf. They always come accompanied by a male, a husband or a brother, and the men always circle worry beads, gems of amber and agate, in their dark-skinned hands. I think back to the small private clinic in Harley Street where I went for my nose job. It too was filled with Arabs, some of them resident in London's West End, others flown in from Abu Dhabi and other Middle Eastern countries. They would entertain tens of visitors in their private rooms and I'd see them sitting on the floor as I passed by. When I was recovering from the eight-hour surgery, I remember smelling the delicious aroma of charcoaled lamb and hearing the sound of drums coming from the next room, as well as the cries of the nursing staff: 'They've got a whole sheep in there!' Here in Hadassah, only the smell of overcooked beans permeates the air.

On the third floor, in Surgery, I am put to bed but cannot sleep. I wish Sam could have stayed with me but the nurse asked him to leave. I lie awake and look at the stark walls. I dread the possibility of waking up without a breast as my mother did. I think of her and how she had my father by her side, giving her full love and support and taking care of her every need. I comfort myself as I lie here alone on this night by comparing my plight to that of a traveller. I am at a country railway station. The train I have been travelling on until now, the one with the red plush seats, the dining car with white starched tablecloths and snazzy uniformed waiters offering hot fresh rolls, has come to a standstill and now I must board another train, a sleeper. The upholstery is worn. Only a bar selling crisps and hot dogs is in service. It is headed to an unknown and dark destination. There is something I need to learn now, people I need to meet and situations I need to experience, I am sure of it. I know God is giving me yet another test.

I open my eyes after surgery and Sam is sitting next to me. I reach out for his hand. It takes a few moments for me to realise where I am. Sam looks different. He has shaved his head in solidarity, as he knows that when I start treatment I will be bald.

I slowly lift my hand to my chest but bring it back down again to my side, too frightened to check.

'It's good news,' Sam says. 'He only took a slice.'

I am too woozy to sit up and peek at my breast, even if I dared. Sam rips open the buttons of my gown. 'Looks good,' he says, peeping under the heavy gauze, and then he holds me, appreciating what is left of my mammary gland. I am relieved and let the tears fall. I look at the green curtain drawn between my bed and my neighbour, envying my mother the private hospital room where she recovered from her cancer surgery. I can still conjure up the scene in my mind: my mother sitting up in bed wearing a frosted pink negligee and matching bed-jacket trimmed in satin, an extravagance of flower arrangements surrounding her so that the room looked like a film star's boudoir on opening night. She had put her face on: her lipstick was a shade paler than usual, which gave her smile a pearly sheen. Her hair was set and backcombed into a beehive. I had never seen her look more beautiful. But then I let my eyes wander towards her chest and saw the place on the right side where her bed-jacket lay flat. I turn back to face Sam and whisper under my breath, 'Mummy, Mummy,' finally understanding how broken she must have been when she woke up and discovered what they had taken.

Tonight, my first night home, I squeeze the liquid from the lymph drainage tube in my back into a measuring cup. I am determined not to weave a web of secrecy around my illness as my mother did. I found out about her cancer the night I heard her crying from inside her locked room and found my father reading a book about cancer in his study. With both my parents withdrawn into their own suffering, I rolled into a tight ball of misery, lying on the carpet of my room, sure that I was responsible, since she had always told me I'd be the death of her. I want my children to feel secure and want to assure them I am not dying, so I have told them what is happening. Now I ask Adele to help me measure the pinky juice in the tube, as if it is the most natural thing to register one's bodily discharges. Adele checks the liquid and charts the figures on graph paper. I call the surgeon with the information. Yankele is too squeamish for such a chore but plays his new song on the guitar for me. Leah wants to sleep at Simcha's house. She senses I cannot take care of her as before. I have a stash of grass in my room and openly roll and light up now that I have the excuse of being a cancer patient. Adele can't bear the smoking and has begged me to stop. I understand how she feels and remember being appalled by the crates of Möet and Chandon stacked in the hallway of our London flat and how my mother sipped the bubbling liquid from a crystal glass and giggled stupidly until she collapsed drunk every afternoon in bed. But now I understand my mother and I too need something to take the edge off the anxiety. Like my mother, I want to numb myself and check out. Champagne was her medication of choice; grass is mine.

I sit in Oncology in the chemo lounge, a large room with high ceilings. The walls are decorated with framed photographs of fields in Holland bathed in red tulips, someone's idea of how to soothe the anxieties of all us ugly and bald people who are wondering about whether the chemo will work and how we'll cope when the side effects begin to kick in over the next few days. Orange-red liquid drips slowly into my vein, one drop every five seconds, a treatment my oncologist has told me can reduce the risk of a travelling cancer cell that may have escaped the surgeon's knife when he scraped out seventeen lymph nodes from under my arm. I focus on counting the drops and not on the other patients slouching in black vinyl recliners. The place is as silent as the disease. The only noise audible is intermittent vomiting from adjacent rooms. As the poison drips into me, a nurse gives me a bowl of ice water. I lower my hands into the freezing liquid to prevent my nails falling out. But I cannot leave my fingers in the bowl for long and when I take them out they are red and sore with cold. I ask for ice chips to suck on to prevent the nasty mouth sores common to this treatment. The nurse brings me ice cubes, but when I try to fit them in my mouth, they seem like glaciers that will never melt in a thousand years.

I turn to Sam. 'Can you break these into chips for me?'

He is in a foul mood, probably because he is tired and not used to being awake at nine o'clock in the morning. I sense the heat of his anger strong enough to melt the ice as he takes the bowl from me and walks out of the lounge. A thunderous noise is coming from the corridor. The nurse checking my IV panics, sure a terrorist has found his way past security into their safe haven. I know it is just Sam punching away at the ice, beating the cubes wrapped in a plastic bag against the wall. He brings his offering back to me, smiling now.

My oncologist is blonde. Branching out from her orthodox medical practice, she is trying some New Age healing techniques and experimenting on me. As the chemotherapy drips in to my arm, she straddles a chair next to me and lays her hands on my shoulders. Her dress rides up as her white shapely legs wrap around her chair. Sam averts his gaze and goes off for a smoke. 'Be rest is what you have to do now. Be rest = breast,' she says.

Sam returns after she has left and adjusts his pants to accommodate his swelling hard-on. 'The doctor should be more careful. Doesn't she realise the effect she has?'

I say nothing, but I know what is coming.

'After seeing her white triangle, I want to take her into the toilet now, pick up her dress and fuck her brains out.'

I know the role of caretaker is getting to be too much for him. Now that the treatments have begun, Sam is distancing himself from me and I have overheard phone conversations in which he is ordering drugs, maybe even crack. His adolescent fantasy about the doctor is too painful for me to deal with and I close my eyes and try to concentrate on the healing properties of the poison. I slide my bandanna back over my skull, which is so bald that it has become sensitive to the wind, chafes against my pillowcase and makes me look like an alien. Chemo is a breeze, I think, compared to dealing with Sam.

At home I lie in bed, crashing after the treatment. I cannot move further than the bathroom. My whole system is screaming out from poison. My digestive tract has packed up. I cannot eat a thing. Hard blobs of light-coloured stool are expelled with difficulty from my bowels. My tongue is furry white as if a fungus has grown there overnight. I gargle with salt water to prevent infection and drink sage tea for momentary relief. Electronic waves and high-pitched sounds make me feel as if I've have been hijacked to another planet. A blowtorch has been ignited inside my body. Friends have suggestions for my recovery: healers, alternative doctors, acupuncturists, Chinese mushrooms, tinctures, guided imagery and Reiki practitioners. I try them all. Nothing helps. All I want are Sam's arms around me. Only he can comfort me.

18

Life after Death

Concentrate on three things and you will not fall
into sin. Know from where you came – a putrid
drop. To where you are going – a place of dust,
worms and maggots, and before whom you will
have to give account and reckoning – before the
Supreme King of Kings, the Holy one, Blessed be He.

Ethics of the Fathers 3:1

There are only another seven days to go until my oncology
treatment ends. I have been waiting a year for this moment to
come, but never believed it would. I am weak, exhausted and
unrecognisable from the woman with the chic skinhead look I
was at the beginning of treatment. Now my skin is yellowed
and my eyes bulge out of my face without the protective
contouring of brows and lashes. I have flopped down onto the
couch and turned on the television to watch my favourite soap
opera. But pandemonium is erupting on the screen, the scream
of sirens, panic in the streets, hysteria. A suicide bomber has
blown himself up in the entrance of an electrical appliance
store in a Tel-Aviv mall. Five dead bodies stuffed into black
plastic body bags are lined up on the side of the road. Mobile
phones ring and are not answered. Torn limbs litter the
ground. Human remains are being scooped up from trees,
scraped off pavements and bagged for burial.

I watch the names of the dead scroll across the television screen. Among them, in bold type, is Leib Gordon. Leib, named after his Aunt Leibe, who was raped and killed by Nazis fifty years earlier, smiles out of a recent snapshot, a handsomer version of his brother Sam. He had been blown to smithereens within seconds.

I weep for Sam and his parents, and soon find myself weeping for my own losses: my health, my marriage, my father. The sound of the phone ringing brings me back to the present. It's Simcha, who has just heard the news. '*Baruch Dayan Emet*, Blessed be the true judge, who gives life and takes life,' he says when I answer the phone. 'When's the funeral? I want to go.'

Simcha has often emphasised the importance of the *mitzva* of accompanying the dead to the grave, quoting Ecclesiastes: 'It is better to go to the house of mourning, than to go to the house of feasting: for that is the end of all men.' My illness has caused a lot to change between me and Simcha and Simcha and Sam. Taking care of me has given them a common cause, which has forged a bond. But still I am surprised that Simcha wants to go to the funeral. He has never liked Sam. I can't forget how he cringed the first time he saw Sam walking around the apartment bare-chested, as though to flaunt his tattoo, and how horrified he was that Sam slept in my bed when the children were around. But the death of a loved one through a suicide attack cuts through these differences, for we know that we are all equally at risk.

I wonder how Sam will react when he sees Simcha at the funeral. He used to call the ultra-Orthodox parasites, disgusted by their refusal to serve in the army and the way they live off the state with the excuse that they are uplifting the nation by learning Torah. He never felt comfortable in Simcha's presence and could barely tolerate the awkward hellos and the uncomfortable handshakes when Simcha came to visit, shuffling around in his black Hassidic garb. Lately, since he has seen Simcha's kindness towards me, I think he has come to appreciate him.

I want to go to the funeral too. Even though I am weak from my treatments and have been advised not to expose myself to the sun, I make the effort to dress. This is not easy, as my breast, burnt red from the radiation and still very sore, has to be smeared with a thick white ointment and covered by a big wad of gauze over which I have to wear a large cotton exercise bra. Still, I want to look presentable and try on everything in my wardrobe until finally I decide on a black sleeveless shift, the most comfortable thing I can find. I tie a kerchief over the fuzz that is now sprouting on my bald head, put on my dangly gold earrings and apply lipstick to bring some colour to my washed-out complexion. I am making this effort for Sam because I'm remembering my father's funeral in London two years ago, and how isolated I felt with only my mother and the people from my father's congregation in attendance. The rest of my family and all of my friends were in Israel, too far to offer comfort, so now I want to give to Sam what I needed for myself that day.

Simcha and I drive together to the cemetery at the entrance to Jerusalem. We walk into the grounds and find Sam locked arm in arm with his parents in a tight circle. It is only hours since he had the agonising task of identifying his brother at the forensic institute. Since the body was mutilated beyond recognition, he had to identify him on the basis of a square of blue knit fabric taken from the remains of a knitted vest Leib had worn, which he recognised as the present he had given his brother for his last birthday.

On a slab of marble lie Leib's remains, wrapped in a *tallis*, ready for his journey to the next world. Earth from the holy land cannot be sprinkled on his forehead and genitals and the ceremony of *tahara* cannot be performed as there is no whole body to wash or dress in the simple white linen *tachrichim*, the burial clothes consisting of trousers, tunic and head-dress fashioned after garments worn by the high priest in the Holy Temple. The only rite that is performed is laying a handful of earth on top of the *tallis*. I think of my father's *tahara* and how the *chevre kadisha* assured me that my father's body would be treated with the utmost modesty and care, only one part uncovered at a time for the ritual washing and cleansing. They promised to accord him the same respect in death as he was given in life as an important leader of the Jewish people. Their words didn't comfort me. I couldn't bear to think of my father zipped up in a bag that looked just like his own carry-on luggage.

I look away from Leib's remains and turn to where Sam is standing. I yearn to go over and hug and comfort him, give something back and support him the way he has taken care of me. But the ring of family members is closed in on itself and can't be penetrated, so I hang around until Sam comes over to greet us. When I see him approaching, I hold out my arms, but he brushes me aside and falls into Simcha's embrace. 'Is there really a God?' he asks, resting his head on Simcha's chest. 'If so, how could He have done such a thing?'

I watch Simcha holding on to Sam and feel humiliated that it is Simcha Sam wants, instead of me. But I cannot judge him.

I cannot compare the suffering that he is feeling now with my own experience at my father's death. After all, my father was an elderly man, not a young man with his life ahead of him, and his passing was a beautiful one, which left me in awe of the magnitude of God's presence. I knew that what I had witnessed at his bedside was the natural conclusion to the cycle of life, and as sad as I felt over my loss, I also recognised it as inevitable and even felt liberated by it. But Sam could never feel a sense of awe or rightness about the tragedy of his brother's passing. It is only horror he feels now, and he may live with this suffering forever. He is looking to Simcha, desperate to make sense of the cruel loss.

'Life is like a tapestry,' Simcha explains. 'In this world, we only see the knots and the threads, but in the next world, we will see the whole clear picture.'

I look at Sam shyly, but he hardly notices me. In his grief, it is Simcha he wants now. I want to butt in and claim my rightful place, but a member of the burial society is striding towards us with a razor blade in hand. 'Mourners cut their clothing before burying their dead,' Simcha explains, noticing how Sam winces as the official takes hold of his collar.

I remember when my black shirt was torn that cold wintry day at Willesden Jewish cemetery and I realised I had lost my father forever.

'Let me.' Simcha carefully takes the razor blade from the man. 'I'm going to make a small cut in your shirt,' he says quietly, and makes an incision the size of a thumbnail into the collar of Sam's T-shirt. 'Repeat after me,' he soothes. '*Baruch Dayan Emet.*'

Simcha approaches Sam's parents and offers to cut Dr

Gordon's shirt. The Gordons prefer to deal with this soft-spoken rabbi rather than the rough burial official. I can see their bodies slump with relief.

Mrs Gordon's plump figure is visible through the sheer cloth of her sundress. Wisps of grey hair fall out of the fraying brim of her straw hat and spider lines web under her eyes. Simcha looks for a place to cut her dress. He chooses the patch of material near the strap, which he cuts gingerly, trying not to reveal her bra. Simcha cuts Dr Gordon's shirt at the collar, revealing liver spots. I notice the blue number stamped on the inside of his forearm peeping out of his shirt sleeve as he circles his arm around his wife's shoulder.

'Simcha . . . will you say a few words of Torah?' Sam begs through his tears.

'Would you?' the Gordons chime.

Simcha is surprised. He has never met Leib Gordon and has only come to pay his respects. But, seeing the earnest look in Sam's teary eyes, he agrees and sits down on a wooden bench to make a few hasty notes in preparation for his address. I feel small and insignificant. I want to give to them too, but there is nothing they want from me.

At the graveside, the speeches begin and the tears flow, as friends and close relatives speak about the man whose remains lie before them on a stretcher. They note his accomplishments. He has, in his thirty-eight years, published a novel and a book of short stories and had recently written a collection of poetry. Sam reads a stanza from Leib's latest work and recounts how his brother wrote many of his poems on paper napkins in purple ink. It's funny what you remember about people when they're gone. When I think about my father, I think about his modesty. I never saw him undressed, but always dignified in his dressing-gown belted at the hips.

The secular crowd, the women dressed in an array of halter-neck tops and mini-dresses, the men bareheaded, look surprised when a Hassid in a long black caftan and sidelocks shuffles towards the gaping hole in the earth.

Simcha has never addressed a crowd of non-fearing Jews. He averts his eyes from the mass of bare skin around him and concentrates on Sam. 'Your shirt is torn as a sign of mourning and by stripping away the cloth, your broken heart has been revealed.' Sam's muffled sobs sound like a wounded animal, caught in a trap.

'The soul hovers around the body before it enters the purely spiritual world.'

Where is my father's soul? I think. Is it with God? Did he make *tshuva* before he died? Did he repent?

'The righteous sit in the front row seats in the godly arena, enjoying the radiant light emanating from the source, the light we can only access on *Chanukah*.'

I glance over at Sam, remembering our trip to Sinai, but he doesn't look my way. He is listening intently to Simcha, hanging onto his every word.

'The sinners are further away, in the cheap seats, unable to fully enjoy the performance. This, Sam, is the Jewish definition of hell.' Simcha lowers his voice to a whisper. 'Your brother has died as a pure sacrifice for the Jewish people. He is right up there among the righteous, basking in God's light.'

Out of his mouth dance the graceful words of Torah, of solace and comfort, about a man he has never met, would probably not have liked and who would not have liked him.

Sam embraces Simcha in gratitude. Both men wear black and they become a dark blur with four white hands patting and confirming, encouraging and loving. I cannot tell which hands belong to whom as I stand back, excluded.

Leib is being lowered into the earth. Sam reaches out. I don't dare step forward to stand by his side, as I feel rejected now. I know he doesn't want me any more. I cannot concentrate on the horror of this burial, on the waste of this life, as the misery of a future without Sam is sinking in and all I can think about is how I will cope when he is gone. I weep for my own loss. Simcha is right beside Sam and lets Sam's quivering hand cling to him for support.

Here in Israel there is no coffin. Seeing the body wrapped in the shrouds and *tallis* lowered into the dirt is not an easy sight. I imagine worms and maggots burrowing into the flesh. But I have learnt that burying the body without a coffin symbolises our return to the earth and dust.

As people surround Leib's immediate family, Mrs Gordon finally notices me. 'Reva,' she says, gesturing toward the swatch of gauze sticking out from under my arm, 'what are you doing here? You should be lying down at home.'

In her grief, her concern for my health is touching. But I know she has wanted me out of the way since she heard the chemotherapy treatments terminated my menstrual cycle, disqualifying me as a potential child-bearer and suitable partner for her son. I can understand. Sam should have kids of his own. All his family were wiped out in the Holocaust. Now more than ever it is vital that he perpetuate his family name. I am hurting. I can deal with being temporarily bald and having a mutilated breast with an ugly scar over bunched-up skin and a nipple that veers off to the left. But being unable to bear children, due to a change of life that has come years before its time, is the cruellest side effect of the treatment.

Death always brings about a moment of truth; a tragic death like this even more so. I can feel the shift that has taken place. Sam and I are finally over.

Simcha and I visit the Gordon home the day after the burial when Sam and his parents begin to sit *shiva* for the customary week. Deep down I am still hoping that Sam will want me by his side. This is the first time I have been in Sam's parents' home since a Friday night dinner before I became sick, which was the only time I met Leib. He was classically handsome and sexy too, but to my taste he had nothing on Sam. The table was covered by a plastic tablecloth that felt cold to the touch and the meal of boiled skinned potatoes, chicken, also skinless, and sliced white bread wrapped in a plastic bag made me think of war rations. As I look over at the table, I remember putting my knife and fork down, leaving only a cube of chicken and a sliver of potato on my plate. When Sam gobbled it up fast before his father could see the waste, I had my first glimpse of what it must have been like to grow up in this Holocaust-haunted home. I understood that there were reasons for Sam's substance abuse, felt the pull of his gravitation to the dark underground world of porn and seedy nightlife. He needed an escape, a place to forget the unbearable silence of unanswered questions, of not knowing, of not wanting to know, yet knowing all.

I look around. Fake leather sofas and a jumbo television screen are the only furniture in the room. There are no paintings on the walls. A few photographs lean up against the mantelpiece and an arrangement of dried flowers sits neglected in an old earthenware vase.

The mourners sit on low stools and eat the customary hardboiled egg, its roundness symbolising the cycle of life. Friends filter in to pay their respects and Simcha covers the mirror in the hall to enable the mourners to focus inwards. Dr Gordon seems calm and is passing round photos of Leib. Sam's mother cannot lift her head. She sits looking at her hands. I cannot imagine her pain. I think of my own children and pray for their health.

My mother kept up a brave face at my father's *shiva*. She entertained the congregants with tea and cakes and fond memories of my father. It was only when the week of mourning was over, when there were no more callers, that she finally broke down. Then she talked aloud to my father as if he were still around. In the weeks and months that followed, she kept him with her and his memory alive by taking her religious obligations more seriously. She became the *rebbetzin* she had never been, praying and keeping the *Shabbes* laws strictly. I didn't miss my father at that time. I felt relieved at being able to enter the flat without first trying to anticipate all the strict rules that I had to abide by, and I was more relaxed there than I'd ever been, now that my every word wouldn't come under his scrutiny. But as this year has progressed and I have borne these difficult treatments, I have missed his warmth and dreamt about him repeatedly. In my dreams, I see him with his *tallis* covering his head and I feel that he is with me, supporting me through my cancer.

To ease Leib's passage into the world to come, Sam and Simcha read the holy psalms and the *Mishnah* tractates that begin with the letters of Leib's name. Simcha is a magnet to whom the mourners and their friends cleave for comfort. His name is on everybody's lips. They all want to talk to him, offer their appreciation for his speech at the grave, and ask his advice.

A week later, the day after the *shiva*, I pay my final respects to the mourners. This coincides with the end of my radiation treatment. For the past three months I have lain on the cold surgical table every day and seen the radiation doors slide shut and dared not move lest the beam hit a healthy piece of skin unmarked by the purple ink that has to be redrawn each time. I thought of my mother then, as the machine moved forward buzzing onto my chest, and wondered how she dealt with the daily dose of hell. Every day I was fearful that the door would not reopen and the red light that zoomed in on my chest leaving a mark as if an iron had stamped my skin would just keep buzzing and burn me to cinders. But now I have had my last blast.

I have imagined this moment for months – how I would celebrate the end of a year of treatment, throw a party and invite the medical staff. But without Sam next to me, there can be no celebration, no party. Nevertheless, I am mentally celebrating my recovery, looking forward to getting my life back, and in this positive frame of mind I visit Sam and his family for the last time.

I enter the Gordon apartment and I find Simcha busy winding the black leather straps of his *tefillin* around Sam's freckled arm. Round and round he goes, circling Sam's arm. Sam is completely absorbed in the performance of the *mitzvot* and reciting prayers that sound strange to me coming from his mouth. During the *shiva*, under Simcha's direction, Sam adhered to the laws of mourning: he did not wash or shave, nor did he wear leather shoes, but instead, his tattered carpet slippers which are torn at the toe. Today, he wears the barmitzvah *tallis*, which looks like an old scarf, stained and creased, which only partially covers his tank top. The silky material slips off his shoulder revealing his tattoo. There were many occasions when I tried to engage Sam in a conversation about our religion, show him the beauty there, but he always scoffed. He never wanted to hear a word about it.

'Goodbye.' I say approaching the family. I know it is time to walk away forever. I have understood that I have no place here any more, with Sam or with his family. I am glad that the last time I am seeing Sam he is enveloped in *tallis* and *tefillin* with prayer on his lips. I will always remember him like this. The jealousy that I feel towards Sam and Simcha, who have excluded me from their spiritual adventure, is waning. I have come to terms with the knowledge that I don't belong with either of them. They both represent extremes that are destructive for me. Leaving them together is the best way out, for me, and perhaps for all of us. I even consider that they may heal each other. They nod goodbye to me politely and resume the binding of *tefillin* and bonding of friendship. Sam looks into my eyes. He says nothing, but his face tells me that our separation is hard for him, too.

I leave the mourners and step out into the sunlight. I cannot shake the image of the two men and their unlikely camaraderie, which seems emblematic of the quest I have been on, the attempt to fuse my two worlds. I walk away, hopeful that at last I am on the course to find the middle road, the way of balance, the golden mean.

19

The Final Release

Cast me not off in the time of old age.

Psalms 71:9

'I just can't go on.' My mother's voice is crazed with pain that bolts across the miles between us in the darkness of the night.

She has woken me from a deep sleep and it takes me a few moments to react. 'Mum,' I slur, 'I know it's hard, but it'll get better.' Two years have passed since my father died and I am not sure she will ever be able to cope alone. I try to comfort her even though I am annoyed that she has called so late. I need to be up early for the morning shift at work.

'I want to die. Please God take me . . . Take me soon.'

Here we go again. My mother has often threatened suicide. When I was a child she used to perch herself by the window ledge as though to jump in order to manipulate me into good behaviour. Then I was terrified. But now I am not impressed. I have heard it all before.

'Muuuuummm.'

'I can't cope with it all, the banking, the bills, the accountants. Daddy took care of everything. I don't know where I am when the bills come in. I start shaking.'

'Don't you have a friend who can help?'

'What friends? They're all no good. They loved Daddy, but

now he's gone they can't be bothered with me. A dog has a better life.'

'What about *Shabbes*?'

'I make *kiddush* and then eat a *challah* sandwich in bed. I can't be bothered with anything any more. I don't want to live, Reva . . . I just can't.' Her voice sounds desperate.

The melodrama has woken me fully and I sit up in bed. The alarm clock on my bedside table reads 1.30 a.m. 'Mum, think about coming over here to be with us.'

'Don't be ridiculous. I can hardly get off the bed. Come to Israel! You don't realise what a state I'm in. You don't know what you're talking about. It's no use.'

'Mum, do you want me to come to London?'

'Who will take care of the children?'

'I'm sure Simcha will.'

'What about your health?'

'I'm feeling fine now.'

'You can't give up work.'

'I'll ask for a week off.'

'Then come.'

I am sad to find my mother lying in a bed strewn with crumbs and snotty tissues, wearing a stained nightgown and with her hair all askew. Now that Father is not here to give her strength, it seems her manic–depressive cycle has become a steady downward slide into the abyss. She cannot seem to pull herself out of it.

'I'm afraid to go out of the house. I may fall in the street, but then I won't die, just break a leg or a hip, so how will that help me?'

'You can't be alone any more,' I tell my mother. 'We need to find you a live-in who can shop and cook.'

'I've called the Hemlock Society and asked them to send me something. I could do something terrible, terrible.'

'There is nothing left in England for you now. Come to Israel to be near me and your grandchildren.'

'What? Leave England? Leave Michelle?' I feel her guilt surfacing again. It is years since she has seen Michelle. She hires someone to visit Michelle and take her for a walk.

I do not say that Michelle will not know that she has left the country. Instead I reply, 'I'll help you move.'

'I couldn't. It's too much for me. What about packing up the flat, the arrangements?'

'Mum, I'll deal with it. It may be hard for you but it isn't for me.'

After only a moment's hesitation, she perks up. 'OK,' she says, 'I'll come. But you'll have to take care of everything, absolutely everything. I can't do a bloody thing.'

Feeling as if I have dug my own grave, I am already sinking under the heavy burden of caring for her. But there is no way out. I am doomed to take care of her now and for the rest of her life.

With the journey to look forward to, Mother moves into high gear. Operating from her bed, she sells the flat to a neighbour. When I am not busy finding her a place to live in Jerusalem, sorting out her possessions, dealing with immigration papers, packers, movers, doctors, prescriptions, insurance and, most draining of all, listening to her constant chatter, I give her a manicure and snip off the dry skin growing from her cuticles and bring light meals to her bed. Anything heavier than a slice of toast, yogurt or ice cream just 'won't go down'. She wants me to help with her bath, too, but even though I have been through breast cancer myself, I still cannot bear to see her mastectomy scar and refuse. This is old business between us. After her surgery her nightly ritual when she undressed was to remove her bra, heavy with its fake breast, and wrap it in a towel which she placed on her night table. If I was accidentally caught in the room with her when she started to disrobe, I had to avoid witnessing this at all costs lest I see the mutilation, which terrified me. But I never wanted her to notice me averting my eyes or looking down at the long beige shagpile carpet, just as now I don't want her to know why I won't come into the bathroom to heave her out of the tub.

In Israel she will live in her own apartment in an old age home, a five-minute walk from my home. There she will have twenty-four hour care in a friendly environment where there are many European residents, some who speak English, many who speak German. My mother majored in German Literature at university and graduated *cum laude*. I expect she will fit in well.

After a busy two weeks, we say our final goodbye to the flat where I grew up. It is painful for me to leave behind my father's books, boxed and stored in his study, which we have donated to the synagogue. The dismantling of the library makes me feel I have torn him limb from limb. Mother doesn't seem at all sad to leave. She is in top form, impatient to get away.

Mother and I cannot stop giggling on the plane ride to Tel-Aviv. Everything amuses us. We joke about how she clutches her carry-on bag filled with sleeping pills and medicaments with all her might. We chuckle about our snoring neighbour who sounds, according to my mother, like 'a steam engine'. We laugh as I stand on the tarmac and watch her descend the plane in an outdoor wheelchair lift. When I see her mood darkening and worry lines deepening on her forehead, I assure her that she will love her new apartment. She rests her heavily veined hand on mine. She trusts me now.

A security button on the wall next to her bed and another in the bathroom of her new home allows Mother to call the nurses' station any time she needs something. Three nutritious meals a day are served in the dining room. Maid and laundry service are available. She has only to walk down to the lounge or out into the manicured garden to find company.

Euphoric, she raves to everyone she meets. 'It's just wonderful, marvellous. What staff. I've been saved. I don't need to go out. Everything is under one roof: exercise classes in the morning, a library with English books and a synagogue on the ground floor. I can go to *shul* when I have *yartzeit* and for the festivals. I don't need to wear a hat and get all dressed up here. I can throw on my long cotton skirt that hides those clunky orthopaedic shoes of mine and a wear *shmatte* on my head. There's even a hairdresser on the premises but of course I can't trust anyone but Robert to get my colour right. I could go grey; no I don't have the face for it. The food is delicious, but I can't eat all they give me. My bowels are working better than ever. I remember my German. It paid off having my textbooks in the toilet: Schiller in the upstairs bathroom and

Goethe in the downstairs cloakroom. Most of all I have my grandchildren nearby. Why have I never realised how wonderful they are? I love Adele best. She comes over after school to do her homework and watch TV. And Reva, Reva, what a wonderful daughter I have. All these years and I never really appreciated her. What a great girl! How she takes care of an old woman like me, you can't imagine.'

I don't cringe any more. I have accepted her and she has accepted me. I am happy. Now that I am her caretaker, my mother wants to hear my news. If she has a good day and is not completely self-absorbed, I confide in her about problems I have with the children. She has a special connection with Adele and takes an interest in her – more, I feel, than she ever did in me. We invent a secret nonsense language, another source of laughter. I love having my mother here, even if I am the one doing the mothering.

The past month has been glorious. My mother has assimilated her new environment with ease. Three mornings a week are taken up with exercise classes. Mother, a former linguist, is learning Modern Hebrew and using her new vocabulary at every opportunity. On *Shabbes* I accompany her to the little synagogue and to the *Kiddush* afterwards where she can mingle. In the afternoons, I collect her and walk her to my flat. The children are delighted to have a grandmother around, a family member who is more lenient with their behaviour than I am.

The shipment has arrived from London and the furniture has been arranged to replicate her living room at home. The oil painting of my father in his clerical cap and gown hangs dignified above the couch. The tea service is stacked in the kitchen cupboards and the little walk-in closet is filled with her designer clothes. But now Mother isn't happy. She cannot sleep. Her eyes itch from the dry climate and she has to lie down in a darkened room with damp pads on her lids. Nothing helps – neither the air-conditioning nor the cooler. Her legs won't work. Even though she could cling to the bars that run along the corridors, she doesn't make it down to meals. She wants lunch brought up to her room, but the social worker refuses. There is little sympathy for depression here. Residents are encouraged to socialise. The charming widows at my mother's dining table welcome her to Israel, but she spent so many years with my father in the forefront, casting a shadow for her to hide under, that even simple everyday social interactions are difficult for her. She feels that she has nothing to contribute, that she is inferior to the others. I know this isn't true. Mother has a fine brain and wicked sense of humour, but her attention span is short and she prefers to deal only in superficialities. She was never comfortable in her role as rabbi's wife, always anxious she wouldn't know the answer if asked a question about religion, or even about what page we were reading from in the prayer book. Her Torah education was limited. Although she had been an avid scholar at university, my father didn't teach her much. She was versed in the Grace after Meals and the stories from Genesis, but little beyond that. I think my father preferred to keep her in the dark, dependent, and following his lead.

Years of hiding behind a façade have made her fretful and feeble. I am sure her psychosomatic symptoms indicate a deeper pain. She pops anti-anxiety pills like sweets. Often of a morning she will admit, 'I just had to take a Valium. Look, I'm shaking like a leaf.'

I must find a psychiatrist and seek professional help.

Dr Goldstein has been recommended as a sympathetic geriatric psychiatrist. His clinic in Hadassah Hospital is just down the corridor from the Oncology department where I was treated. Mother is leaning on my arm. She is taking little pigeon steps. 'I can't see where I'm going,' she cries.

'I'm leading you,' I tell her. 'It's going to be fine.' Passing Oncology, I think to myself how well I feel now, how successfully I have recovered from the debilitating treatments.

Mother doesn't like me leaving her in the room alone to talk with the handsome doctor, but I insist. I sit outside his office, pleased with myself for arranging her first therapy session, chuffed that she will finally receive treatment. As a girl, I begged my father to get her help, but he ignored my request, afraid of the stigma on our illustrious family name. I have achieved what he could not, I think, as the door opens and the doctor beckons me to come inside.

My mother is dropping down onto one arthritic knee and grabbing my hand as if she never wants to let me go. 'I've never appreciated what a wonderful daughter I have,' she cries, tears flowing down her cheeks. 'I was only interested in Daddy and the community.'

'Mum! Get up.'

'Forgive me.' She kisses my hand with quick smacks like a devotee to her guru, beseeching and begging. 'Forgive me.'

I pull her up and she collapses back into the armchair.

'Tears,' she says. 'I haven't had tears for ages . . . incredible . . . even when Daddy . . .'

I look to the doctor in bewilderment. What has happened here while I was waiting all unawares outside his office?

'An epiphany! Yes, that's what it is. Just talking to the nice doctor, getting things off my chest to someone who understands, has made me feel better.'

Mother looks beautiful to me at this moment: her skin bare of make-up radiates light, her furrowed brow is relaxed and her hands are at peace, not incessantly twirling her diamond ring around her finger.

I cannot believe how quickly the change in her has come about. I allow myself to imagine her getting well and becoming the strong mother I have always needed, one who can talk to me and guide me. I'm in denial, stupidly willing myself to believe in the absurdity of her being able to free herself of suffering in only half an hour.

The day following her 'enlightenment', I am eager to see my mother but, as I enter her little flat, I notice the glow in her cheeks has been extinguished. Her face is dark. The curtains are drawn. She is still in her nightgown at three o'clock in the afternoon and has not eaten lunch.

'Come on, Mum,' I say, opening the drapes and bringing in the glorious summer day. 'Get up.'

'Close those curtains immediately! You know the light hurts my eyes. Are you deliberately trying to upset me, after all I've been through, after everything that's happened to me?'

She is going rapidly down again and my radar tells me that she senses my disappointment at her relapse. I know a tirade of snide remarks is about to be unleashed. Her tongue lashes venomously and accuses me. 'You've never really loved me, have you? It's only Adele who is worth anything; only she really loves me.'

I cannot wait to get away. This burden has become too much for me. The mood swings are getting to me. I will not put up with more abuse.

'Mum,' I say, trying to keep my voice calm, 'I'm going now. I'm leaving your bananas on the counter and the *Shabbes* candles for you to light here on the table.'

Mother turns her head to the wall. I leave the room and head for home. I cannot take it any more.

It is *Shabbes*, only a day after I left my mother to stew in her depression. The phone is ringing. I recognise the voice of the head nurse from the old age home.

'Reva?'

Why is she calling me? This is the first day in the two months since Mother arrived that I haven't visited. Why can't my mother give me some space? 'Is everything all right? Has my mother fallen?' I ask coldly.

'Your mother has passed away. I'm so sorry.' Nurse sounds shaken.

I hear the words, but cannot absorb their meaning. I say nothing for a few seconds while my rapid heartbeat becomes a deafening roar.

'I saw her yesterday, she was alive, breathing.'

'She's dead.'

I cannot grasp it. People don't die without warning.

'She's committed suicide. I think you'd better come.'

It cannot be. This cannot be happening. She couldn't have really done this. I never took her seriously. And on *Shabbes*. It's all my fault.

'The police are here. They want to talk to you.'

Leah is shrieking, running away from my outstretched arms. She understands her grandma is dead. 'Don't run away from me,' I beg. 'I need you now.' Yankele hugs me close. 'Did she kill herself?' he whispers. I nod yes. The children have often heard her voice a desire for death. Adele is inconsolable. She truly loved my mother and is the only one of us who was able to see past her madness.

I call Dr Goldstein on his mobile. 'You're not going to believe it,' I wail. 'She's killed herself.'

'Oh no . . . no. Reva, I'm on my way. We'll go to the home together. Meet me downstairs. Ten minutes.'

My body is lead. I am guilty. I have killed her just as she always said I would. I need a drink or a smoke or even a fix. Dr Goldstein is sitting next to me in the office at the old age home signing medical forms. 'There's nothing you could have done,' he says. 'Nothing at all.'

I cannot bear the pain. A police officer is holding a folder containing the plastic bag my mother tied around her head along with thirty empty packets of sleeping pills. I recognise the bag as the very same one that I used to carry her bananas from the grocery store only the day before. I have supplied the tool for her suffocation. The policeman is burly and handsome and I stare at his tanned arms. I think of sex – anything not to feel. Nurse brings me a brandy and I sip. How could I have entertained the idea that I had outdone my father by taking her to therapy? I am worried that the burial society will not give Mother a Jewish funeral and she will be buried on the outskirts of the cemetery with the sinners. The policeman assures me they will hush up the cause of death. I gulp the brandy. There are so many details to think about. I am terrified this pain will cause another cancerous growth in me. She may be killing me too.

Simcha is helping me with the funeral arrangements. He calls close family and a few friends. Mother knew no one here. If we were in London she would have a grand funeral, but I know deep down she would have preferred it this way, intimate.

I never thought I'd be back here at the funeral home so soon. This is the very spot where Sam stood with his parents. Like Sam, I too am turning to Simcha for support. My mother's Hebrew name, Dvorah bas Reuven, Dvorah the daughter of Reuven, is scrawled on a board at the entrance to the funeral home. This is her true essence, not mother or rabbi's wife, but the youngest of seven daughters of Reuven, a darling man who died too young.

The burial official requests that I, as next of kin, identify my mother's body, which is lying in an ante-chamber. It is impossible. 'I cannot do it,' I stutter, but the rabbi tells me I must. Simcha moves forward and takes it upon himself to pass into the small room, unfold the white sheet that is tucked around her head and nod his recognition that the corpse is my mother.

Yankele holds my hand at the funeral. He is my comfort. Family members stand around the grave and praise my mother. They tell me that only the righteous die on *Shabbes*. How ridiculous their words sound. Simcha has one arm around Adele, who is weeping terribly, and he holds Leah close with the other. The service is simple. I have requested my mother's favourite *Shabbes* melody to be sung, the one my father used to sing to her on a Friday night, '*Eshet Chayil* – A woman of valour'.

We stand by the tilled earth of her grave. I am joining in with the chorus:

> Favour is deceptive and beauty is vain;
> A god-fearing woman –
> She should be praised.

I am singing for her, hoping she has finally found peace.

Simcha is with me when I enter my mother's flat a week later. A glass of water stands stagnant on the night table. Probably the same glass from which she drank to take the pills. It makes me think about the moment when she must have gagged, when she didn't rip the plastic bag off her face, when she allowed herself to die. I find it hard to breathe. I search frantically for a goodbye note like the ones I have seen in the movies, but find none. I cannot believe she didn't say goodbye.

We have work to do. Her belongings have to be packed and moved. These are the same items I packed up and sent from London only three months ago. Touching them makes me remember my childhood and I feel nauseous. I look over at Simcha carefully stacking up the crockery. I know I am blessed with his friendship.

Clearing out my mother's possessions is an inner cleansing

process. I am wrapping up my past. With every box of her clothes that I tape shut, I am closing her out of my life. With every suitcase that I load, I make a vow to rid myself of every shred of her that I have naturally absorbed, every nuance of the insanity that has been ingrained in me since childhood. I want to make myself a healthy woman, a strong mother for my children, the mother I never had. Now that the dishes are boxed and the paperwork sorted, I sense her madness cannot touch me any more. It has died and been buried along with her. Four hours of work later, all that remains of my mother is a pile of crates and boxes.

'You can't take it with you,' Simcha says. 'All we take to the next world is our good deeds.'

I sit down on a crate and stare at our handiwork. Everything is organised. But I know there is still one thing left undone. The time for me to visit Michelle has surely come.

20

Michelle

*If you believe that it's possible to ruin something,
you must always believe it's possible to mend it too.*
Rabbi Nachman of Breslov

The thirty-five degree heatwave hits me as I roll down the car window. It is similar to the desert temperature of the Judean hills, but rare here in the British Isles. Flanked with oak trees and thick shrubbery, the country road to Ravenswood is familiar. This is the road I travelled with my parents every week after Michelle was institutionalised. I recognise the way, even though twenty years have elapsed since I was last here. On the seat next to me is a fluffy pink poodle, a toy with ropey handles that doubles as a bag. I remember Michelle needing to clutch onto something all the time. Even though she is approaching her forty-fifth birthday, I think she will like the toy.

I ask myself how I could have abandoned my sister for so long, ignored her for so many years. She was thirteen years old and I was eight when she was sent to Ravenswood. Every time we went to visit her, my mother wept the whole way in the car, repeating the words, 'Harrowing, just harrowing,' while moving her diamond ring back and forth over the raw, red psoriasis sores that had erupted the night before. My father always sat rigid, silent and stationary. With my parents so wrapped up in their own misery, I felt afraid and alone. And I missed my sister, too. Even though I always knew she was different, I had never found anything upsetting about her. My parents had explained that her brain was damaged, but all it meant to me was that I had a perfect playmate who allowed me to instigate all our games and let me boss her around. Of course I sometimes took advantage of her weakness. One time in a game of 'house', where she was the wayward daughter and I the strict mother, I pulled down her pants and made her bend over while I lightly, oh, I am sure it was ever so lightly, smacked her bare bottom with a cane. I knew it was wrong, but Michelle didn't seem to mind. Or at least I hope she didn't. I loved her and wouldn't have wanted to hurt her, even though I liked it that she would do whatever I told her to.

But once Michelle moved to Ravenswood, and I saw her among her new friends, the water-on-the-brain children with their grossly oversized heads like veiny balloons and bodies thin like matchsticks, I started to dread seeing her because it meant seeing her playmates too. Their swollen faces would invade my sleep and make me scream at night. The word my mother used over and over, 'harrowing', became true for me as well.

And then when my mother became sick with breast cancer, our visits stopped permanently. She couldn't cope with any added stress. Michelle had become a taboo subject at home, as any mention of her triggered my mother's depression, so I never asked about her and even put her out of my mind.

It is only two months since my mother's death, and I remind myself that I have begun a journey of my own. I want to be the person my parents couldn't be, accomplish what they found too difficult, be strong where they were weak. It's wrong to keep Michelle out of my life. She is my flesh and blood and must be treated so. My visit is also a declaration that I, Reva, am not afraid like my mother was. She can no longer infect me with her fears or keep me from visiting Michelle by convincing me that I won't be able to handle it emotionally. Her death has released me from all that.

I wonder if I will recognise Michelle and if she will remember me. The last time I saw her, I was just as riddled with guilt about going home with Mum and Dad and leaving her as I had been the first time I had visited her there.

At the sight of the 'Welcome to Ravenswood' sign up ahead, a snake of fear writhes in my gut. Driving up the gravel road, I see the pastoral landscape spreading out before me. The grounds are dotted with houses, each with its own garden. Exteriors are painted in primary colours. Pansies and geraniums smile from window boxes. Squirrels scatter down a path. The neighing of horses is audible from across the fields. I am so nervous I'm almost shaking as I get out of the car.

I am looking for the Coppice. A part of me wishes my mother were here beside me. Then I could be the strong one, noble and kind and generous next to my weak snivelling mother. But I soon retract that wish, remembering how I used to hate the way Mother called the residents 'inmates'. I couldn't bear to have to put up with that now.

'Hello!'

I jump, taken aback.

A young man with Down's syndrome calls to me as he approaches. 'Who have you come to visit?' I remember how my mother often said, 'If only Michelle would have had Down's syndrome, then we could have kept her at home.'

'Michelle,' I answer. 'Michelle Mann.'

'Is it her birthday?' he asks.

'No. I've just come for a visit.' Fear is creeping up from my gut and crawling into my chest.

'Shall I show you where she lives?'

'It's up here, isn't it?' I say, remembering the way to the Coppice.

Joan, Michelle's carer, greets me at the door. She is just as I imagined from our telephone calls, healthy looking with an open face and honest smile. My heart is beating double time as I enter the house. The carers, one for each resident, come to say hello. Their cheery talk calms me. Lunch is being prepared and a succulent aroma drifts toward me from the kitchen. A cacophony of strange noises and some shouts is coming from the bedrooms. This is it. I am back among the most severely handicapped in Ravenswood, the leading Jewish home for the mentally challenged in England.

'Michelle's doing fine,' Joan says, leading me towards the cosy lounge. I sit down on a comfortable couch. There is a thin sheet of plastic laid underneath the throw cover. 'She can express verbally what she needs most of the time, except of course when she gets agitated and then she doesn't sleep, rants and raves and grabs at people.'

As a child, I could decipher Michelle's strange noises. I understood her language when my parents could not. Yet I remember her awful moods, the nervous waving of her arms and garbled speech that sounded as if she were swearing. I think of my mother and how upset she would be to hear Joan's descriptions.

'Where is Michelle?' I ask Joan, as a blonde autistic girl

comes up to me and offers her hand. I give my hand in return but I'm unnerved by the gesture. I never know what to expect from the handicapped. I am never sure if a gentle clasp will become an unintentionally hurtful squeeze, or worse. There are no social boundaries here. My body is on guard, adrenalin discharging into my bloodstream.

'She's just having her clothes changed,' Joan says. 'She won't be a moment.'

I remember my mother saying, 'The care at Ravenswood is exceptional and the inmates are treated with dignity. They never let Michelle walk around with a stained shirt or wet trousers.' I thought she was trying to make herself feel better for not keeping Michelle at home, but now I see her words were true.

I need the bathroom and enter the narrow hallway. A young girl with brown ringlets shouts in gibberish and jerks from side to side within the confines of a caregiver's arms. A man in a wheelchair is navigated across the landing to the living room. His head hangs down and his arms fall limp by his sides. A hunchbacked man sits on the floor clutching a wad of Monopoly money. Every few minutes he bursts into laughter.

The bathroom is spotless. Special handles are attached to the white ceramic tiles along the bath and the wall next to the toilet. As I squat down to pee, I wonder how they bathe Michelle. I remember how difficult it was for my mother to wash her once her body developed. I was never present for this daily chore, but remembering my mother's loud moans and heavy sighs, I realise now how hard it must have been for her to see Michelle developing physically into a woman, while her brain stayed at the level of a small child. I am as scared now as

I was as a young girl when I needed my father to sit with me in the middle of the night and soothe my anxiety. I want to stay in here where it is safe, away from the damaged and deformed. I take time washing my hands and splashing water on my face. When I finally open the bathroom door, I look out into the hall with trepidation, afraid of what I might see.

There she is. Michelle is walking towards me with her funny little walk. She hangs her head down and off to the side. In the flopping motion of her head, I see a resemblance to my mother. Michelle is grunting her wonderful grunts. They are the sounds of my childhood. She is wearing navy cotton trousers and a turquoise short-sleeved T-shirt. Her red hair is cut short like a boy. She looks younger than her forty-five years, not one grey hair visible, no wrinkles on her skin. I notice her bottom lip is swollen and parched. It must be from the medication. She grips a battered teddy in her hand that trails behind her and is spilling its stuffing. 'Michelle!' I run over to my sister. I am surprised by how lovely she is. Why couldn't my mother appreciate her translucent blue eyes, her thick red hair and most of all that cheeky look on her face? I want to hug her, but twenty years cannot be bridged so fast. Instead I touch her arm and hand her the fluffy pink poodle. She grabs it from me by the ropey handles and grinds her teeth. Now she is turning around in circles. I can tell she is happy with the gift. Any question I had about whether Michelle understands what is happening around her is immediately dispelled as she pushes her chapped hand into mine. It feels cold and rough against my skin. She may not know I am her sister, or remember the time when we both lived at home, but she knows I'm someone special to her. I recognise the birthmark on her left arm as I lovingly hold her hand.

'We've got something for you,' Joan says, handing me a book of A4 paper bound together with blue ribbon. It is a collection of Michelle's artwork. It reminds me of the end-of-term offerings Leah brings home from kindergarten.

'Thank you,' I say, taking the portfolio. There is a photo of Michelle stuck onto the cover. It has been snapped at an angle that shows none of her beauty, only her swollen lip and abnormal expression. It makes me think of our first visit to see Michelle after she had been moved to Ravenswood thirty-two years ago. My mother, myself, Michelle and her carer, are standing in Michelle's new bedroom admiring the curtains and the carpeting, trying to make my sister feel proud of her new room. On the wall hangs a photo of Michelle at ten years old. She is wearing a paisley dress. Her features are fine, before puberty distorted them. There is no dribble drooling from her mouth and she is smiling. It is to this picture that my mother points. 'This is Michelle!' she announces to the carer, articulating her fantasy of having a perfect and beautiful daughter. My sister looks at the floor and I hear her grinding her teeth in a menacing way. Years later, I confronted my mother about this insensitivity. 'Michelle doesn't have any feelings at all,' she told me. 'The doctor told me so.'

Opening the portfolio I find smudges of red and yellow under headlines that read 'Michelle chose the colours'. Turning the pages, I find the words 'Michelle likes to stack pots,' written above another colourful splotch. A photo depicts Joan helping Michelle hold a paintbrush. I know I am supposed to make a fuss and praise Michelle, but I don't like this attempt at proving her abilities. I am not interested in the charting of her stacking and painting. I want to see Michelle as she is, grunting and waving, ranting and raving.

'Michelle has much more confidence lately,' Joan tells me. 'She likes to wear nail varnish and use hand cream and she's very fussy about her clothes.'

Just like Mum, I think, looking down at Michelle's pink nails. I hadn't noticed them before.

Joan points to the picture on the back cover of the book. Michelle is all dolled up in a red silk shirt. 'We had a disco here one night and Michelle had a fine time sitting on all the boys' knees. Definitely not behaving as a rabbi's daughter should!'

I cringe as Michelle pulls me towards the door.

'Why don't you two go for a walk?' Joan says. 'Michelle loves her walks. Don't you, Michelle? If she had her way, she'd walk all night, wouldn't you, Michelle?'

Michelle seems excited as she mischievously leads me into the garden. I want to get away from the baby talk. I sense Michelle doesn't like it either. I feel it is demeaning, but connecting to my sister is no easy task. Michelle is stronger than she looks and she is yanking my right arm almost out of its socket. 'Take the other arm,' I say, shifting to her other side, as my right armpit is still sore from surgery and radiation.

'Over there in the garden there's a plaque in memory of your father.' Joan is walking towards us and points to a rectangle of bronze that is embedded in the grass with the help of a metal prong. The words 'For my dad. Love Michelle' are engraved in Edwardian script. I stand still and stare at the epitaph. I must tell Michelle about our mother's death, but this is not the time. Mucous leaks out of her mouth and she wipes it away with her arm still holding the poodle. I sense Michelle understands that our father has gone and is sad as she doesn't want to look at the plaque but fixates her gaze on the grass.

'Have a nice walk, you two,' Joan calls after us.

Out onto the grounds we sisters run, past the stables and the art therapy clinic, past the rabbit hutches and towards the forest. Michelle's legs are sturdy, despite her flat feet collapsed over the arch of her sneakers. I can hardly keep up with her. On and on we go, down the country lanes towards the open fields.

'Hold on, I need to slow down.' I stop, sweating. When did it ever get this hot in England? I wonder, wishing I had brought my Israeli summer clothes. Michelle tightens her grip on my hand. She doesn't stop.

I wish Joan had come with us. I don't want to be alone with my sister any more. I feel I cannot control the situation. There must be a way to steer Michelle back towards the Coppice. 'Michelle, do you remember Daddy's *Shabbes* songs?' I ask, trying to slow her down.

Michelle kicks at the stone path and a cloud of dust rises up in front of her. Maybe she recognises the word 'Daddy'.

'*Lecha dodi*,' I begin, imitating how our father sang at the *Shabbes* table with the melody of exile and the yearning for redemption in his heart. '*Likrat callah*.' Could Michelle remember the songs from home? I ask myself, as she flaps her arms up and down and tries to sing along. '*Pene Shabbat, nekabelah*,' I continue the first stanza. Michelle keeps chirping. I imitate her. Michelle sings louder. I flap my arms in unison with her. We look like birds flapping their wings. Our father's refrain is transformed from a holy psalm to a mating call. We are both laughing now. Michelle is getting excited. I open up my arms. Now is the time to hug. Our long separation is over. I hold her thin body in my arms. Michelle's arms lie quietly by her sides. Her head weighs heavily on my shoulder, and the pressure of her body against my breast hurts a little, but I don't move away. I am savouring every second of our closeness.

The bell for lunch is ringing after only ten precious minutes of our crazy duet. We can hear it out here in the open. Michelle releases herself from my hold, turns around and stomps back to the dining room. I follow in her footsteps.

Six misshapen men and women sit around the table, their carers among them. The autistic girl is moaning. The man in the wheelchair is being spoon-fed. Michelle tucks into the meat stew and mashed potatoes dolloped onto her plate. When she stuffs the food in her mouth I notice that her bottom teeth are missing. Her swollen lip covers up the cavity in her mouth. This must explain the incessant drooling.

I stand in the dining room, looking around the lunch table that as a child I would have found so distressing. Today I can see that the mood is festive. The carers are chatting. Everyone is enjoying themselves.

I have had my reunion with my sister and it is time to go. I take Michelle's forgetting I am here as my cue to leave. I kiss her on the top of her head. 'Goodbye, my darling sister,' I say. She doesn't take her eyes off her plate.

'Goodbye, Joan,' I say. 'Thank you for taking such good care of Michelle.'

I slip out of the house, feeling as if I'm running away. I roll my shoulders and stretch my arms. I have held tension in my muscles for the past two hours. Exhaling, I try to relax.

Getting away is all I can think of, but in that same thought I am also planning the next visit. I will bring nail varnish and body lotion. The impossible has become possible. The mountain I thought I could never climb has been reduced to a small molehill. I feel wretched that it took me this long. Why have I carried such a deep fear of the handicapped for so many years? I think of Sam and how he told me it was time for me to visit Michelle and make a *tikkun*. So much time has been wasted. I have robbed myself of a relationship with my only sibling. Michelle is not the ideal sister. There is so much that I can never share with her, the burden of our parents, the joy of having children. Yet I am weeping, because despite her constraints and limitations, she is my sister and I love her.

Epilogue

I am sitting on the steps of the ghat by the Ganges in the city of Rishikesh in northern India near the Maharishi ashram, where the Beatles lived in their post-psychedelic phase. It is *Diwali*, the festival of lights. My children are by my side. Adele is taking photographs of the orange-robed swamis. She has grown into a responsible young lady. I could never have made this trip without her. She shares the responsibility for travel planning and, when making decisions, I am often led by her high moral code. Next year she will volunteer for her National Service with the handicapped. My parents would have been so proud. Although at first they might have tried to deter her, wanting to protect her from what they found so impossibly painful, her inner strength would have won them over. She will be doing what we could not, healing the trauma of the past generations.

Yankele and Leah are holding hands, looking out at the sacred river flowing past them. They have a special sibling love for each other and whisper in a secret tongue. Yankele is always looking out for his little sister. His hand is often searching for hers, or cutting up the food on her plate. Leah idolises her big brother and boasts to her friends that he is the coolest guy around. And cool he is. I look at Yankele and remember the day of his *upsharin* haircut, when I imagined my three-year-old son grown up and playing electric guitar with his blond curls falling over his face, which I was sure would never happen because I thought I'd lost him forever to the yeshiva world. Today his hair is long and music is his passion. He has found a way to express his pain in angry rap lyrics. I never dreamed I would experience a generation gap with my kids. I always thought I was a hip mum, so unlike my parents, but I have not escaped being on the other side of the rift that thirty years brings. Just like my parents before me, I find myself cringing in horror as I look at my child, his jeans worn so low on his hips that the hems sweep the ground, which here in India is so much filthier than anywhere else.

A teenage boy slithers on the ground towards us. He wears flip-flops on his hands and thick leather patches are sewn around the knees of his trousers. Yankele insists I give him money. He cannot bear the sight of poverty. The boy looks up at me and smiles. His face radiates happiness. Seeing his spastic legs, my thoughts turn to Michelle.

Visits to Ravenswood have become part of my annual routine. I have been blessed with Lisa, an old school friend, who accompanies me there. She mingles among the residents with ease. A visit once a year for a couple of hours may seem minimal, yet it demands courage every time. When I am with Michelle, acting now in my capacity as her guardian, I realise the burden my parents carried, and my harsh judgement of them dissipates into sympathy for the hardships they faced.

Despite her exasperating personality, I miss my mother most. Though I know that even five minutes of being in her company would infuriate me, I find myself feeling nostalgic for those rare moments when she emerged from her solipsistic state long enough to mother me. My father I miss most acutely when I pray in synagogue during the High Holidays, which brings back the sound of his operatic voice singing the liturgy and the eloquence of his moving sermons. I usually find myself crying my way through the service, missing them both.

It will get dark soon and the *Puja* ceremony will begin. Candles and flowers are placed in the water. They look like coloured sequins floating by. Chants of '*Hare Krishna, Hare Rama*' are intensifying, reminding me of the days when my Indian school friend Amita taught me to wrap saffron threads around miniature statues in her West Hampstead home. She and her family decorated their hands with intricate patterns of henna before the ceremony, and accompanied it with a chant that I still remember:

Shantakaram bhujagashayanam Padmanabham suresham Vishawadharam gaganaa sadrusham meghavarnam subhangam.

These foreign words are on my lips as the burning of incense begins, and the sweet smell takes me back even more vividly to those visits long ago with Amita and her family, which inspired in me a dream of one day visiting her in her homeland. I am so glad to be here at last.

There are thousands of Israelis travelling in India and many here in Rishikesh. They all seem to desperately want to be part of the Puja ceremony and, eager for enlightenment, they cling to the shiny brass arms of the lighted candelabras that are being circled in the air above our heads by the Hindus. But they seem to me to be so misguided, searching for God through this idolatrous form of worship. I know Jewish souls can only find true closeness to God through the Torah. However, there are many lessons to be learnt here in India and that is one of the reasons I have come. I want to learn acceptance from the beggars, who, no matter how poor or deformed, appear to me to live in a state of grace. I want my children to observe life far removed from the fast-food, high-tech materialistic world we live in. There are other things too. I have always wanted to see the regal India that Amita told me about, the bright colours of Rajasthan, the poise of the Indian women wearing saris, gliding along barefoot with perfect deportment. I want the romance of Bollywood and more of the enchanting remnants of the British Empire that I so enjoyed on our train ride here from Delhi, when uniformed waiters ran up and down the carriage selling Cadbury's fruit and nut chocolate bars and ladling out 'tomato soooouup' and calling me 'Madam'.

We cannot stay for the entire ceremony as tonight is *Shabbes* as well as the first night of *Succoth*, the autumn harvest festival, and we must head to our Jewish observances. I steer the children away from the pulsating crowd. We navigate our way over the Laxman Jhula Bridge, which is chockablock with cows, pilgrims, motorbikes, limbless beggars and malevolent looking monkeys swinging on their long arms. The crossing is hard for Leah. She is frightened of the animals and clutches on to Yankele for protection. In the distance I am relieved to see the words 'Chabad house' lit up in the gathering twilight.

Tables are set up in long rows in the *succah* booth, a rudimentary structure topped by palm branches spread across wooden slats that criss-cross to form the roof. Paper Chinese lanterns and tissue flowers hang down from the centre. Indian waiters are carrying trays of food to the tables on their heads. My children are delighted to see hummus and pitta breads and Israeli salad chopped up fine. They have had enough of rice and curried dhal. There must be over two hundred Israelis here tonight, many of them young men and women travelling after army service, everyone swapping travel stories and advocating hotels and trains. Most wear the simple cotton clothes sold here. Their Indian bangles clink as they help themselves to dinner.

The rabbi, originally from Crown Heights, is on a mission. This is his third year in India. Not an ideal environment in which to educate his three small children, but as part of the international Chabad movement, which seeks to provide a home away from home with free hospitality and a warm welcome to any Jew who arrives on their doorstep on *Shabbes* or during any of the Jewish holidays, he is bringing Torah to many who would never otherwise be exposed. He stands up to address the crowd. I am all ears.

'This week, during the Feast of the Tabernacles, we leave our permanent residence for the temporary dwelling of the *succah*, an unprotected booth. In doing so, we stretch our faith by looking out at the heavens through the foliage above and realise that the true source of our protection is God above.'

I feel so comfortable here. It's as if I am back in a yeshiva atmosphere but with the added bonus of being able to wear shorts and a tank top and spend time in India with my kids. If we had stayed in Jerusalem, I might not have sat in a *succah* or heard such beautiful words of Torah because the holidays still sometimes trigger a deep sadness within me. With my family broken and no man by my side, I feel fragmented. But here on holiday, exploring and discovering India with my children, the four of us bonded together by this new experience, I feel whole again.

As the rabbi continues his discourse, I muse on my complicated relationship to God. I still believe in Him and His holy Torah, but am unable to follow many of the laws. Like many Jews before me, I live in a spiritual exile. Eating kosher, praying and studying the Torah are organic parts of my life, but ever since my mother took her life on a Friday night, keeping the Sabbath has been harder than ever for me. The old unhappy memories of tense dreary Sabbaths in my parents' home have been eclipsed by a new wave of negative associations, and I find the loneliness that I have always felt on *Shabbes*, with no distractions from the telephone, the DVD player or the Internet, hard to bear. But tonight, I welcome the opportunity to join in with the festivities, and to share the Sabbath with all these other travellers.

The Chabad rabbi breaks into song and two hundred pairs of hands clap along with the tune. '*Mitzva Gedolah* . . . It is a *mitzva* to be happy always.' The men have formed a circle and are dancing around the tables. I think about my father and how he loved to sing this melody on a Friday night. I think about Simcha, who often quoted these famous words of Rabbi Nachman of Breslov.

Bottles of wine are passed around, but I decline. Water is my drink of choice since my clean out. After Mother died I began a detoxification of body and soul. I knew I had to change and grow. There was so much poison to get rid of. The combination of chemotherapy, radiation, caffeine, dope and a bottle of wine a day had made me highly toxic. I kept to a strict diet: protein, rice and carrots. I delved into my yoga practice and began the arduous journey into myself. Without the amelioration of mind- and mood-altering substances, I had nothing to band-aid my hurting, and for the first time in my life, I allowed myself to feel the existential pain I had always run away from. Every time the pain erupted, instead of reaching for a joint, a glass of wine, or loveless sex, I put up with the disease. It was hell. But I was surprised to discover that hell is not an infinite suffering, simply a transient anguish that has to be waited out.

As part of the clearing out of the negative elements in my life, I had to let go of many people too. There have been no men since Sam. I live the life of a nun and worry I am once again going to an extreme, this time of sexual abstention. But it is not easy to find a man with whom I connect as deeply as I did with Sam. I think of him often, but will never allow myself to enter into such an unhealthy relationship again. I work on myself by concentrating on well-being and healing and I stay away from self-destruction. I focus on what I have and not on what I lack. The project of maintaining health anchors me. I don't believe one can control cancer, but by keeping clean in body and soul, I know I am doing my best to keep it at bay.

The meal is over. We manoeuvre our way back to our hotel. The way is steep, down a muddy road. The juxtaposition of the Chabad *succah* celebrations with the pagan Indian festivities makes me think back to the scene of Simcha binding *tefillin* around Sam's freckled arm after the *shiva*. I remember how I left them bonded together in friendship, creating a synthesis of the sacred and the secular. This is how I must live if I am to find peace, bringing together the holy and the profane, merging them instead of ricocheting from one to the other.

Dodging the racing rickshaws, I think about the Rambam's golden path of balance. I laugh at myself and how, in my yeshiva days, I thought I had found that path. I had no idea what a lengthy journey was ahead of me. Now that I have begun the task of building within myself a receptacle that will be able to contain His light, I am beginning the true process of repentance. I keep humming the tune 'It's a *mitzva* to be happy always'. As I look around me, at my three beautiful children, and at myself realising a lifelong dream, I feel that tonight I am at last fulfilling that *mitzva*.